1995

RACIAL POLITICS IN AMERICAN CITIES

RACIAL POLITICS IN AMERICAN CITIES

Rufus P. Browning
San Francisco State University

Dale Rogers Marshall
Wellesley College

David H. Tabb
San Francisco State University

Longman
New York & London

RACIAL POLITICS IN AMERICAN CITIES

Longman, 95 Church Street, White Plains, N.Y. 10601

Associated companies:
Longman Group Ltd., London
Longman Cheshire Pty., Melbourne
Longman Paul Pty., Auckland
Copp Clark Pitman, Toronto

Senior editor: David J. Estrin
Production editor: Camilla T. K. Palmer
Cover design: Kevin C. Kall
Production supervisor: Kathleen Ryan

Library of Congress Cataloging in Publication Data
Racial politics in American cities / [edited by] Rufus P. Browning.
    Dale Rogers Marshall, David H. Tabb. — 1st ed.
        p. cm.
        Includes bibliographical references.
        Contents: Introduction : can Blacks and Latinos achieve power in
    city government? / Rufus P. Browning, Dale Rogers Marshall, David H.
    Tabb — Minority mobilization in ten cities / Rufus B. Browning,
    Dale Rogers Marshall, David H. Tabb — Biracial coalition politics
    in Los Angeles / Raphael J. Sonenshein.
        ISBN 0-8013-0178-5
        1. Afro-Americans — Politics and government.   2. Hispanic
    Americans — Politics and government.   3. United States — Race
    relations.   4. Municipal government — United States — History — 20th
    century.   I. Browning, Rufus P.   II. Marshall, Dale Rogers.
    III. Tabb, David H.
    E185.615.R214   1990
    323.11'96073—dc20   89-36784
                                                                     CIP

ABCDEFGHIJ–AL–99   98   97   96   95   94   93   92   91   90

Contents

Preface

This book on racial politics illustrates the contribution that a professional association for professors, particularly the American Political Science Association, can make to scholarship.

In 1985 our earlier book on minority organizing in California cities, *Protest Is Not Enough,* won two prizes from the American Political Science Association for the best book in American policy and the best book on ethnic relations. In response to those prizes Cathy Rudder, now the Executive Director of the Association, invited us to organize a forum for the Association's magazine, *PS*. We asked distinguished scholars to write articles applying the ideas explored in *Protest Is Not Enough* to other major American cities. That forum, published in *PS* in Summer, 1986, was the catalyst for this book.

It was interesting to compare minority politics in American cities using a common framework. The forum was well received, so we decided to expand it by adding cities and to revise it so as to reach a larger audience.

Now that the task is finished, we wish to express our thanks to all the authors who shared their expertise, the University of California Press and the American Political Science Association for permission to draw heavily on earlier work, and to David Estrin, Camilla T. K. Palmer, Cynthia Farden, Victoria Mifsud, and others at Longman who have worked with skill and commitment on the book.

We dedicate this book to our children and we hope that their generations will continue to give priority to the struggle for racial justice:

Marla, Ross, Charles, and Mark Browning
Jessica, Cynthia, and Clayton Marshall
Kevin, Lisa, and Jonah Tabb

About the Authors

Rufus P. Browning is professor of political science at San Francisco State University. He has written on political psychology and computer simulation as well as on the politics of race and ethnicity. In his current work, he is applying the framework of *Protest Is Not Enough* to other American cities.

John G. Corbett is associate professor of public administration at Lewis and Clark College, where he teaches courses on comparative and local politics and administration. He has a continuing research interest in comparative community politics. He has published widely on community and urban issues.

Charles P. Henry is associate professor of Afro-American studies at the University of California at Berkeley. He holds a Ph.D in political science from the University of Chicago. He has two books forthcoming: *Culture and African American Politics* and *The Search for Common Ground: Jesse Jackson's Campaigns for President.*

Richard A. Keiser holds a Ph.D. from the University of California, Berkeley, and is assistant professor of political science at the University of Denver. He is completing a book on the political incorporation of blacks in Philadelphia, Atlanta, Chicago, and Gary.

Dale Rogers Marshall is dean of the college and professor of political science at Wellesley College. She has published widely on urban politics and policy and has served as a vice president of the American Political Science Association.

John H. Mollenkopf, associate professor of political science at the Graduate Center, City University of New York, recently edited *Power, Culture and Place, Essays on New York City.* He is completing a book on the question—Why does a city with a liberal tradition and a white minority have a conservative white government?

Carlos Muñoz, Jr. received his Ph.D. in government from the Claremont Graduate School and is associate professor, Department of Ethnic Studies, University of California, Berkeley. He is the author of *Youth, Identity, Power: The Chicano Movement* and is working on a biography of Dr. Ernesto Galarza.

Huey L. Perry is professor of political science at Southern University. He is the author of several journal articles and book chapters on black politics in the South. He is co-editing a book on blacks and the American political system.

Michael B. Preston is professor and chair of the Department of Political Science, University of Southern California. He has published many articles, monographs, and books including *The New Black Politics* and *The Politics of Bureaucratic Reform*. He has been president of the National Conference of Black Political Scientists, vice president of the Midwest Political Science Association, and chairperson of the American Political Science Association's Committee on the Status of Blacks in the Profession.

Raphael J. Sonenshein, associate professor at California State University, Fullerton, received his Ph.D. degree from Yale University in 1984. His articles have appeared in several journals. His current research interest is the politics of biracial coalitions, particularly the relationship between minority incorporation and liberalism. He is completing a book on the biracial coalition in Los Angeles.

John F. Stack, Jr., is professor of political science at Florida International University, where he teaches international and ethnic politics. He is the author of *International Conflict in an American City: Boston's Irish, Italians, and Jews, 1935–1944*. He is also the editor of three other books on ethnic and international politics. He is presently working on a book on the internationalization of Miami.

Robert T. Starks teaches inner city studies and political science at Northeastern Illinois University, where he is associate professor. He has published many articles on black politics and urban politics and served as an issues adviser to Harold Washington and the Rev. Jesse Jackson. He is working on a book on Harold Washington.

Clarence N. Stone, professor of government and politics at the University of Maryland, College Park, has authored several books and articles on urban politics, including two books on Atlanta—*Economic Growth and Neighborhood Discontent* and *Regime Politics: Governing Atlanta, 1946–1988*.

David H. Tabb, professor of political science at San Francisco State University, has written on ideology formation and social welfare as well as on the politics of race. His current work focuses on a comparison of the politics of race in Great Britain and the United States.

Toni-Michelle C. Travis (Ph.D., University of Chicago), assistant professor of government and politics at George Mason University, writes on the impact of race and gender on American politics. Her current research examines the role of women and blacks who have served in the Virginia House of Delegates.

Christopher L. Warren is associate professor of political science at Florida International University, where he teaches urban and American politics. His research and publications have focused primarily on the politics of ethnicity and class, Miami politics, the reform of local governmental structures, and local school system politics.

RACIAL POLITICS IN AMERICAN CITIES

PART I
Problems and Possibilities

Can Blacks and Latinos Achieve Power in City Government? The Setting and the Issues

Rufus P. Browning, Dale Rogers Marshall, and David H. Tabb

The long, sad history of racial domination in the United States has twice led to great, ultimately irresistible national movements, prolonged political conflict, death and destruction. The movement to abolish slavery, finally achieving its goal in the Fourteenth Amendment, failed to secure for blacks the rights of citizens and legal and political equality. Nearly a century later, the civil rights movement addressed the gap between American ideals of democracy and political equality and the practice of extreme inequality and exclusion with respect to the most fundamental rights and liberties of black people—the right to vote, to equal treatment before the law, to freedom of speech and assembly.

THE CIVIL RIGHTS MOVEMENT AND BLACK PROTEST

From the late 1950s to the mid-1970s, the United States and its cities were caught up in a turmoil of protest and demand around issues of political, social, and economic equality for blacks and, to a lesser extent, Latinos.[1] The assault on

---

[1] We use the term "Latino" to denote groups which are Spanish speaking but of Caribbean, Mexican, or South or Central American ancestry. Although "Hispanic" is commonly used in government, the media, and scholarly writing to refer to these groups, that term means literally "pertaining to Spain or Spanish culture," yet very few "Hispanics" in the United States have anything to do with Spain other than a shared language. "Hispanic" ignores and obscures the reality of Mayan or other native American ancestry, and it obscures also the political identities expressed in such terms as La Raza and Latino. For further comment on this issue, see Chapter 10 by Muñoz and Henry in this volume.

However, usage varies among Latino (Hispanic) groups in ways that reveal their diverse identities, and among the authors of this book. Cubans in Miami use the terms "Latin" or "Hispanic"; among them, the name "Latino" is often associated specifically with Mexican Americans.

3

traditional patterns of dominance and inequality was felt to one degree or another in all cities with significant black and Latino populations. First came the civil rights movement, challenging the exclusion of blacks, etching scenes on the American consciousness—National Guardsmen escorting black children past mobs of taunting white parents, lunch counter sit-ins, Governor Wallace—"segregation today, segregation tomorrow, segregation forever"—blocking the doorway to the University of Alabama to federal officials, Martin Luther King, Jr.'s impassioned plea for equality from the steps of the Lincoln Memorial, the marches in Selma and Birmingham, Alabama, the murder of civil rights workers, the burnings of black churches. The challenge of the civil rights movement spread to cities across the nation, leading both to protest and to the organization of more traditional electoral and lobbying efforts. The shock waves were felt in city after city.

Mass violence erupted in the mid-sixties. Riots in Los Angeles, Detroit, Newark, and other cities aroused fear, anger, and hatred as leaders struggled to control events and prevent cities from burning. The riots were followed by recriminations, investigations, and heightened demands.

The federal government initiated programs aimed at poverty, racial inequality, and discrimination. President Lyndon Johnson pushed aggressively for the passage of the Civil Rights Act of 1964, the Voting Rights Act of 1965, and the "war on poverty": the Economic Opportunity Act of 1964. These were followed by Model Cities and a great array of other programs in employment, housing, education, and health, most of which impacted the agenda and resources of city governments and of minority groups. Under the Nixon administration, the federal grant system was reorganized but continued to expand with the institution of general revenue sharing and block grants.

Since the 1970s, the civil rights movement, which had earlier generated enormous passion and commitment, has lost access to national governmental circles and is less visible. The number of minority officeholders, blacks especially, has grown nationwide; the dramatic protests that so gripped public attention in the sixties have now virtually ceased. In cities where blacks have risen to positions of authority, the politics of administration, implementation, and planning—and sometimes crises of competence and corruption, as in governments generally—have replaced the politics of mobilization and mass action. Open conflict within minority groups now represented in some city governments has on occasion replaced the unity that could prevail when the city was the common enemy.

THE STRUGGLE FOR ACCESS
TO CITY GOVERNMENTS

A significant part of the political mobilization of blacks and later of Latinos and others, including women, aimed to gain access to city governments—to positions of authority and influence, to city jobs, and to the potential benefits of city programs and policies. The civil rights movement and local mobilization efforts became critical tests not only of the ability of minorities to sustain a high level of political activity but of the American political systems itself, tests of the proposition that hitherto excluded groups could realize the democratic promise of the American political tradition.

The continuing struggle of blacks and Latinos for access to government and for responsive policies in the cities, and the responses of local political systems and city governments to their efforts, are the subjects of this book. As we shall see, this struggle has achieved changes that are striking in their scope and significance. On the other hand, its gains remain subject to attack, the value of the benefits it has produced is questioned by some, its momentum has greatly slowed, and its successes have been uneven over time and from city to city.

There is no question that the number of blacks and Latinos elected to public office in American cities has grown dramatically. From none in 1960, there were, in 1985, twenty-seven black and three Latino mayors of cities with populations over 50,000 (Joint Center, 1985; National Association of Latino Elected Officials, 1986). The mayors of three of the largest cities in the country were black at the time of this writing—Los Angeles, Chicago, and Philadelphia. So many blacks and Latinos hold important offices that it might seem to an observer obvious that minorities have indeed achieved their full and secure place in local politics.

While the trend is obvious, its significance is disputed. Many cities with substantial black or Latino populations have no minority representation in city council and mayoral offices, or very little. Even where minority officials hold office, how much power do they have? Can minority officeholders really make city governments responsive to minority interests? And even if we concede that they can control local governments, perhaps in only a few cities, can even these minority officeholders make any headway against the central minority problems of unemployment and poverty, now higher than in the early 1970s, as help from the federal level is dismantled? In a period of fiscal stringency and reduced federal spending, can they carve out a larger piece of the municipal pie for minority populations? Can they strike a better bargain for minorities with the investors and financial institutions on which local economies depend for development? Although the growing number of minority officials suggests the achievement of access to government, do the limited powers of cities in a federal system and a capitalistic society render that apparent gain more symbolic than real? And is the favorable trend likely to continue at all, or can we already see signs of reversal, of a mobilization of conservative whites that is retaking control of city halls around the country, as the Republican Party took control of the presidency in 1980?

In short, can blacks and Latinos achieve meaningful participation in city government?

This book addresses these questions by bringing together thirteen articles on the political mobilization and political power of blacks and Latinos in nineteen cities, among them the four largest cities in the country—Los Angeles, Chicago, and Philadelphia, all with black mayors, and New York—and other major cities in diverse regions, including Boston, Atlanta, San Francisco, San Jose, Oakland,

Miami, San Antonio, and Denver. In this group, Atlanta and Oakland have black mayors; Miami, San Antonio, and Denver, Latino mayors.

Blacks and Latinos are the two largest minority groups in the United States, composing 18.1 percent of the national population in 1980 and much larger proportions in many states and cities. The quality of their mobilization and their capacity to sustain political power in cities are crucial to their ability to gain continuing access at the national level of government as well as their ability to have a voice in the governance of cities. And because many contenders for national office learn from their first and formative experiences in city politics, it is important to understand the diverse lessons those experiences teach.

The movement to establish minority political strength in cities has implications as well for the constitutions of city governments: in many cities, minorities and their allies are changing the charters of city government, strengthening mayors and city councils and changing election systems to their advantage. As we shall see in city after city, these constitutional differences between cities alter the conditions of politics. They have an impact on minority mobilization and on the ability of groups that resist minority influence to construct institutional barriers to it. Constitutional structure thus affects the ability of minority groups to gain incorporation into city government and ultimately the responsiveness of city government to minority interests.

But most important, this book offers a current report on struggles of minorities for access to city government—continuing experiments in American democracy.

HOW THIS BOOK WORKS

To understand minority political mobilization and to assess its chances for success—and for failure—require attention to two issues. First, we need to address values. What of value has been or can be achieved by the minority political movement in cities? What should we look for when we seek to gauge the success or failure of the movement? What vision guides the movement itself? The questions raised above about the effectiveness of minority officeholders suggest some but not all of the central concerns.

We need also to focus on explanation. We need to understand how minority groups mobilize and why they are able to do so in some cities but not in others. We need to identify the barriers to participation in governance, what it takes to overcome them, and the conditions for successful participation. We need to explain why it is that a few city governments became vigorously responsive to some demands of the movement, while others yielded much less or hardly at all.

Chapter 1 lays out the guiding conceptions—the theoretical framework— applied in the following chapters to the cities under study. But it starts with the story of the struggle for minority access to government in ten cities. The theoretical framework partly guided but also partly arose from a study of ten northern California cities over the period 1960–1980. Proceeding from the concrete to the abstract, we aim to show the interplay between the events and conditions of that period, as we found them, and our developing conception of minority mobilization and government response.

In the following chapters, other authors apply this framework to other cities, testing its adequacy against new evidence and extending it, as they encounter patterns not observed in the first ten cities. By the end of the book, we should understand not only how the movement unfolded in some of the largest and most important American cities, but also the present and the possibilities of the future: the adequacy of minority political incorporation as it really is, the extent to which minority-governed and minority-oriented regimes pursue the broader goals of the movement, and what they might do in pursuit of those goals.

Taking the framework we present in Chapter 1 or other perspectives you bring to the task, join us in the interplay between evidence and understanding as we study the uneven and problematic emergence of minority power in city governments.

REFERENCES

Joint Center for Political Studies. 1985. *Black Elected Officials: A National Roster*. New York.

National Association of Latino Elected Officials. 1986. *The National Roster of Hispanic Elected Officials*. Washington, D.C.

CHAPTER 1

Minority Mobilization in Ten Cities: Failures and Successes

Rufus P. Browning, Dale Rogers Marshall, and David H. Tabb

Why did blacks and Latinos mobilize strongly in some cities but not in others? Why did mobilization lead to significant minority representation in some city governments but not in others? Where representation was achieved, why was it transformed into power and responsive policies in some settings but not in others? Overall, was the movement successful?

We present in this chapter a framework for understanding why minority mobilization unfolded in diverse ways, and with notably different results, in various cities.[1] We do this by examining patterns of evolution in ten cities in northern California, first for the 1960s and 1970s, then for the 1980s. Study of these cities enables us to assess the successes and failures of minority mobilization in local settings and the conditions that led to success or failure; this assessment, valid for cities in northern California, is then a set of hypotheses about the achievements and evolution of the minority movement in other regions and in cities with very different characteristics and histories.[2] To understand the emergence and evolution of the national movement in the cities is to understand why it evolved in different ways, depending on social, economic, historical, and political factors that varied, and still vary, from city to city.

Understanding variation is essential for political action as well. Political action in cities occurs in the presence of each city's distinctive shaping characteristics. To make our understanding relevant to action, we must understand variation—change in particular cities as well as change measured across all cities.

---

[1] Portions of this chapter are drawn from the authors' *Protest Is Not Enough* (1984).

[2] Without intending to diminish in any way the significance of political effort by other groups, we use the term "minority" to refer, for ease of expression, to blacks and Latinos, the subjects of this book. We also do not mean to imply by this shorthand that blacks and Latinos are generally united or have identical goals and interests.

8

REPRESENTATION—WHY IT IS NOT ENOUGH

The goal of representation has been at the center of the struggle for political equality of blacks and Latinos. Viewed from the perspective of their virtual exclusion from city governments in the late 1950s, it must be seen indeed as a striking achievement now to have numbers of minority mayors and councilmembers. As important as representation is, however, it does not guarantee minority interests or minority power. The mere presence of minority people in office does not ensure that they will seek to fulfill a particular vision of minority interests or that they will be able to influence their governments.

To change the direction of city government in the face of opposition requires control of local legislation, programs, spending, governmental structure, and governmental personnel, starting with the city manager, over an extended period of time. This means that blacks and Latinos, if they are to achieve their political goals in any city, have to secure the support of a majority of the city council over a period of years. Thus the key to control of city government in favor of minority interests has to be a *dominant coalition*—that is, minority participation in a coalition that is able to dominate city council and secure repeated re-election. Such a dominant coalition does not have to consist entirely of blacks and Latinos, but it does have to have a strong commitment to their interests if they are to obtain the changes in city government policies that they want.

With only one or even with no minority representatives, a dominant coalition strongly committed to minority interests might still be able to turn a city government around. Conversely, even substantial minority representation—three or four minority members on a council of nine—might have little or no effect if minority members are opposed at every turn by an entrenched and intransigent dominant coalition. Where minority groups fall short of 50 percent of the voting-age population, as they usually do, coalition between the groups and with liberal whites is a possible way to replace a resistant dominant coalition. Thus, representation alone is not enough to control city government, and the formation of biracial and multiracial coalitions takes on great significance in the struggle for political power.

We use the term *political incorporation* to refer to the range of possibilities. At the lower end, we have no minority representation; then some representation, but on a council dominated by a coalition resistant to minority interests; finally—the strongest form of incorporation—an equal or leading role in a dominant coalition that is strongly committed to minority interests. The higher levels of political incorporation are likely to afford substantial influence or control over policy.

TEN CITIES AND A FRAMEWORK FOR ANALYSIS

We have studied the largest cities in the region—San Francisco, San Jose, Oakland, and Sacramento—and a group of smaller cities with substantial black or Latino populations: Berkeley, Stockton, Richmond, Hayward, Daly City, and Vallejo. In

1980 their total populations ranged from 75,000 to 679,000; combined black and Latino populations ranged from 26 percent to 58 percent—large enough in all of these cities to have substantial influence in city politics, if they could unite or form an alliance with liberal whites and other groups. (See Table 1.1 for city by city data on population and other variables.)

Constitutionally, all these cities are in the progressive reform tradition, with nonpartisan elections, city managers, and professional civil service systems. All had at-large elections for city council in the early 1960s, but the larger cities later changed to district elections, typically as part of efforts to secure the representation of minorities. The authority and prominence of the mayor's office is much greater in the larger cities.

What Did Blacks and Latinos Want of City Governments?

First, they wanted to end their exclusion from government and the political process. Specifically, they wanted respect from government, access to it, position in it, and real influence over policies and programs of special interest to them. They wanted to be able to get the attention of city government, to have their concerns taken seriously. They wanted to hold office and to shape city policies and spending priorities.

Second, they wanted a share of the benefits of government and an end to discrimination. They wanted increased minority employment in city government (starting from nearly zero in many cities). They wanted to see minority administrators in top city jobs. They wanted minority businesses to get some of the city's contracts and purchases. If economic development funds were considered, they wanted minority business districts to get a share. They wanted police to stop shooting and beating minority suspects. They wanted low-income housing, parks and recreation programs, police protection, libraries, and health and other services in minority neighborhoods.

They wanted, in short, government that included them and that was responsive to a broad range of deeply felt demands. But because racism was pervasive, not rare; because whites controlled all the functions of city governments and discrimination was accepted practice; because people in power hold onto it and do not willingly give it up, a prolonged struggle would be necessary if minority demands were to be satisfied even partly.

What Form Would the Struggle Take?

Groups pursue political objectives in two ways: they petition government from outside (the interest-group strategy) or they achieve representation and a position of influence inside (the electoral strategy). These are not mutually exclusive approaches, and large groups (such as blacks and Latinos) typically pursue both. Which strategy is dominant in a given setting however, might strongly affect the

TABLE 1.1. MINORITY POPULATION AND REPRESENTATION IN TEN NORTHERN CALIFORNIA CITIES

City	Population, 1980			Electoral system[1] (year of adoption)	City Council					
	Total (1000)	Percent			Size[2]	Percent black and Latino				
		Black	Latino			Mean, 1975–1978		June, 1988		
						Black	Latino	Black	Latino	
San Jose	637	4.6%	22.1%	D (1980)	11	0%	14%	9%	9%	
Hayward	93	5.7	20.2	A-L	7	0	0	14	14	
Stockton	150	10.4	22.1	D (1971)	9	22	11	33	11	
Daly City	79	10.7	19.3	A-L	5	0	0	0	0	
San Francisco	679	12.7	12.3	A-L[3]	11	9	9	18	9	
Sacramento	276	13.4	14.2	D (1971)	9	11	6	0	11	
Vallejo	80	19.1	8.5	A-L	7	0	0	0	0	
Berkeley	103	20.1	5.1	D (1986)	9	38	0	22	0	
Oakland	339	46.9	9.6	D (1981)	9	17	6	55	0	
Richmond	75	47.9	10.3	A-L	7	28	6	57	14	
Mean	251	19.2	14.4			12.4	5.1	19.7	6.8	

[1]A-L, at-large; D, district elections.
[2]Councils include mayors except in San Francisco, where the mayor does not sit on the board of supervisors. Size of council in San Jose was 7 until 1980.
[3]Voters chose district elections in 1977 but reverted to at-large elections in 1980.

success or failure of the effort—the ability of the group to achieve its political objectives.

We can represent a successful interest-group strategy in this way:

Group mobilization	⟶	Demand and protest activity	⟶	Appointments and minority representation	⟶	Governmental responsiveness

The group organizes and produces a substantial amount of demand and protest. The dominant coalition in city government may respond by appointing one or more minority representatives to vacancies as they occur on city council; in any case, the coalition responds positively to some of the group's demands.

A successful electoral strategy may be diagramed as follows:

Group mobilization	⟶	Electoral activity	⟶	Group representation and incorporation	⟶	Governmental responsiveness

In this scenario, the focus is on electoral mobilization. Protest is carried out, but its primary function is to arouse minority populations and their potential supporters, to raise the level of anger and the determination to act. The position in city government achieved by minority officeholders, rather than outside pressure on the city, leads to responsiveness. There is nothing inevitable to these scenarios, however: the coalition in power may be utterly unresponsive to minority demands or electoral effort may lead to no victories and no representation.

By the late 1950s, blacks in several of these California cities already had considerable experience both with electoral mobilization and with moderate forms of protest. Blacks in Berkeley in the 1930s focused on picketing and on increasing black voter turnout to demonstrate opposition to discrimination in public accommodation and employment; black candidates ran organized campaigns for city council, not with the expectation of winning but as a way of registering protest (Nathan and Scott, 1978, p. 10).

With the rapid influx of blacks to work in defense plants during World War II and the continuing migration afterward, their electoral prospects improved. Blacks became active in the state Democratic party and were instrumental in selecting black delegates to the 1948 Democratic convention. In that year as well, the Black Caucus was formed in Berkeley, and W. Byron Rumford became the first black elected to the California State Assembly, from a district of predominantly black neighborhoods in north Oakland and south Berkeley. The Caucus screened and selected black candidates so that multiple candidates would not split the black vote (Nathan and Scott, 1978, p. 133).

As the civil rights movement gathered force in the late 1950s and early 1960s, the electoral strategy in particular was already at least well practiced, if not well established, where leadership and conditions were optimal in parts of the San

Francisco Bay Area. As the movement spread to Bay Area cities generally, it was testing elsewhere the boundaries of the rights of assembly and petition with non-violent protest. These gatherings were peaceful, usually intensely unwanted or forbidden by local authorities, and sometimes disruptive or costly to their targets, such as large-scale marches and rallies, boycotts, and sit-ins. Nonviolent protest became civil disobedience, and organized nonviolent activity was increasingly overshadowed by spontaneous violent protest.

Thus a range of strategies was being acted out by the late 1950s, extending to widespread violence in the mid-1960s. What path would blacks in northern California act upon? Would it be a peaceful path, focused on voter registration and turnout and the recruitment of minority candidates? Would it follow the direction of traditional interest-group effort, concentrating more on articulation of interests and demands than on elections? Would it take the more threatening stance of sometimes violent protest?

The answer was not one path but many, and the movement unfolded in different cities. The dominant effort in a given city was shaped by characteristics of the minority community, of the white population and historical race relationships, and of the local political system and its response to minority mobilization.

The Structure of the Situation

For both white and minority activists, a fundamental political condition was the size of minority populations. Black and Latino populations varied greatly in these cities: in 1970, from a mere 2 percent to 36 percent, and from tiny communities of less than 2000 to groups of more than 100,000.

Both the magnitude of protest and the importance of group voting are contingent on the numbers of people who can be mobilized, but protest and voting factors depend on different aspects of these numbers. The ability to mount large-scale protest depends on the absolute number of people who can be mobilized to demonstrate. In contrast, the ability to mount a powerful electoral challenge depends not on numbers but on the percentage which those numbers constitute of the electorate. In these cities, numbers and percentages of minority populations are not closely related. For instance, San Francisco's large black population in 1970— about 96,000—constituted only 13 percent of the city's population, somewhat less of the voting-age population; but Richmond's 29,000 blacks were a potent 36 percent of its population. So minority groups in these cities varied with respect not only to their basic population resources but also to the extent to which those resources equipped them for protest or for electoral mobilization, for neither, or for both.

As minority populations increased in the post–World War II era, so too the partisan balance in these cities was shifting. Democratic voter registration was increasing rapidly. By 1962, it ranged from 53 percent to 73 percent of registered voters, but Republicans still constituted majorities on half of these city councils. At the same time as the civil rights movement was gaining momentum, Democrats in these cities were moving to capitalize on Democratic majorities among voters. For Democrats, the task was to mobilize Democratic voters to replace Republicans; blacks and Latinos were likely sources of such support. For blacks and Latinos, the task was to mobilize minority voters, liberal whites, and others to replace all-white, conservative coalitions that had no intention of responding positively to minority demands; racially liberal whites were likely to come from the ranks of Democrats.

These tasks were related but not identical. They were not identical because many Democrats were not sufficiently liberal on the racial, social, and economic issues important to blacks and Latinos to support a minority-oriented coalition. Even those who were willing to accede to some minority demands often preferred not to share leadership with minority leaders. The extent to which white Democrats were eager or willing to work closely and cooperatively with blacks and Latinos varied.

As black mobilization intensified, local political leaders faced quite different structures of political opportunities and problems. In addition to group size and ideological commitment, what especially affected the responses of white politicians to minority mobilization was the extent to which they depended on minority support. In San Francisco, for example, Democrats had already won the mayor's office before the first concerted black protest campaign in 1964. In Sacramento, in contrast, blacks and Latinos were increasingly well organized and outspoken at the time that liberal whites sought to form a challenging electoral coalition. A Democratic mayor who had already demonstrated his ability to win an election without making major, long-term concessions to minority supporters, as in San Francisco, was in a much stronger position to resist fundamental commitments than a potential mayoral candidate who believed he needed the active support of vocal and strongly organized minority groups in order to win office in the first place, as in Sacramento.

Both the ideological commitments of liberal activists and the structure of the situations in which they sought control of city government powerfully shaped their incentives to actively seek minority support and to make significant concessions in order to get it.

PATTERNS OF MINORITY MOBILIZATION

We can summarize the evolution of the movement in these ten cities by describing minority initiatives and white responses that had various consequences, ranging from continued exclusion of minorities from city government to some form of inclusion in a governing coalition, often in a subordinate role, occasionally in an equal or dominant role.

Demand–Protest

The pattern of minority mobilization in a given city was indeed very strongly shaped by the nature of the fundamental resource of group size, but was shaped also by the extent of political support from white liberals. Where black or Latino populations were large in an absolute sense, intense, sustained demand and protest activity developed. Figure 1.1 shows the very close relationship between population size and level of black demand–protest mobilization.

The measure of demand–protest was constructed from ratings by well-informed observers and participants and from contemporaneous accounts in the media. (See Browning et al., 1984, Appendix C.) At the high end of the scale, both San Francisco and Oakland experienced substantial racially related rioting and other violence, in addition to organized and persistent pressure on city government, including rallies, marches, sit-ins, picketing, and numerous dramatic and successful efforts to focus media attention on issues. At the low end of the scale, local minority groups generated some demand activity, such as meetings with city officials to request their consideration of problems, but typically not enough activity to get into the media.

Although the relationship between black population and level of black demand–protest is very close, this correlation does not mean that size of black population was the only factor involved in the production of intense demand–

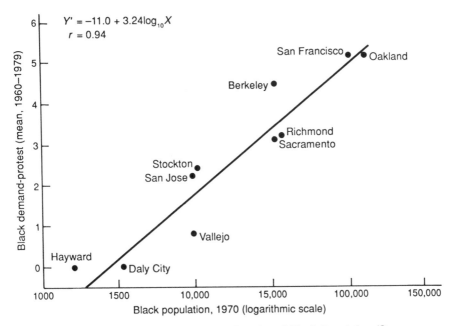

Figure 1.1. Black Demand–Protest as a Function of Black Population (Source: Rufus P. Browning, Dale R. Marshall, and David H. Tabb, *Protest Is Not Enough*. Berkeley: University of California Press, 1985 [Reprint], p. 88.) This scale is based on informants' rating of the level of minority demand-protest directed at city hall and on the reconstruction of events from interviews, newspapers, and other published sources. Ratings for each year were combined, then the combined ratings were averaged over the twenty years 1969–1970.

protest. Cities with large black populations were also large cities, and organizers gravitated to them with size of city and the availability of media attention in mind. A very large, vociferous rally in San Francisco, with clever arrangements to involve the mayor as the target of demands, would almost certainly hit the San Francisco media, would be distributed throughout the greater Bay Area, and would stand a chance of making the national media. Events in the larger cities were intrinsically more interesting to the media.

The impact of liberal support may be seen in the pattern of cities above and below the regression line that summarizes the relationship. In cities below the line, where blacks generated less demand–protest than we would predict on the basis of black population alone, liberal support for black interests was typically noticeably lower than in cities that had greater than predicted black demand–protest. White hostility to black political interests typically diminished demand–protest; liberal support encouraged it, no doubt by raising expectations that demand–protest would be effective.

Electoral Mobilization

The electoral mobilization of black populations was shaped by a different calculus of resources and opportunities. Numbers generate massive protest, but percentages win elections. And because black and Latino populations in all of these cities fell well short of electoral majorities in 1960 and 1970, electoral victory depended on the support of liberal whites. The most successful electoral efforts therefore always involved the creation of cohesive electoral coalitions of blacks and whites, some-times with Latinos as well. Such coalitions formed slates of candidates, carefully recruiting and controlling the number of minority and white candidates so as not to split the minority vote, developed common platforms, shared funds, and organized common publicity and canvassing; sometimes they established continuing citywide, partylike organizations.

In the often tense atmosphere of minority protest in the 1960s and 1970s, conditions did not always permit formation of such coalitions. Nevertheless, the extent of coalition formation efforts by blacks was strongly shaped by the combina-tion of black population and liberal support (by whites, Latinos, and other groups). Figure 1.2 shows the relationship. The percentage of black population and the percentage of liberal support are represented by their product on the horizontal axis of Figure 1.2 because their effects on coalition formation were interdependent. An example makes this clear. Consider a black population that made up 25 percent of a city's electorate. With no liberal support for black candidates, that 25 percent could not elect sufficient councilmembers to control city government. In this situation, blacks had little incentive to expend a great deal of energy in a futile effort to contest elections. On the other hand, if liberals other than blacks also constituted 25 percent of the electorate, both groups stood an excellent chance of winning control of city council, if they could unite around a common slate of candidates. In that situation, the incentive to organize a cohesive biracial slate and to establish partylike control

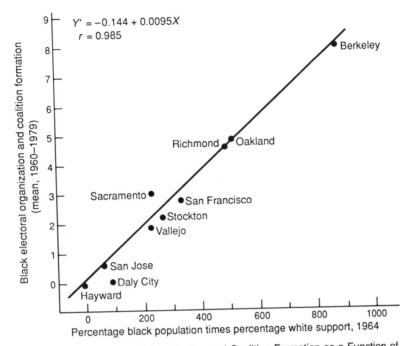

Figure 1.2. Black Electoral Organization and Coalition Formation as a Function of Black Population and Liberal Support (Source: Browning, Marshall, and Tabb [1984], p. 100.) Key to electoral mobilization/coalition formation scale: 8-black leaders conduct centralized recruitment of black candidates on bi/multiracial coalition slates; 6-coalition formation: negotiations between black and white organizations over black candidates on coalition slates; 4-recruitment and endorsement of black candidates by black organizations, no bi/multiracial coalition; 2-endorsements of black candidates by black organizations; 0-occasional black candidates run without significant endorsements.

over minority candidacies was very strong. Thus, the impact of both black population and liberal support depended on the level of the other factor.

In those cities where blacks and liberals together accounted for nearly half, or more than half, of the electorate—Berkeley, Oakland, and Richmond—blacks did indeed consistently take the long step from recruitment and endorsement of black candidates to negotiations with white activists over the formation of biracial coalitions.

Latino Mobilization

Latinos also mobilized in many cities, but typically less vigorously than blacks. For many reasons, Latino mobilization not only occurred later, for the most part, but was also usually not so unified, so well organized, or so intensely pursued. Latinos, more recent arrivals in these cities, are on average better off than blacks. In some cities, they are culturally and politically fragmented into several nationality groups

(Central and South Americans as well as Mexican Americans). Significant numbers are not citizens. Some consider themselves culturally but not racially different from whites and are therefore less inclined to insist on an autonomous group political role. The political experience of Mexican Americans in particular may predispose them not to turn to government for solutions to problems. Finally, Latinos are more evenly distributed in these cities than blacks are (see Table 1.1), probably because housing discrimination is not so intense for Latinos as for blacks, but concentrating a group's population in a few cities is politically advantageous in those cities.

Latino mobilization, because it came later and because black mobilization was already under way, also depended on black mobilization to some extent. In particular, in a given city, the occurrence of black demand–protest tended to stimulate Latino demand–protest. And just as black coalition formation depended on the presence of liberals (including Latinos), the ability of Latinos to participate in electoral coalitions was contingent on the presence of sizable black populations.

PATTERNS OF COALITION AND POLITICAL INCORPORATION

From minority mobilization, four qualitatively different patterns of coalition and levels of incorporation emerged. In ascending order, these were

- Weak mobilization and exclusion
- Protest and exclusion
- Co-optation and partial incorporation
- Biracial electoral alliance and strong incorporation

Weak Mobilization and Exclusion

Minority mobilization was weak in three cities: Vallejo, Daly City, and Hayward. They appear in the lower left quadrant of Figure 1.3, which shows combinations of coalition formation and incorporation for blacks. These cities lacked the conditions of minority-population size and liberal backing to support either strong demand–protest or the formation of a successful challenging coalition. Vallejo's black population, for example, is about as large in percentage terms as Berkeley's, and its Latino population is slightly larger. But Vallejo's white population is largely blue collar and, on a measure of support for black interests in 1964, only 16 percent supportive compared with Berkeley's 46 percent. In spite of some electoral effort, therefore, no liberal, multiracial coalition formed, and blacks won election to city council only occasionally. Consequently, very little was achieved in the way of minority representation and political power. Vallejo and Daly City had no minority representation in 1988 (Table 1.1).

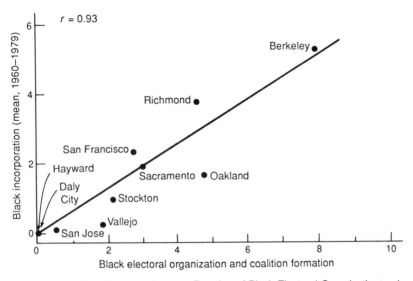

Figure 1.3. Black Incorporation as a Function of Black Electoral Organization and Coalition Formation (Source: Browning, Marshall, and Tabb [1984], p. 119.) Key to political incorporation scale: very strong (6 +)-black mayor leads and blacks hold an equal or dominant place in a cohesive liberal dominant coalition; moderately strong (3-5)-blacks participate in a liberal dominant coalition led by a white mayor, blacks do not dominate it or it is loose; weak (2)-blacks are represented in city council but not in conservative dominant coalition; very weak (0)-no black representation on city council.

Protest and Exclusion

In three other cities—Stockton, Oakland until 1977, and sometimes San Jose—blacks and Latinos generated substantial protest and some electoral mobilization, but these efforts were thwarted by a tenacious dominant coalition that did not include minority group members and largely ignored minority demands.

The histories of these cities are quite different, but they attest to the importance of leadership and the difficulty of overcoming rivalry and fragmentation among potential allies. Blacks in Oakland might have been able to form an alliance with Latinos and liberal whites and take control of city government years before they did, but they were badly split. The unusual intensity of protest in Oakland and the extreme militance and violence of the Black Panther Party in that city disrupted and postponed the unity among blacks and between blacks and whites that was necessary for a successful challenge to the conservative dominant coalition. The Panthers pursued an increasingly moderate electoral strategy in the 1970s, finally participating in an uneasy alliance that elected Lionel Wilson mayor. Wilson was a black, moderate judge who had been the chairman of the city's first antipoverty board.

In San Jose, a coalition of minorities and liberal whites formed around Mayor Norman Mineta, but when Mineta ran successfully for Congress, city hall was retaken by a group less sympathetic to minority concerns.

In Stockton, a successful initiative led to the adoption of district elections, which in turn permitted the election of three minority councilmembers. However, the leadership that conducted the district-elections campaign was not re-created in the subsequent electoral and city council process, and minority groups and liberal whites were unable to form a viable challenging coalition.

All of these are cases in which some of the fundamental resources for a minority-oriented coalition were present—in particular, sufficient numbers of minority population and liberal supporters—but coalitions did not form or could not be sustained because of conflict among potential partners or lack of unifying leadership.

Co-optation and Partial Incorporation

This pattern characterized San Francisco, Sacramento, Richmond, and San Jose during Mineta's administration. In these cities, more or less liberal coalitions under white leadership made significant commitments to minorities in response to minority protest in the sixties. The degree of commitment and the motivation for it varied.

San Francisco had experienced increasingly militant minority mobilization, including marches, boycotts, and picketing, and a riot in the Hunters Point district. Mayor Joseph Alioto won election in 1967 by assembling a diverse coalition of minorities, labor, and business, defeating both a Republican opponent and a more liberal Democrat. In an effort to convert some of the demands emanating from highly factionalized black and Latino leadership into electoral support and to fend off further protest, Alioto promised jobs and programs in both Latino and black areas of the city (Kramer, 1969, pp. 251–252). Although some major programs with significant collective benefit were carried out, in particular the redevelopment of Hunters Point, they were often better arranged to reward and co-opt supporters and split the opposition than to achieve lasting benefits. The mayor used federal programs, appointments, contracts, and other benefits not to unify minority leadership but to keep blacks and Latinos fighting among themselves and with each other. The policy of establishing programs separate from the regular departments of city government often served to insulate these departments from minority demands rather than to institutionalize minority interests.

Whereas by the mid-sixties minority activists had achieved some political cohesion in their opposition to city hall, Alioto's strategy induced many of them to become entangled in program administration and in competition for funds and jobs rather than in the building of a strong minority presence in a governing coalition. Once they had program jobs themselves and had come to rely on program funds to reward their own supporters, Alioto made it clear to them that continued support of his administration was the price of continued funding. Alioto's strategy was classic co-optation, pursued with the temporary resources of federal funds rather than with the permanent control over regular city jobs that supported political machines in some eastern cities. There were gains for minorities in this policy, in jobs and other benefits, but the commitment to blacks and Latinos was less broad and less well institutionalized in some respects in San Francisco than in other cities with minority and liberal populations of similar size.

The process in Richmond was different but also co-optive. Richmond is a small city with small-city expectations. In the reform tradition, the mayor is the chair of the city council, and the city manager is the chief executive. A liberal Democratic coalition with no blacks on its slate won control of city council in 1963 and appointed a liberal city manager. Under his leadership, city staff worked in the late 1960s to obtain federal Model Cities money and to bring moderate blacks into active roles in the Model Cities program—a good thing to do in itself and a good way of separating moderates from militants, reducing support for protest, and perhaps reducing the impetus for vigorous electoral mobilization. A clearly defined liberal biracial coalition did not form. Subsequently, Richmond's black population continued to grow, and blacks are now a majority of the city council as well as of the electorate.

In Sacramento, white activists were organizing a liberal electoral challenge simultaneously with peak minority demand–protest in the late sixties. Sacramento's minority population is modest and about evenly divided between blacks and Latinos. The coalition formed under white leadership included minority leaders: the coalition's slate included one black and one Latino candidate. It also made explicit commitments to minority interests, channeling funds to improvements in minority neighborhoods, aggressively increasing minority employment in city government, and instituting other programs. Although minorities were not entirely equal partners in this coalition—for example, the coalition's candidates for mayor have always been whites—they have had a solid place in it, perhaps proportional to their size, and the coalition's commitments to minority interests have continued in periods when there were no blacks on city council. The coalition has promoted, not undermined, the cohesiveness of minority leadership. This pattern stands in contrast to the San Francisco experience, where city politics aims more to manage, and manipulate, diverse, fragmented groups than to create and maintain coherent coalitions.

In the four cities in this group, white responses to minority mobilization began as co-optations but with different structures of opportunity, different degrees of commitment to minority interests, and different evolutionary paths. In Sacramento, where liberals and minorities were mutually dependent in their effort to overturn a dominant conservative coalition, the co-optive initiative has matured into a long-lasting multiracial coalition.

Biracial Electoral Alliance and Strong Incorporation

As noted earlier, Berkeley's black population was already protesting and running candidates in the 1930s. When a group of idealistic Democrats inspired by Adlai Stevenson's presidential campaign in 1952 began to talk of mounting a political effort in Berkeley, both their ideological commitments and the realities of the situation led them to join forces with black leaders, and in 1955 the biracial Berkeley Democratic Caucus was established. Like a party, the caucus screened and limited the number of liberal candidates, both black and white; its leaders were committed to the ideal of racial integration, and white and black leaders agreed to accept each other's candidates for a common slate. An effective coalition had been formed, based on the premise of equal partnership rather than white leadership. In 1961, after 6 years of competing in elections, this coalition succeeded in capturing a majority of city council and in electing the first black councilmember in any of these cities. By 1964, Berkeley voters registered much stronger support for black concerns than voters in any other of these cities. By 1969 three blacks sat on the council. By 1980 the mayor, the city manager, and a high proportion of department heads were black.

The early integration of blacks into Berkeley city government meant that they were already part of the power structure when black protest swept across the country in the second half of the sixties. Consequently, protest by blacks in Berkeley did not come so close to the edge of violence as it did in other cities.

In Oakland also a biracial challenging coalition eventually formed and won control of city council in 1977, after delay brought about by the intensity of racial conflict and the split of black electoral mobilization between the Black Panther Party and moderates. Blacks were appointed to the city manager's post and many other high administrative and commission positions, and the coalition effectively controlled city government.

Did Coalition Formation Produce Incorporation?

To summarize the achievement of political incorporation and its relationship to electoral organization and demand–protest, we have developed a scale of incorporation that captures not only representation in the sense of officeholding but also the strength of the group's position in dominant coalitions. Figure 1.3 shows the relationship of this measure, for blacks, to black electoral organization; however, because black electoral organization responded so precisely to the resources of black population and liberal support, the graph really shows the relationship to those factors as well as to black electoral effort. The graph steps back from the city-by-city patterns we have described in this section to examine the relationship between initial fundamental conditions and mobilization efforts, on the one hand, and the results in terms of minority political strength in city government, on the other.

Figure 1.3 shows that the strength of black political incorporation, on the average in the years 1960 to 1979, was closely related to the extent of biracial coalition formation and the resources that supported that effort. On the average, and with variations due to other local factors, *fundamental resources of black population and liberal support approaching majorities did lead to the formation of biracial or multiracial electoral coalitions. In turn, these coalition efforts did produce proportional gains in black political incorporation, and the strongest political positions were achieved only with cohesive coalitions. Electoral mobilization of this kind was the key to strong political incorporation.*

It is also clear from Figure 1.3, however, that local conditions could delay or thwart incorporation, even where some of these fundamental resources were favorable and there was effort, as in Oakland and Vallejo.

Did Demand–Protest Also Produce Incorporation?

In spite of the appointment of black councilmembers in some cities in response to black protest, the average net effect of demand–protest on black incorporation was negligible. For Latinos, the picture was somewhat different. Remember that Latinos constituted smaller proportions of the population than blacks in these cities, in part because the Latino population was more evenly distributed and was inversely related to black population. A consequence was that Latino electoral effort was likely to be less determining. Analysis showed that Latinos got more of their representation in the years 1960 to 1979 by appointment in response to Latino demand–protest than from autonomous electoral effort. This result was typically less desirable than officeholding generated by the group's own effort, because the appointer would appoint to maximize his or her own interests rather than the interests of the group. (On the other hand, some minority officeholders who arose out of an autonomous electoral process were also not strong representatives of their groups.) The strength of the Latino presence in city government depended also to some extent on the strength of black incorporation; Latinos tended to be stronger where blacks were stronger.

In summary, the minority mobilization movement was an engine that ran everywhere on the available fuel of minority population and liberal support; the demand–protest or electoral mobilization (coalition formation) it generated corresponded to the resources available. Where the elements of support for the movement could be held together and applied to the political tasks at hand, mobilization was intense and sustained. The task was more difficult where minority populations were divided between blacks and Latinos or within each group, and both minority and white leadership and the dynamic of their interaction determined whether those divisions were overcome or exploited. Although demand–protest produced some significant victories for both blacks and Latinos, blacks especially achieved much greater long-term political incorporation through coalition formation and associated electoral effort and officeholding. Of the two scenarios diagrammed in the first section of this chapter, the electoral strategy was by far the most effective: electoral mobilization and coalition formation ultimately determined the ability of minority groups to reshape city government.

DID MINORITY INCORPORATION MAKE CITY GOVERNMENTS MORE RESPONSIVE?

Some commentators have answered this question in the negative, arguing that the protest of the sixties and a few black and Latino officeholders in the seventies did not really make much difference in what city governments did. Cities are, after all, severely constrained by economic pressures and by the limits and mandates of federal and state governments (Peterson, 1981). The politics of city governments are also strongly influenced by a formidable array of local forces, including the rules and operating procedures established by bureaucrats (Levy et al., 1974; Lineberry, 1977). Under such limitations, how can we expect demonstrations, the efforts of a few minority officeholders, or even a change of dominant coalitions to have much impact?

The simple—and true—answer is that minority incorporation did make city governments more responsive, and Figure 1.4 provides a simple demonstration. Here we have taken the averages of city government responses to minority demands in four key areas: establishment of civilian police review boards, appointment of minority members to city boards and commissions, provisions for minority shares of city contracts, and minority employment in city government. Figure 1.4 shows a close relationship between these average responsiveness values and black political incorporation. City governments in which blacks had achieved strong incorporation

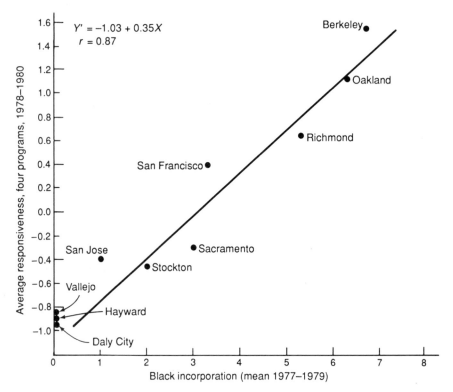

Figure 1.4. Average Responsiveness as a Function of Black Incorporation (Source: Browning, Marshall, and Tabb [1984], p. 166.) This measure is constructed by calculating the standard scores of measures of city government responsiveness in four policy areas: minority employment, police review boards, minority representation on commissions, and contracting with minority businesses. The measure is the mean of the four standard scores; its mean is 0, and its units are standard deviations.

were more responsive on this measure, and, for the most part, only such governments were responsive.

The lesser but still significant effects of black and Latino demand–protest and of Latino incorporation can also be read from individual cities in Figure 1.4. San Jose was more responsive than predicted on the basis of black incorporation alone because of the vigorous demand–protest efforts by its large Latino population; San Francisco, because of both black and Latino demand–protest.

At its strongest, the governmental response to minority interests extended across the programs and agencies of city government and permeated routine decision making and service delivery. At its weakest, the response was sporadic, halfhearted, undertaken only under duress, and limited to verbal assurance and an occasional, isolated action.

Across a wide range of issues and routine actions that never became issues, the responsive governments were pervasively different. Economic development funds were channeled to minority business districts. Senior centers were deliberately located in minority neighborhoods, which were also beneficiaries of programs for street tree planting, sidewalk repairs, and the undergrounding of utility lines and poles. City-supported and minority-oriented health services were located in minority neighborhoods, such as sickle-cell anemia and blood-pressure control programs. Major parks were developed or improved in minority districts. Support was given to dozens of community-based organizations that offered employment, health, educational, social, and cultural services to residents. Even city libraries developed responsive programs, such as the tool-lending office behind the South Berkeley Branch, where residents of low-income neighborhoods were able to borrow tools for nothing or at modest cost. Major city projects such as housing and redevelopment were developed with minority participation in the more responsive cities.

Although the picture was uneven from city to city, it is clear that demand–protest produced some responsiveness and that strong incorporation, as in Berkeley and later in Oakland, could produce across-the-board change at the highest levels of city government and significant changes in the allocation of neighborhood improvements; the prevention of unwanted change in minority neighborhoods; the provision of new social services; the redistribution and reorientation of traditional city services, including police; and minority employment. Where minority incorporation was less potent, substantial gains were made in at least some of these areas.

The presence of minorities on councils changed decision making to include minority people as a matter of course and sensitized whites to minority concerns. Blacks and Latinos talked about how different it was to be "on the inside," to attend council meetings and see minority representatives on the council, and to be able to call them on the telephone. Councilmembers talked about a new atmosphere and new pressure on the council once minorities were members. As one city official said, "When minorities talk to the city council now, councilmembers nod their heads in agreement rather than yawn."

Measured by the standards of the dream of integration and an end to poverty, these gains still fall short. They were nevertheless of enormous importance to minority people and dramatically different from what had gone before.

155,020

SINCE 1980: BACKSLIDING, STAGNATION, OR PROGRESS?

The account to this point of the fruits of minority mobilization in ten northern California cities applies to the period 1960 to 1979. It reflects conditions that shaped local responses to an extraordinary chain of national forces: the eruption of the civil rights movement into protest and the black power movement; the special conditions and legislative outpouring of Lyndon Johnson's presidency; rapid, sustained growth of real income and governmental revenue during the 1960s; the readiness of some whites to support the political incorporation of blacks and Latinos.

How have blacks and Latinos fared in these cities in the 1980s, when so many of the fundamental conditions have changed? Many developments have threatened minority incorporation and policy responsiveness: the decline and confusion of the inheritors of the civil rights movement, the growth of opposition to government spending and taxation and minority-oriented programs, and the relatively hostile stance of the Reagan administration toward minorities and cities. Are the political achievements of the movement being undermined and reversed in these cities?

Representation

Minority representation has continued to advance (Table 1.1). Average black representation on councils, in percentage terms, was in 1988 equal to average percent black population in 1980. In the period from 1975–1978 to 1988, blacks increased their representation by more than half and won additional council seats in San Jose, Hayward, Stockton, San Francisco, Oakland, and Richmond; Oakland's mayor is black, and Oakland and Richmond have black majorities on city council. There were also losses in this period. The mayor's office in Berkeley, which was held by two successive black mayors in the seventies and eighties, was won by a white woman in 1987, and council seats held by blacks have been lost in Berkeley and Sacramento (where a black councilmember ran successfully for county board of supervisors, as in Vallejo). In 1988, blacks sat on city councils in seven of the ten cities.

Latino representation has increased slightly. Latinos hold no mayoral offices but are found on six city councils. Average Latino representation (6.8 percent) is about half of average Latino population as of 1980.

Coalitions, Incorporation, and Responsiveness

In several cities, dominant coalitions were by 1988 perceptibly more liberal than in 1980, including San Jose, where a black woman is a councilmember and vice mayor, and Vallejo, where the minority presence is still weak and an effective biracial or multiracial coalition has yet to form.

The stronger biracial and multiracial coalitions are intact, although they are typically not so cohesive as they were. Coalitions between groups depend on some combination of similarity of interests and exchange of support for each other's separate goals. Many of the central issues of city government have changed considerably since the 1960s, with sometimes adverse consequences both for the unity of minority–liberal coalitions and for the capacity of city governments to respond to minority interests. Shifts in issues stemmed from the rise of other claimant groups (women, gays, environmentalists) and the leveling off or decline in city revenue, the consequences of the state antitax movement—which in California succeeded in passing Proposition 13 in 1978, sharply reducing local property tax revenue—and of the severe drop in federal funding to cities.

The dramatic decline in federal funding for community-based programs forced liberal coalitions in power to drop many minority-oriented programs, saving and improving only the strongest. The shift in funding also compelled a shift in agenda. If federal funding was not available and the ability of California cities to increase their own revenue had been sharply limited, what could cities do for their minority populations? In the 1980s, minority-oriented coalitions typically focused on job creation for minorities. Mayors and councils argued for increased downtown development in order to generate jobs for minorities. This occurred both in cities where blacks were in the majority, such as Oakland and Richmond, and in cities such as San Francisco and San Jose, with coalitions dominated by white liberals.

Economic development is of course not a new strategy for city governments, nor does it benefit only minorities. What was new was that economic development became a principal strategy of minority-oriented coalitions. Revenue constraints enacted at both federal and state levels compelled these coalitions to embrace the classic development policy of vigorous city governments generally. What was different about their implementation of development was the extent to which they extracted commitments for minority business participation and minority hiring from developers.

In several cities conflict has arisen within minority groups over the direction of development activity. Older minority leaders, often aligned with city employees, stress the need for downtown economic development as well as aggressive efforts to implement city affirmative action plans. Following an earlier lead of the dominant coalition in Berkeley, younger dissidents in Oakland and San Francisco have sought to build new multiracial coalitions that emphasize neighborhood community development and affordable housing rather than downtown development (Deleon and Powell, 1989). Except in Berkeley, however, these efforts have not been successful at the polls.

Minority-oriented coalitions that support downtown development have also been weakened by the rise of groups concerned with gender, gay, and environmental issues; such groups have generally favored slower growth. In Sacramento, for example, disagreements have surfaced between these groups and the older liberal coalition over the implementation of affirmative action programs and the focus on downtown development. The older alliance has claimed that recent affirmative action effort has favored white women at the expense of minority hires, and criticizes a lack of commitment of those they call "nouveau yuppies" to the creation of jobs for the minority labor force.

Coalitions have tried to manage conflicts among these claimants, sometimes successfully. In Sacramento, for instance, labor and ethnic groups have been brought together with environmentalists to work for the enforcement of the minority hiring provisions of state environmental law. Temporary alliances have also been developed in San Francisco over issues of land-use planning. The consequences of historical coalitional patterns emerge in this phase: in San Francisco, whites have historically taken the lead in the management of issues to create and sustain coalitions; now blacks and Latinos tend to lack coalitional-issue management skills.

The management of issues is crucial to the formation and maintenance of coalitions. How issue management shapes the survival of multiracial coalitions is skillfully developed and elaborated by Raphael Sonenshein in Chapter 11 of this volume.

In these changing circumstances, cities with strong minority incorporation still accord minority interests substantially higher priority. When cutting expenditures and generating new revenue, they attempt to minimize negative impact on minorities. When negotiating for major development, they build in strong requirements for minority contracting and employment. Berkeley continues to devote resources to the renewal of a minority business district; several cities have moved to create more low-income housing. Commitments to affirmative action in city government employment typically remain in place.

Despite these programs, there is no denying the fiscally strained circumstances of California cities in the 1980s. Prenatal and community health clinics that provided significant services to low-income minority populations have been closed with the termination of federal and state funding, and it has not always been possible to find other resources to keep them open. Homelessness, a problem not only for minorities, has grown much more rapidly than funds to alleviate it.

The legacy of decades of minority mobilization is the realization of their right to participate in the governance of cities. It is also the institutionalization of their interests and more responsive policy than would otherwise be the case, under much tougher revenue constraints. The earlier goals of equity and redistribution of resources have not disappeared, and they continue to shape the responses of most of these cities to their new problems and diminished shares of both federal funds and local taxes.

The political resources of blacks and Latinos remain unevenly distributed; governmental commitment to their interests therefore varies considerably from city to city. Nevertheless, undeniable gains have been made in most cities and certainly in the largest ones, where most of the minority population lives. Successful protest, governmental sensitivity to minority interests, officeholding, participating in coalitions, and governance were once unheard of but are now common indications of political equality. The impact of racial discrimination on city government employment, contracting, and services has been greatly reduced.

To be sure, racism is still a potent force that finds frequent expression, and the list of painful and intractable problems experienced disproportionately by minority groups remains long. Unemployment, poverty, welfare dependency, drug abuse, and crime are conditions that were on the policy agenda in the 1960s, and they remain there.

QUESTIONS FOR OTHER CITIES

The assessment of minority mobilization and incorporation in ten northern California cities that we have presented in this chapter constitutes a set of hypotheses or questions about the minority movement in other cities in the United States.

Variation and Explanation

Do the same conditions and resources explain differences between other cities as they do between these ten cities? Did the same patterns of minority population and liberal support produce similar levels of minority incorporation, or were other factors at work—other barriers or other advantages that produced different results in similar circumstances?

Strategy and Its Results

Is the relationship of strategy and outcome the same as it was in northern California? Is the formation of biracial and multiracial coalitions the key to strong incorporation and to governmental responsiveness elsewhere?

Progress and Its Limits

Were the same kinds and degrees of progress toward political equality and the reduction of discrimination in city government achieved? Do we find the same levels—and limits—of mobilization, incorporation, and responsiveness in other cities? Did minority populations of similar size achieve the same gains as in the ten California cities?

Beyond questions of similarity and tests of the descriptive theory lie questions of value and tests against a normative standard. We have argued that protest alone is not enough and that even representation is not enough. We have also argued that the gains of political incorporation and policy responsiveness achieved in the California cities were genuine and substantial. Compared with what went before, they were indeed substantial. But we must still ask whether those gains, and similar achievements in other cities, are enough—whether they meet, or promise to meet, the goals that minority mobilization efforts set out to achieve. Despite our positive assessment of the California cities, we have not addressed this question. In their studies of other cities, some of the authors in this book do address this issue, and we will come back to it in the concluding chapter.

REFERENCES

Browning, Rufus P., Dale R. Marshall, and David H. Tabb. 1984. *Protest Is Not Enough*. Berkeley: University of California Press.

DeLeon, Richard E. and Sandra S. Powell. 1989. Growth Control and Electoral Politics: The Triumph of Urban Populism in San Francisco. *Western Political Quarterly* 42 (2, June): 307–331.

Kramer, Ralph M. 1969. *Participation of the Poor: Comparative Case Studies in the War on Poverty*. Englewood Cliffs, N.J.: Prentice-Hall.

Levy, Frank, Arnold Meltsner, and Aaron Wildavsky. 1974. *Urban Outcomes*. Berkeley: University of California Press.

Lineberry, Robert L. 1977. *Equality and Urban Policy: The Distribution of Municipal Public Services*. Beverly Hills, Calif.: Sage.

Nathan, Harriet, and Stanley Scott, eds. 1978. *Experiment and Change in Berkeley*. Berkeley: Institute of Governmental Studies, University of California.

Peterson, Paul E. 1981. *City Limits*. Chicago: University of Chicago Press.

PART II

Successes

CHAPTER 2

Biracial Coalition Politics in Los Angeles

Raphael J. Sonenshein

Editors' Note

In Los Angeles, the second largest city in the United States, blacks constitute only 17 percent of the population (see Table 12.1). Yet Los Angeles elected a black mayor, Tom Bradley, in 1973, and has reelected him three times. How is that success possible when blacks constitute such a small proportion of the population? Why are blacks so much stronger in Los Angeles than we would expect? Why are Latinos, who significantly outnumber blacks, significantly weaker?

In this chapter Raphael J. Sonenshein argues that a carefully constructed coalition of liberal whites, particularly Jews, with blacks was the key. Putting together and maintaining a coalition in which blacks are a minority yet the leading figure is black is surely a difficult feat. What special conditions and special arts of political leadership account for it in Los Angeles?

Even when a coalition takes over city government, the conditions and context of its success may limit policy change. Is it possible for a substantial but still relatively small group of blacks to make city government highly responsive to their interests? In nonpartisan Los Angeles there are no party machines to stand in the way of a liberal coalition. Do other requirements of coalition limit the policy and organizational options of the winning coalition? Sonenshein discusses the problems of maintaining a biracial coalition as new issues emerge and new groups mobilize. How can a coalition of

33

> blacks and liberal whites, including many Jews, remain unified
> when a prominent Black Muslim publicly criticizes Jews as a
> group? As rapidly growing Asian and Latino groups push for
> political power, how can blacks maintain their own influence? Can
> a biracial coalition transform itself into a multiracial or rainbow
> coalition? If it cannot, defeat at the polls and the ascendancy of a
> coalition less responsive to minority concerns are likely.

In their 1984 book *Protest Is Not Enough*, Browning, Marshall, and Tabb suggested that biracial coalitions are powerful vehicles for achieving minority incorporation in the political life of cities. Their optimistic view of biracial and multiracial coalitions contrasts strikingly with the more common pessimism about cross-racial politics. Racial polarization in such major cities as New York City and Chicago (as well as in a number of medium- and smaller-sized cities) has fed the belief that the black protests and white backlash of the 1960s doomed biracial politics.

In this light, the success of biracial coalition politics in Los Angeles is extremely significant. In Los Angeles, the urban center of traditionally conservative Southern California, a small black community has won a major share of political power through membership in a biracial coalition with white liberals. Latinos, who significantly outnumber blacks in the city, have been junior partners in the coalition and have been less successful than blacks in winning political incorporation. The Los Angeles case illustrates the potential of coalitions between blacks and white liberals, but also shows some of the obstacles to the creation of "rainbow coalitions" composed of blacks, white liberals, Latinos and other minority groups. Recent strains within the dominant liberal coalition also suggest that even a successful biracial alliance cannot easily surmount the tensions that inevitably characterize the politics of interracial coalitions.

BACKGROUND

Los Angeles is the prototype of the newer western city. Its expansion began in the 1880s and continued well beyond World War II, as its population rank among cities rose from 135th in 1880 to second in 1982. Los Angeles has grown another 10 percent in the 1980s. During the period of the city's greatest growth, Los Angeles was dominated by white Protestant migrants from the Midwest who hoped to create an urban model of the heartland life-style (Fogelson, 1967). Their explicit intention was to avoid the political "fate" of the big eastern and midwestern cities, dominated by Catholic immigrants, labor unions, and minority groups.

Midwestern values helped create and sustain the nonpartisanship of California cities. In both formal structure and actual practice Los Angeles has been a strongly nonpartisan city (Adrian, 1959). As a result, party organizations have been virtually nonexistent. Despite a clear majority in party registration, Democrats failed for many years to take over city hall (Mayo, 1964; Carney, 1964) until the rise of the liberal coalition in the early 1970s.[1]

The homogeneous community ideal of the midwesterners' new city implicitly excluded such minority groups as blacks, Jews, Mexicans, and Japanese. However, the steady migration of minorities into Los Angeles before and after World War II slowly eroded the predominance of whites. Until the 1980 census, whites were a majority of the city's population. By 1980, whites made up only 47.8 percent of the city's nearly 3 million people. The second largest group was Latinos, 27.5 percent of the city; blacks represented only 16.7 percent as can be seen in the following list:

1980 City Population (Percent)

Whites	1,419,413	(47.8)
Latinos	816,076	(27.5)
Blacks	495,723	(16.7)
Asians	235,638	(7.9)

Jews (included in the white category by the Census Bureau) are an important and distinctive group in the city, representing about 7 percent of the population. Highly mobilized, Jews composed an estimated 15 percent of the local electorate in 1973 (Halley, 1974). A 1979 survey of Los Angeles area Jews showed that 89 percent were registered to vote. They were also heavily Democratic and liberal. Nearly 80 percent were Democrats, 41 percent were liberals, 5 percent were radicals, and only 16 percent were conservatives (Beyette, 1979; Sandberg, 1986).

The political and cultural exclusion of Jews from the homogeneous community in the first half of the century suggests that despite their economic success, they experienced the feeling of being a minority group (Vorspan and Gartner, 1970, Chap. 5). This sense of being an out-group combined with their liberalism and activism, established the basis for political coalition with blacks and Latinos.

In addition to its large and liberal Jewish community, Los Angeles has shared in the surprisingly high level of racial liberalism characteristic of the far west. While Los Angeles culture was by no means attuned to the idea of the melting pot, its residents have been less likely than people in other states and regions to hold racist opinions. Antiblack attitudes have been more likely to take the form of "symbolic racism," in which blacks are perceived as unsettling to community norms valued by whites (Sears and McConahay, 1973).

ELECTORAL REPRESENTATION

Los Angeles blacks have been more successful than Latinos in winning political representation. Blacks have held three of the fifteen council seats since 1963. (The

---

[1] According to County of Los Angeles figures, in 1962, Democrats represented 60 percent of the city's registered voters compared to 36 percent Republicans. By 1980 the Democratic edge was 63 percent to 27 percent.

Los Angeles City Council has been elected by district since 1925.) In 1973 black City Councilman Tom Bradley was elected mayor, with support from blacks, Jews, and Latinos. He was easily re-elected in 1977 and 1981; and in 1985 he obtained 68 percent of the vote and swept all fifteen council districts in 1985. Bradley narrowly won a fifth term in 1989.

Latinos were unrepresented on the city council between 1963 and 1985, a period of more than two decades. In 1949, Latino Edward Roybal was elected to represent the Ninth Council District with Latino and Jewish liberal support. When Roybal went to Congress in 1962, the city council appointed a black, Gilbert Lindsay, to fill the seat. Since defeating a Mexican American challenger in 1963, Lindsay has easily won re-election.

In 1985, Mexican American Assemblyman Richard Alatorre (Democrat, Los Angeles) was elected in the overwhelmingly Latino Fourteenth District. Despite its large Latino population, the district had been represented by a white conservative for many years. Large numbers of minors, noncitizens, and unregistered voters greatly reduced the potential Latino base in the district.

Many Latino activists felt excluded from city hall both before and after the rise of the liberal coalition in 1973. The city faced lawsuits charging discrimination against Latinos after each of the last two decennial reapportionments (Regalado, 1986). A federal suit contesting the 1982 reapportionment led to a redrawing of district lines in 1986. The new plan created an additional Latino district, resulting in the election of Gloria Molina.

Blacks gained entry into the dominant citywide coalition through Bradley's mayoral victory in 1973. Despite their three council seats between 1963 and 1973 (and the rise of black Councilman Billy Mills to council president pro tem), blacks had been very much on the outside of city policy. The administration of Mayor Sam Yorty, initially rather liberal, became increasingly conservative and unresponsive to blacks after the Los Angeles riots of 1965. On such issues as police brutality in the black community, Yorty steadfastly backed Police Chief William Parker (whom he had promised to fire in a successful attempt to win black votes in his 1961 mayoral victory). Yorty avoided seeking federal grant funds for programs to benefit blacks and generally aligned himself with the white community. Ironically, Yorty gave considerable attention to upwardly mobile, conservative Latinos; despite their lack of direct representation, these Latinos enjoyed some incorporation into the Yorty regime.

Tom Bradley, a lawyer and former Los Angeles police lieutenant, was the key figure in the shift to a citywide biracial coalition. He was elected in 1963 to represent the multiracial Tenth Council District, the westside area to which upwardly mobile blacks moved from the crowded central city. Bradley had a solid black voting base, middle-class black allies, and links to Jews, Asian Americans, and Latinos. Bradley provided a key link between the often separate black and liberal reform movements in Los Angeles. Unlike other Los Angeles black politicians, the majority of whom were active in the regular wing of the Democratic party, Bradley was an early leader in the reformist and white-dominated California

Democratic Club (CDC) movement. Blacks had been generally ignored by the CDC, suggesting a weakness in its scope (Wilson, 1962; Jones, 1962). Bradley became president of the integrated Leimert Park CDC club. The CDC played an important role in Bradley's first council campaign, supplementing a major grass-roots effort in the black community. Thus, Bradley was in a unique position to link blacks with party reformers, who had a much better chance than the party regulars of taking over the nonpartisan city government.

Bradley was not alone. As a candidate for office with links to all sides, he had a special role. But he was backed by a network of black and white liberal activists who were coming to know and trust each other. For instance, such black leaders as Rev. H. H. Brookins and such white organizers as Maurice Weiner played central roles in the growth of the coalition. Rev. Brookins had originally organized a convention to nominate a black community candidate for the tenth council seat; Bradley won the endorsement. But from that point on, Brookins advocated a campaign strategy that crossed racial lines. He helped frame Bradley's campaign to appeal to white liberals, Asians, and Latinos (Patterson, 1969). Weiner, a Jewish liberal active in the CDC, coordinated a grass-roots effort in the council campaign that drew liberal political groups from all over the city. Other black and liberal activists came out of the biracial Leimert Park Democratic Club to help Bradley. Ten years later they composed the core of the Bradley regime in city hall.

Once in office, Councilman Bradley formed an anti-Yorty alliance with liberal Councilwoman Rosalind Wyman of the heavily Jewish fifth district. Brookins helped bring the two together (Willens, 1981). After Wyman lost her seat in a Yorty-led purge of opponents in 1965, Bradley became the main liberal spokesman against Yorty.

In August 1965, a major disorder broke out in the neighborhood of Watts. A routine traffic arrest of a black man set off conflict between blacks and police; the trouble soon escalated into four days of looting, burning, and shooting (Conot, 1967). When the smoke cleared, thirty-four people, all but three black, were dead and there was an estimated 40 million dollars of property damage (Sears and McConahay, 1973, p. 9).

The Watts uprising revealed the overwhelming black hostility toward Chief Parker and Mayor Yorty. According to one survey, Sears and McConahay (1973), many blacks saw the violence as the beginning of a new era of white awareness of black problems. By contrast, whites and Mexican Americans were highly unsympathetic to the black protest and heavily supported the response of the police. The dissimilarity between black and Latino responses indicated that a strong black–Latino electoral coalition was unlikely to develop immediately. In the long run, the Watts rebellion did help build black unity and political activism, but it certainly did not plant the seeds for cooperation between blacks and Latinos.

Watts also provided a new public agenda for blacks and white liberals. The response to the riot was less negative among liberals, and among whites who lived far from the affected area, suggesting a wider base for biracial politics (Morris and Jeffries, 1970). The seeds of a biracial alliance had already been planted several years before in the Tenth District; furthermore, the fact that liberals were out of power at the time of the riots meant that they were not the target of the protests. In fact, surveys of those arrested revealed high levels of support not only for black elected officials but also for white liberal politicians (Sears and McConahay, 1973). Increased federal funding under the Johnson Administration, partly in response to the violence, gave blacks and white liberals a vehicle to promote new programs for minorities and the poor without raising local taxes. Bradley often used his council forum to attack Yorty for failing to seek federal funds. Thus, while racial protest polarized the city and generated a backlash, it also helped create a conscious citywide alliance between blacks and white liberals.

When Bradley ran for mayor in both 1969 and 1973, he drew on an aroused and unified black community, and on a generation of white liberals shut out of state leadership by the party regulars and out of city policy by Yorty. The Bradley campaigns provided a common symbol for blacks and white liberals. The campaigns were managed by an inner team of Tenth District allies. Bradley's links to white liberals gave him access to citywide strategists and campaign money; in both races, he outspent the incumbent mayor.

By blatantly capitalizing on fears of black militancy and student antiwar protests, Yorty defeated Bradley in 1969. In that conservative election (several other liberal candidates and ballot propositions were defeated), Bradley ran a rigidly liberal campaign aimed at blacks, Jews, and Latinos (Maullin, 1971). Yorty's campaign cut heavily into Bradley's base among the latter two groups. Bradley won just over half the Jewish votes and lost a majority of Latinos to Yorty (Maullin, 1971; Pettigrew, 1971). Some class division appeared among Jews. The better-off voted more heavily for Bradley, but even the less well-to-do were much more pro-Bradley than other whites (Maller, 1977). Combined with Yorty's huge edge among non-Jewish whites, the erosion of Bradley's three-sided coalition ensured his defeat.

Yorty's victory reflected both racial prejudice and a fear of crime and social disorder. For elderly Jews in the lower-middle-income Fairfax area, the direct threat of crime in a transitional area cost Bradley votes (Wilson and Wilde, 1969). By contrast, Sears and Kinder found that feeling personally threatened by blacks was less relevant to conservative white voters in the San Fernando Valley than symbolic concerns about the decline of community order and values (1971).

Bradley's inability to stem the crime issue reflected the difficult balancing act of holding his coalition together. His enthusiastic liberal backers felt that crime was a code word for racism. Therefore, to take a strong law-and-order stance would be to betray a key part of the Bradley movement (Maullin, 1971). Bradley's defeat stunned his backers; one conclusion drawn within the inner circle was the need to move toward the center (Weiner, 1981; Rothenberg, 1982).

In 1973, Bradley ran a more moderate campaign in a more moderate time. He called for political reform and a ban on offshore oil drilling in the affluent Pacific Palisades. In addition, he prominently featured photographs of himself in his police uniform in citywide television commercials and in so doing tried to assure the city's voters that he would strengthen community order. He vigorously attacked Yorty for weak and ineffective leadership.

Bradley's black support, as in 1969, was immense. This time, however, Jews turned out in large numbers to vote for Bradley. A precinct analysis by Bradley's strategists found a 62 percent to 44 percent difference between Jews and white gentiles of the same socioeconomic status in their support of Bradley (Halley et al., 1976). Moreover, the precinct analysis probably understates the difference, because Jews provided an estimated one-third of the Bradley vote in some predominantly white gentle precincts (Halley, 1974). Overall, Bradley won 46 percent of white votes in 1973, compared to 37 percent in 1969 (Hahn et al., 1976). Both totals far exceeded the presumed limits on white support for black mayoral candidates.

Bradley won a bare majority (51 percent) of the less mobilized Mexican-American vote in 1973 (Hahn et al., 1976). Unlike the highly unified black vote, the Latino vote was apparently divided among class lines; Bradley did better in low-income Latino neighborhoods (Hahn et al., 1976). This was the opposite of the class relationship among Jews. Latinos were substantially more likely than white non-Jews to back Bradley and therefore made up an important part of his electoral base.

Bradley's popular appeal helped elect Jewish liberal Burt Pines as city attorney by bringing him black votes. In turn, Pines may have brought Bradley some Jewish votes (Hahn et al., 1976). Within a year of taking office, Bradley had helped elect two black allies to city council seats, each backed by Bradley's black and white liberal campaign associates. Since 1973, white liberals with vote-getting ability among blacks and Jews have won the city attorney and city controller spots. Younger and more liberal councilmembers were elected in other districts, and Bradley's allies eventually gained control of the council presidency.

In 1985 Asian Americans gained their first council member and Mexican Americans ended their 22-year drought. A second Latino was elected in 1986. All three new members are liberal Democrats. Currently, the council consists of eleven Democrats and four Republicans; its members now include three blacks, two Latinos, one Asian American, and four women.

Biracial liberalism has triumphed in Los Angeles as an electoral phenomenon. But as a policy vehicle, biracial liberalism has been marked by caution and incrementalism. Some significant changes benefitting minorities have been made. But the very circumstances that led to electoral success have placed limits on policy change. And the difficulty of devising policies acceptable to all groups within the coalition has led to a weakening of the coalition in recent years.

POLICY UNDER BRADLEY'S LEADERSHIP

The norms of political reform are publicly revered in Los Angeles. Consequently, centralized government is seen to smack of machine rule; leadership moves that would hardly be noticed in New York City or Chicago bring loud cries of "bossism'' in Los Angeles. Even a fairly unified Los Angeles government must move carefully to implement sweeping, redistributive policies.

The 1969 and 1973 elections provided a further constraint against redistributive programs on behalf of racial minorities. Bradley had to work hard in both campaigns to dispel Yorty's charge that Bradley would bring a black–leftist regime with radical programs into city hall.

The imperatives of incumbency in a weak-party city have drawn even liberal politicians into the embrace of local business, the main source of long-term campaign money. Growth rather than redistributive politics produces new city resources and large campaign war chests. As in other cities, Los Angeles minority and liberal politicians have increasingly turned toward the business community to fulfill their policy agenda (Swanstrom, 1985).

Bradley's coalition now found itself at the center of city power. Trusted activists from the Tenth District were placed in top mayoral staff posts, as well as in the leading city commissionerships. In the process minority representatives achieved significant incorporation into the regime.

Maurice Weiner was appointed Deputy Mayor. Warren Hollier, a key black activist in the 1963 council campaign, became President of the Board of Public Works. Stephen Reinhardt and Frances Savitch, Jewish liberals long associated with Bradley, were named President of the Police Commission and Executive Assistant to the Mayor, respectively. Bill Elkins, an early black activist, was another executive assistant. Manuel Aragon, a Latino businessman, was chosen second Deputy Mayor. An increasingly liberal city council became incorporated into the governing regime. Bradley's white liberal ally Pat Russell ascended to the council presidency backed by Tenth District councilman David Cunningham, whose own election to the council had been engineered by the Bradley forces. The Tenth District network, augmented by younger activists recruited during the mayoral campaigns, became a fairly unified regime around Bradley.

Led by Bradley, the coalition moved cautiously but steadily. The pressure to make redistributive choices was anticipated and eased by an emphasis on increasing overall resources. In this sense, the federal funding boom of the 1970s was a godsend. Using federal money, the city undertook a wide range of new social service programs, hardly tapping the city treasury. Many, although not all, of these programs were in poor and minority communities.

Using federal and private dollars, the administration pursued a major economic development program. Bradley's Los Angeles received a greatly increased share of federal economic development funds and millions of dollars were invested in the redevelopment of downtown Los Angeles (Saltzstein et al., 1986).

On controversial policy issues, Bradley distanced himself from day-to-day decision making. The depth of his governing coalition allowed him to use his allies to take the heat on tough decisions. Most city departments are run by commissioners appointed by the mayor and confirmed by the council. Bradley filled these commissions with liberal allies (including many blacks, Jews, and Latinos) and remained publicly aloof from their hard policy choices.

For instance, the liberal police commission established civilian control of the police and transferred officers from low-crime white areas into high-crime minority areas. When asked about the police transfers in his televised 1985 campaign debate with Councilman John Ferraro, Bradley said he had had nothing to do with the decision.

Bradley's appointees to the public works and civil service commissions—long-time political allies—took the lead in pursuing affirmative action in city hiring and contracting. Eisinger (1983) has shown that with the exception of police hiring of blacks, Bradley's administration has made progress in affirmative action comparable to black-mayor cities with larger percentages of black population.

More specifically, an analysis of city figures (Table 2.1) reveals that significant gains in city hiring were obtained by blacks, Latinos, Asians, and women. On a per-capita basis, however, Latinos were still below parity while blacks and Asians stayed ahead of their population percentages. All four groups registered solid gains in the two most desirable categories: officials/administrators and professionals (Table 2.2).

Even though blacks were declining as a share of the city's population, they were holding their position in city hiring. Despite a lower degree of political incorporation, Latinos and Asians were markedly increasing their positions. In a quiet way, the regime seemed to be doing a respectable job of developing a secure occupational base for some elements of minority communities.

On such tinderbox issues as school busing, Bradley has been utterly invisible, making no pronouncements and suggesting no policy alternatives. A prodevelopment mayor downtown, he has been (at least until 1985) proenvironment on the coastline; this is feasible in a city of Los Angeles' physical size. He collects tens of thousands of campaign dollars from local business and still gets liberal support.

Meanwhile, Bradley floats above it all, attending numerous civic events, quietly monitoring the council and his commissioners and keeping in touch with

TABLE 2.1. PERCENTAGE OF COMMISSIONERS AND CITY JOBS 1973 AND 1984

	Commissioners		City Jobs	
	1973	*1984*	*1973*	*1984*
Whites	67	56	64.1	50.1
Blacks	15	19	21.9	23.6
Latinos	9	16	9.3	16.8
Asians	7	9	4.0	8.9
Women	32	33	16.0	22.9

Sources: On commissions: Doug Shuit, "Bradley Names 140 to Commissions, Retains 21 of Yorty's Appointees," Los Angeles Times, August 8, 1973; Janet Clayton, "120 Commissioners Named in Major Bradley Shakeup," Los Angeles Times, August 2, 1984. On jobs: City of Los Angeles, Department of Personnel, "Numerical Progress, 1973–1986."

TABLE 2.2. SELECTED CATEGORIES

	Officials and Administrators		Professionals	
	1973	*1984*	*1973*	*1984*
Whites	94.7%	77.5	81.4	62.7
Blacks	1.3	9.2	5.0	10.2
Latinos	2.6	7.2	4.6	8.9
Asians	1.3	5.3	8.0	17.9
Women	3.0	9.8	11.9	25.7

Source: City of Los Angeles, Department of Personnel, "Numerical Progress, 1973–1986."

federal funding officials, members of key congressional committees, and local community leaders. This gives Bradley a certain "Teflon" quality unavailable to a more publicly active political executive.

Nevertheless, Bradley and his close associates generally take the lead when intergroup tensions threaten to break out. He and his allies mediated a bitter conflict over President Carter's 1979 firing of black United Nations Ambassador Andrew Young for unauthorized contacts with the Palestine Liberation Organization. Nationwide, blacks and Jews exchanged very angry words. In Los Angeles, members of the biracial network met behind closed doors under the joint chairmanship of two Bradley aides: Ethel Narvid, Jewish, and Bill Elkins, black. Angry feelings were vented privately and a conciliatory joint message was issued to the press. The incident seemed to do little long-term damage to the coalition.

Narvid and Elkins had previously formed the Black–Jewish Coalition to pursue joint community projects, among them an interracial housing program. Later, an exchange of pulpits between black ministers and Jewish rabbis took place. Thus the regime's pattern of conflict resolution called for immediate meeting within the coalition leadership, the private expression of bitter feelings, and resolution through joint activities in a formal organization.

Bradley used his mayoral prestige and powers to defuse intergroup conflict. For instance, when two members of the school board, one black and one Jewish, got into a public shouting match, Bradley called them privately to his office and convinced them to settle their differences. In another case, Bradley backed an unsuccessful ballot proposition to increase the number of council seats, in hopes of winning spots for Latinos and Asians. When the council passed a reapportionment plan in 1986 that disadvantaged Asians, Bradley vetoed it. In the process, he overrode the objections of a number of minority and liberal councilmembers interested in protecting incumbents.

When the coalition is in good form, the challenges of outsiders can be easily repelled. Outsiders include black leaders with a working-class black base, Jewish leaders with a lower-middle-class base, and conservatives. The black politicians associated with Congressman Mervyn Dymally represent the first group of outsiders. Linked to the Democratic party regulars, the Dymally forces have been shut out of city politics by the Bradley coalition. The rhetoric of reform in the hands of the dominant coalition places the Dymally forces at a disadvantage. The Bradley people even challenged Dymally candidates in state senate and assembly primaries between 1975 and 1978, winning one seat and nearly winning two others. The network of black and liberal activists helped fund and manage these campaigns among black candidates.

The second group—the Jewish grass roots—is exemplified by councilman Zev Yaroslavsky. From his base in the Fairfax district, Yaroslavsky upset Bradley's aide Frances Savitch in a 1975 special election for the fifth council seat. Yaroslavsky won by appealing to the lower-middle-class Fairfax Jews who had been open to Yorty's appeals against the well-to-do liberals friendly to Bradley and Savitch. On the council, however, Yaroslavsky found it wise to make peace with the dominant coalition. Without the numerous and powerful high-status liberals, Yaroslavsky was unable to develop a base equal to the dominant coalition.

The third group of outsiders—conservatives—can be seen in the police chief Darryl Gates. Drawing on San Fernando Valley whites, some conservative Jews, and middle-class Latinos, Gates' base is much like Yorty's. Frequently mentioned as a mayoral candidate, Gates has been hamstrung by Bradley's police commission. When he sought to take a leave of absence to run against Bradley in 1985, the commission refused his request. In effect, he would have had to give up his job in order to risk the campaign. Not surprisingly, he stayed out. More generally, the prospect of a Gates candidacy unified the liberal coalition against a common enemy.

Beginning in 1985, a series of new challenges arose to the dominant coalition that have made it less stable and more open to attack. Mistakes at the leadership level could be blamed, but some of the problems were inherent in the process of maintaining a biracial coalition.

To blacks and white liberals, the original building blocks of the biracial coalition, policy results have often been disheartening. Black activists express irritation at the slow pace of change under the regime and some have quietly suggested that Bradley takes the black community for granted. Limited progress in the hiring of blacks by the police and fire departments has been particularly frustrating (Littwin, 1981). Bradley's closeness to white liberals and his coalition style of leadership leave him open to charges of insufficient race consciousness.

White liberals sometimes express their displeasure at what they perceive to be Bradley's conservatism and lack of public leadership. As Bradley drew closer to business, environmentalists were alienated by what they saw as the regime's too attentive regard for development. As Eisinger (1983) has suggested, black mayors have often chosen business over the white middle class; Bradley's regime has depended on finding ways to have the support of both.

In normal times, these problems seemed to do the Bradley regime little damage. Blacks and white liberals have had too great a stake in the survival of a regime that has brought them political incorporation. Unlike business, blacks and white liberals are also susceptible to the symbolic appeal of the Bradley coalition.

For blacks, Bradley is an admired symbol regardless of his acknowledged policy limitations for the black community. For white liberals, Bradley symbolizes the dream of biracial harmony, which touches a very responsive chord. These symbolic appeals have continued to bind each group to a slow, cautious, and often frustrating policy program.

But now, after a decade in power, the coalition faces the simultaneous demands of Asian Americans and Latinos for greater incorporation and a new slow-growth movement based among affluent and middle-class whites. The aging and attrition of the coalition's government and a few missteps by leaders have allowed these problems to become serious threats to the coalition's future.

Incorporating two new groups into the dominant coalition has become essential for the regime to survive. Latinos have long been ambivalent to the liberal coalition. Despite their support for Bradley, Latinos did not obtain a council member until 1985. During the council's 1986 debate on Latino representation, black councilman David Cunningham made several remarks about Latino political activism that rankled Latinos and aggravated black–Latino relations. Finally, in a process that the council wisely assigned to Latino councilman Richard Alatorre, a plan was devised that allowed a Latina, Gloria Molina, to be elected in 1986. Through Bradley's use of the veto, a seat for newly elected Asian American councilmember Michael Woo was saved. But the bitter fight over reapportionment showed how difficult it would be to link three ethnic groups and white liberals when there are only limited political resources available. In addition to these direct interest conflicts, ideological differences among blacks, Asians, and Latinos could impede the development of a multiracial coalition (Cain et al., 1986).

At the same time that the coalition confronted the need to expand to four groups, trouble began to brew within the core black–liberal relationship. As the Bradley regime expanded its ambitious redevelopment program, the boom in city construction eventually expanded to the west-side neighborhoods. In affluent Westwood and middle-class Westchester, new office buildings led to traffic congestion, increased smog, and inflation of housing costs. At the grass-roots level, a slow-growth movement was catching fire. To some minority politicians, the liberal enthusiasm for slow growth seemed to imply that the economic growth deemed essential for minority advances would be halted. The beginning of an interest conflict between blacks and white liberals could be seen.

In 1985 Bradley decided to approve oil drilling in the Pacific Palisades. This highly controversial decision reversed Bradley's own longstanding opposition to the drilling as expressed in his 1973 mayoral campaign. Bradley's contention that the oil drilling plan had been changed to meet the city's environmental concerns was to little avail. The reaction to Bradley's decision, which was bitterly opposed privately by many of his closest advisors, did not immediately hurt Bradley at the polls. It barely dented his 1985 re-election campaign. Calls for Yaroslavsky to run against Bradley in 1985 were rebuffed by the Fifth District councilman with a vigorous defense of the mayor as a coalition builder. But the oil-drilling decision spurred a slow-growth movement with Bradley as its target, and Yaroslavsky now had an issue with which he could link his constituency to the more affluent westside liberals. With the cooperation of Councilman Marvin Braude of the Eleventh District wherein the Pacific Palisades are located, Yaroslavsky steadily moved into a leadership position on the slow-growth issue.

In 1985 as well, black minister Louis Farrakhan came to Los Angeles; with his well-known anti-Semitic views, Farrakhan was anathema to local Jews. But his economic message and emphasis on black consciousness brought him a base among lower-income blacks. Jewish leaders asked Bradley to denounce Farrakhan before his speech. To their great surprise, Bradley refused, noting that he had reached an agreement with Farrakhan to keep anti-Semitism out of his speech. A number of local black leaders had met with Bradley and asked him to follow this course—again bitterly opposed by some of his key advisors. For a long and painful week, Bradley was the target of cross-pressures from blacks and Jews; for once, he was not the solution to a black-Jewish problem, but was himself seen as the problem by both groups. When Farrakhan indeed voiced anti-Semitic comments, Bradley denounced him.

The problems came together in the 1987 council elections, when Bradley's coalition suffered a set of crushing defeats. A slow-growth initiative sponsored by Braude and Yaroslavsky passed overwhelmingly. The resignation of Councilman David Cunningham in Bradley's Tenth District led to a bitter battle between two black candidates, only one a Bradley ally. The anti-Bradley candidate, Nate Holden, easily won the election in Bradley's own backyard. Council President Pat Russell was defeated for re-election by a slow growth candidate. In the absence of Bradley's two key council allies, the council voted to install Bradley's last mayoral opponent John Ferraro as council president. The council members then successfully defied the mayor's position on the police budget, and councilmembers for the first time began taking public, verbal potshots at the mayor. Bradley's reputation for invincibility had already been tarnished by two gubernatorial defeats in 1982 and 1986. Yaroslavsky announced that he intended to run against Bradley in 1989.

Bradley's popularity, however, proved surprisingly resilient. He revamped his staff and adjusted some of his policies to address environmental concerns. Ultimately, Yaroslavsky withdrew from the race and Bradley won a fifth term in 1989 (although by a reduced margin). No sooner had Bradley retained office than he faced a potentially devastating conflict of interest scandal regarding his personal finances.

Overall, the post-1985 weakening of the coalition may have been influenced by the aging of the coalition. One by one, the key members of the network have left city government. While they remain in close touch with Bradley, they do not have the day-to-day access of the past. The regime has not excelled at the process of bringing in new people who would engage in coalition building or coalition maintenance.

Bradley's popularity, the power of his incumbency, the benefits of political incorporation for blacks, Jews, Asian Americans, and Latinos, and the lack of effective opposition now hold the coalition together. Regardless of the outcome of the municipal investigation, the long-term problems of coalition maintenance remain.

SUMMARY AND IMPLICATIONS

What does the Los Angeles case tell us about the prospects for biracial coalitions? Minority incorporation was achieved and maintained through biracial coalition. Clearly, under certain conditions the presumed limits to biracial politics can be overcome even in a big city. The pattern of minority incorporation in the largest western city confirms the model outlined in *Protest Is Not Enough.*

Successful biracial politics was not inevitable in Los Angeles. In their combined numbers alone, blacks and white liberals did not represent a majority of the city. However, in unity and ideological affinity, they formed an extremely powerful force.

A large Jewish population (second only to New York City's) created a major liberal base. A liberal constituency of Jews and other liberals sympathetic to minority aspirations created a strong *ideological* grounding for biracial politics. The liberals of Los Angeles were a political and cultural "out" group before the rise of the biracial coalition. Joint efforts served the *interests* of both blacks and white liberals in their search for recognition and access to city hall.

In addition to ideological and interest alignment, *leadership* played a significant role. Despite traditional Los Angeles' lack of receptivity to minority groups, a large opening was created as minority group leaders expressed themselves in the symbolic language of reform and community. The key element was the linkage between liberal reformers in the black and Jewish communities who pooled resources and strategies for reaching the local electorate. This alliance illustrates the role of elite trust in coalitions (Hinckley, 1981; Sonenshein, 1989).

The roots of this elite alliance preceded the protests of the 1960s and at the leadership level were undamaged by the Watts riot. At key junctures, white liberal and black leaders in Los Angeles have chosen to pursue biracial politics. With Bradley as a leader and unifying symbol, they have reached their mutual goals through accommodation rather than polarization.

If the nonpartisan nature of Los Angeles politics prevented the rise of a traditional Democratic coalition, it also offered an environment conducive to biracial power sharing based on reform. No Chicago-style Democratic party machine mobilized white resistance to minorities or created a huge public jobs system over which groups could fight. The district system of council elections, an anomaly in a nonpartisan system, was a crucial toehold for black and eventually for Latino and Asian American representation.

The Los Angeles case illustrates the difficulty of maintaining a biracial regime over a long period of time. The city's recent experience confirms Mollenkopf's concerns (Chapter 4) that minority gains could face "rollback." The aging and attrition processes as well as new demands for incorporation have weakened the Los Angeles coalition. Black–Latino conflicts have yet to be resolved, and new black–liberal cleavages have emerged. The ability of a flexible liberal ideology to offer multiracial incorporation is essential to any future Los Angeles liberal coalition. The regime's need to maintain constituencies for both growth and the environment will further test its creativity.

Even with its many dilemmas, limitations, and recent troubles, biracial coalition politics has been extraordinarily successful in Los Angeles. This case study provides an important counterweight to the unhappy experiences of numerous big cities and ought to spur further exploration of the prospects for biracial politics. Clearly, minority incorporation through a biracial coalition is workable in a large urban community. Where the conditions are not right, or where leaders pursue other strategies, biracial coalitions are unlikely to arise and endure. But where there is an affinity between groups based on interest and ideology and where leaders choose to do the hard work necessary to link groups together, biracial coalitions can arise, win elections, and govern a major American city.

REFERENCES

Adrian, Charles R. 1959. A Typology for Nonpartisan Elections. *Western Political Quarterly* 12:449–458.

Beyette, Beverly. 1979. Is L.A. Swallowing Up Its Jewish Community? *Los Angeles Times*, November 2.

Boyarsky, Bill. 1987. Old Alliance Loses Ardor for Bradley. *Los Angeles Times*, July 2.

Browning, Rufus P., Dale Rogers Marshall, and David H. Tabb. 1984. *Protest Is Not Enough: The Struggle of Blacks and Hispanics for Equality in Urban Politics*. Berkeley: University of California Press.

Cain, Bruce E., D. Roderick Kiewiet, and Carole Uhlaner. 1986. The Impact of California's Minorities. Paper presented at the convention of the Western Political Science Association, Eugene, Oregon.

Carney, Francis M. 1964. The Decentralized Politics of Los Angeles. *The Annals of the American Academy of Political and Social Science* 353:107–121.

Conot, Robert. 1968. *Rivers of Blood, Years of Darkness*. New York: William Morrow and Company.

Eisinger, Peter K. 1983. The Politics of Racial Economic Advancement. In William C. McCready, ed., *Culture, Ethnicity, and Identity: Current Issues in Research*. New York: Academic Press, pp. 95–109.

Fogelson, Robert M. 1967. *The Fragmented Metropolis: Los Angeles, 1850–1930*. Cambridge, Mass.: Harvard University Press.

Hahn, Harlan, David Klingman, and Harry Pachon. 1976. Cleavages, Coalitions, and the Black Candidate: The Los Angeles Mayoralty Elections of 1969 and 1973. *Western Political Quarterly* 29:521–530.

Halley, Robert M. 1974. Analysis of Ethnic Voting Patterns in the 1973 Los Angeles Municipal Elections. Master's thesis, University of Southern California.

Halley, Robert M., Alan C. Acock, and Thomas Greene. 1976. Ethnicity and Social Class: Voting in the 1973 Los Angeles Municipal Elections. *Western Political Quarterly* 29:507–520.

Hinckley, Barbara. 1981. *Coalitions and Politics*. New York. Harcourt, Brace, Jovanovich.

Jones, William B. 1962. CDC and the Negro Community. *CDC Bulletin* 1:4–5.

Littwin, Susan. 1981. Inside Tom Bradley: The Making of a Mayor, 1981, and of a Governor, 1982. *New West* 6:85–89.

Maller, Allen S. 1977. Class Factors in the Jewish Vote. *Jewish Social Studies* 39:159–162.

Maullin, Richard. 1971. Los Angeles Liberalism. *Trans-Action* 8:40–50.

Mayo, Charles G. 1964. The 1961 Mayoralty Election in Los Angeles: The Political Party in a Nonpartisan Election. *Western Political Quarterly* 17:325–337.

Morris, Richard T., and Vincent Jeffries. 1970. The White Reaction Study. In Nathan Cohen, ed., *The Los Angeles Riots: A Socio-Psychological Study*. New York: Praeger, pp. 480–681.

Patterson, Beeman. 1969. Political Action of Negroes in Los Angeles: A Case Study in the Attainment of Councilmanic Representation. *Phylon* 30:170–183.

Pettigrew, Thomas. 1971. When a Black Candidate Runs for Mayor: Race and Voting Behavior. In Harlan Hahn, ed., *People and Politics in Urban Society*. Beverly Hills, Calif.: Sage Publications, pp. 99–105.

Regalado, James A. 1986. Racial Gerrymandering in Los Angeles, California? Redistricting and the Question of Latino Representation. Paper presented at the convention of the Western Political Science Association, Eugene, Oregon.

Rothenberg, Donald. 1982. Field director for the 1969 Bradley mayoral campaign. Interview with the author, June 11.

Saltzstein, Alan, Raphael Sonenshein, and Irving Ostrow. 1986. Federal Aid and the City of Los Angeles: Implementing a More Centralized Local Political System. In Terry Clark, ed., *Research in Urban Policy*, Vol. 2. Greenwich, Conn.: JAI Press.

Sandberg, Neil, 1986. *Jewish Life in Los Angeles: A Window to Tomorrow*. Washington, D.C.: University Press of America.

Sears, David O., and Donald R. Kinder. 1971. Racial Tensions and Voting in Los Angeles. In Werner Z. Hirsch, ed., *Los Angeles: Viability and Prospects for Metropolitan Leadership*. New York: Praeger, pp. 51–88.

Sears, David O., and John B. McConahay, 1973. *The Politics of Violence: The New Urban Blacks and the Watts Riot*. Boston: Houghton Mifflin Company.

Sonenshein, Raphael, 1989. The Dynamics of Bi-racial Coalitions: Crossover Politics in Los Angeles. *Western Political Quarterly* 42 (June):333–353.

Swanstrom, Todd. 1985. *The Crisis of Growth Politics: Cleveland, Kucinich, and the Challenge of Urban Populism*. Philadelphia: Temple University Press.

Vorspan, Max, and Lloyd P. Gartner. 1970. *History of the Jews of Los Angeles*. San Marino, Calif.: The Huntington Library.

Weiner, Maurice, 1981. Former deputy mayor of Los Angeles. Interview with the author, November 6.

Wilson, James Q. 1962. *The Amateur Democrat: Club Politics in Three Cities*. Chicago: University of Chicago Press.

Wilson, James Q., and Harold R. Wilde. 1969. The Urban Mood. *Commentary* 48:52–61.

CHAPTER 3

The Rise of a Biracial Coalition in Philadelphia

Richard A. Keiser

Editors' Note

Like Los Angeles, Philadelphia is a case of black political success, but there are many contrasts. Philadelphia is a large, old, eastern city with partisan elections and a history of machine politics. Blacks constitute more than twice the proportion of the population in Philadelphia (39 percent) than in Los Angeles (see Table 12.1), but the election of a black mayor came a full decade later—Wilson Goode in 1983.

Why such a long delay? Richard Keiser shows that the Democratic party machine stood in the way of the political incorporation of blacks in Philadelphia. Eventually, however, a moderate, biracial, reform-oriented coalition overcame the machine's dominance of city government. Keiser's account of the origins and evolution of this coalition is worth studying for the light it sheds on the possibilities of leadership, the nurturing of trust, and the avoidance of the more extreme racial polarization of leadership and coalitions that we observe in Chicago.

As in Los Angeles, the problem in Philadelphia now is to maintain the unity of the dominant coalition. Regimes make mistakes, new issues emerge to divide the coalition, and the opposing force—the Democratic machine—regroups and now competes for the black vote. Blacks may be in leading positions in both coalitions, but it may not be possible to keep the more liberal coalition in power.

This chapter presents an analysis of the formation of the biracial, reform-oriented alliance in Philadelphia that was the forerunner of the coalition that elected Wilson Goode as mayor in 1983.[1] The origins of this alliance can be traced to the reform administrations of the 1950s. But the incremental incorporation of blacks into policy-making positions that was a product of this alliance was checked and, in fact, rolled back by a conservative coalition that emerged in the late 1960s and continued to dominate the city's politics throughout the 1970s. By the end of the decade, however, demographic factors, in particular a growing black electorate, combined with a decline in the salience of the antiliberal, antiblack sentiments that had initially catalyzed the reactionary movement, led to the resurgence of the biracial reform coalition and culminated in the election of Wilson Goode. Discussion of the Goode administration focuses particularly on the extent to which his administration has enhanced the status and furthered the political incorporation of blacks and Latinos. This chapter discusses the future prospects for biracial alliances and why such alliances are no longer limited to the reform variety; it also compares the evolution of Philadelphia's biracial coalition with the patterns found in some of the other cities in this book.

THE ORIGINS OF PHILADELPHIA'S BIRACIAL ALLIANCE

In the late 1940s, Philadelphia government was rocked by scandals that disgraced the formerly dominant Republican party. Joseph Clark, a reformer who promised "good government" in the wake of this corruption, led a coalition that ushered in a period of Democratic party domination of the city's politics when he was elected mayor in 1951. This coalition included the Greater Philadelphia Movement (GPM), an umbrella business organization that unified the city's business leadership, the Americans for Democratic Action (ADA), home of the city's liberal activists, as well as significant aspects of the black community. Since then, politics in Philadelphia has been characterized by competition between (1) an amalgam of white liberal activists and "good-government" reformers, including many of the city's business leaders, and (2) the regular organization politicians of the Democratic party (sometimes very loosely labeled a "machine"), many of whom defected, with their neighborhood ties intact, from the discredited Republican organization. The reformers and the organization politicians have battled largely within the confines of the Democratic party (for example, in primary elections); however, when the reformers have been defeated in such battles, they have not hesitated to shift their

[1] I would like to thank the Institute of Governmental Studies and the Department of Political Science at the University of California, Berkeley, for financial support they have provided without which this research would not have been possible. I would also like to thank the Gordon Public Policy Center of Brandeis University both for financial assistance and for providing the stimulating environment in which an earlier draft of this chapter was written.

support to moderate Republicans, periodically resuscitating an otherwise moribund party. One of the major battle lines in this competition has been for the votes of the black community.

Seeking to put machine-style politics out of business, the reformers instituted a new city charter that included a rigid civil service system for the awarding of city jobs. Because of private-sector discrimination, an especially well-educated pool of blacks was available to take the examinations and win city employment (Lowe, 1967; Weiler, 1974). The Commission on Human Relations declared that discrimination in private-sector employment would no longer be tolerated and warned 17,000 companies of penalties if they failed to "tak[e] affirmative steps to guarantee and promote equal employment opportunities" (Lowe, 1967). Mayor Clark and his reform-minded successor, Richardson Dilworth, also began the incorporation of blacks into city government by backing black community leaders (especially clergymen) for elected and appointed offices which heretofore had not been held by blacks. Blacks affiliated with the reform movement were elected as city councilmen, Recorder of Deeds, and Commissioner of Records, and were appointed to prominent positions in such agencies as the Civil Service Commission and as assistant district attorneys. Mayor Dilworth, specifically seeking to remedy police brutality against blacks, created the first civilian police review board in the nation (Rogers, 1971). The reform administrations eschewed high-rise public housing in favor of a program targeted at middle-income blacks that included redevelopment of extant housing and the education of whites and blacks about the integration of neighborhoods (Lowe, 1967). Poor blacks, leaning to the party of FDR already, gave their support to Clark and Dilworth because "for the first time in history [they] were having the pleasant experience of seeing many members of their race work as employees in the offices of the city government" (Reichley, 1959). But this intangible reward would not prove sufficient to maintain the loyalty of poor blacks to the reform wing of the Democratic party.

ROLLBACK AND RESPONSE: THE RESILIENCE OF THE REFORM ALLIANCE

When Democrat George Leader was elected Governor in 1955, the weak Philadelphia Democratic organization finally obtained the means to compete effectively with the reformers for control of the party and the city government. Leader strengthened the organization by placing nearly 3000 patronage jobs at its disposal. The organization cultivated a mass base of support among low-income blacks by distributing patronage jobs—albeit those with the lowest salaries (Reichley, 1959; Strange, 1966). In 1958 the organization co-opted a prominent black councilman, who had until then been allied with the reformers, by promising him the next available judgeship. That same year the organization further increased its black support by slating the first black Philadelphian elected to the U.S. Congress, Robert N. C. Nix.

But even after an organization ward leader and councilman, James Tate, was elevated to the mayor's office in 1962 (because of Mayor Dilworth's resignation to run unsuccessfully for Governor) and elected in 1963, the organization wing and the reform wing of the Democratic party remained highly competitive. The organization did not crush the reformers and come to dominate the city's politics as has been suggested (Banfield, 1965). The organization was weakened by the death of its "boss," Congressman William Green, in 1963. More devastatingly, Republican governors were elected in 1963 and 1967, depriving the Democratic organization of the bulk of its patronage.

Evidence that the regular organization had not vanquished the reformers, and that politics in Philadelphia remained competitive, can be found in the data for the mayoral elections of 1963 and 1967. While Clark and Dilworth had not faced primary challenges in their terms, Tate faced challengers backed by disgruntled Democratic reformers in both 1963 and 1967. Furthermore, as Table 3.1 shows, Tate defeated his 1963 Republican opponent by a narrow margin, compared with his Democratic mayoral predecessors. In 1967, Tate barely defeated Republican District Attorney Arlen Specter (a former Democrat supported by the GPM and the ADA), whose victory in the District Attorney's race 2 years earlier was another indication of the weakened condition of the Democratic organization. Finally, in 1969 the Democratic candidates for District Attorney and Controller were defeated by Republican candidates who received strong support from the white reformers.

That politics in Philadelphia remained highly competitive is significant because it meant that Tate and the regular Democratic organization were forced to court black voters at the same time that they were trying to roll back some of the political achievements blacks had won under the reformers (discussed below). In classic machine fashion, Tate developed a political organization in black neighborhoods by creating new leaders to administer the federally funded antipoverty program and placing patronage jobs at their disposal so they could mobilize others in their neighborhoods (Peterson, 1967). In both mayoral elections, Tate's victory came on the strength of the black vote, largely from poorer black wards (Philadelphia *Bulletin*, 1965; Ekstrom, 1973).

TABLE 3.1. MARGINS OF VICTORY FOR DEMOCRATIC MAYORAL CANDIDATES 1951–1967

Year	Candidate	Margin
1951	Clark	124,700
1955	Dilworth	132,706
1959	Dilworth	208,460
1963	Tate	61,633
1967	Tate	10,928

Source: Philadelphia Bulletin Almanac and Year Book *(Philadelphia: Philadelphia* Bulletin, *1971).*

It is important to recognize that while Tate used particularistic rewards to insure that blacks remained the nucleus of the Democratic organization's *electoral coalition*, they were not part of the *governing coalition*. Blacks who aspired to leadership positions within the organizational structure of the party were rebuffed (Strange, 1969). Moreover, blacks were not slated for visible public offices from which they could influence the formation of policy as they had been under the reformers. Consequently, policy emanating from city hall was less responsive to their needs. For instance, blacks in the party organization and middle-class black leaders who were not beholden to the Democratic organization (for example, many of the ministers) were for most of the 1960s unsuccessful in their efforts to lobby city hall to end discrimination in the school system, halt police brutality, and punish the offending officers, enforce housing codes (created under Clark and Dilworth) that would have raised the quality of housing in black ghettos, and obey existing contract provisions prohibiting discrimination in city building projects.

The growing unresponsiveness to black demands on the part of Tate and the Democratic organization was part of their attempt to halt massive electoral defections by the white working class (Ekstrom, 1973). White voters who viewed black advancement as threatening had been defecting to Republican candidates who promised to "get tough on crime." To increase the party's lagging support among these voters, Tate promoted a charismatic policeman, Frank Rizzo, to the post of chief of police. Tate also moved to shore up white ethnic support by eliminating the city's civilian police review board. Tate was betting that black levels of electoral support for Democratic party candidates could be maintained even as the party adopted a less sympathetic view toward the policy concerns of blacks (Philadelphia *Bulletin*, 1974).

In response to city hall's inattention to their substantive policy concerns, a black protest movement emerged under the leadership of Cecil Moore, the president of the National Association for the Advancement of Colored People (NAACP). Moore led demonstrations against the discriminatory practices of labor unions that were awarded contracts with the city (Fonzi, 1963). He also led the battle to force an all-white orphanage held in trust by the city to open its doors to black children. While Moore and the protest movement which he led did win some battles, city hall remained largely unresponsive to black demands.

Moore also sought to expand his power through the electoral process by promoting black separatism. He argued that only blacks—preferably militant blacks—could electorally represent black constituencies. He argued that cooperating in political alliances with whites was inherently bad and those "so-called Negroes" who did were branded "tools of the white power structure" (Strange, 1969, 1973). But Moore's separatist approach and antibiracial coalition rhetoric was contradicted by the successes that moderate blacks achieved through biracial cooperation.

The white reform community had been working to strengthen alliances with the middle-class black leaders at the same time that Mayor Tate was attempting to insure black support through particularistic patronage rewards and Cecil Moore was trying to catalyze a politics of separatism. After a group of 400 black ministers led a series of well-coordinated boycotts against selected Philadelphia businesses that failed to respond to requests that they hire more blacks, Philadelphia's business community seemed to require no further prodding to begin major efforts to create employment and employment training programs specifically for the black community (Strange, 1973; Reynolds, 1975).

One concerted, well-funded effort to provide employment and training was the Urban Coalition. More than $1 million was pledged to the Urban Coalition by Philadelphia's business community. Together with $4.7 million from the federal government, these monies created the Philadelphia Employment Development Corporation, which provided job training for the hard-core unemployed. In announcing this initiative, Philadelphia's premier business leadership organ, the Greater Philadelphia Movement, echoed the pragmatism for which Atlanta's business leadership has become known by candidly admitting that their motivation for the project was to preclude an escalation from peaceful boycotts to violent riots:

> Most of greater Philadelphia's business and industrial leaders realized that unless the plight of the Black Americans became the central concern for all Americans, there will be no racial peace in this nation for possibly generations to come. (*New York Times*, 1968a, 1968b)

The most notable example of cooperation between the black leadership and the business community was the Opportunities Industrialization Center (OIC). OIC was created in 1964 by Rev. Leon Sullivan and his Zion Baptist Church in order to provide job training and business skills for blacks. After a year of success, money, training machinery and program guidance began flowing in from local business leaders as well as from the Ford Foundation. These are some of the most significant organizational vehicles by which the biracial reform alliance begun under Mayor Clark was continued in the period of rollback that this alliance faced in the Tate-Rizzo years. In the next section we will look at the electoral alliance between white reformers and blacks that was catalyzed by the tenure of Mayor Frank Rizzo.

RIZZO UNIFIES THE OPPOSITION: THE REFORM–BLACK ALLIANCE OF THE 1970s

Because Mayor Tate was prevented by the city charter from running for a third consecutive term, the 1971 Democratic primary became a pivotal contest. Frank Rizzo entered the campaign with the endorsement of Tate and the Democratic organization. Also running were black state Representative Hardy Williams, Congressman Bill Green, Jr. (son of the former party leader), who had broken with the organization and staked out a position as an independent, reform Democrat, and liberal Councilman David Cohen. Green, Williams, and Cohen were all competing for the votes of the biracial reform coalition. Green convinced Cohen to withdraw and lend him his support, but he was unable to convince Williams that dividing the anti-Rizzo vote insured a Rizzo victory. With 48 percent of the vote, Rizzo won, while Green captured 35 percent, Williams won 12.5 percent, and Cohen received the remainder, even though he had withdrawn.

In the general election Rizzo faced Thacher Longstreth, executive vice president of the Philadelphia Chamber of Commerce. Rizzo confined his appearances to working-class white neighborhoods. He promised the residents of these neighborhoods no unwanted public housing projects, opposition to busing children to schools for purposes of racial balance, no tax hikes, and a get-tough attitude toward crime that he boasted "would make Atilla the Hun look like a faggot." Though Rizzo did no campaigning in any black wards, he predicted, "I will win every black ward with the exception of maybe one" (Daughen and Binzen, 1977).

Longstreth campaigned tirelessly throughout the city. He had the support of the Republican organization, much of Philadelphia's business and civic leadership, including the Greater Philadelphia Movement (GPM), former mayors Clark and Dilworth, and the endorsement of the *Bulletin*. However, this was not enough. With a record turnout of 77 percent of the city's registered voters, Rizzo defeated Longstreth by just under 50,000 votes.

Frank Rizzo's 1971 mayoral campaign catalyzed a previously unseen degree of mobilization in the black community. In the primary, black voters demonstrated more willingness to support a white liberal who could win than to support a black who was relatively unknown to white voters. Bill Green won 51 percent of the vote in predominantly black wards; Williams captured only 37 percent. Green, with the help of Cohen's troops, was successful in convincing the majority of blacks that his candidacy offered the only hope of defeating Rizzo. But Green was unable to convince Williams that his independent course guaranteed Rizzo's victory. In retrospect, Williams' candidacy has been viewed as a milestone in independent black politics, both because it represented a first black mayoral candidacy and because Wilson Goode was a staff member (Ransom, 1987). But the salient feature of the 1971 Democratic primary was that together the votes garnered by the liberal-reform candidates and the black candidate would have beaten Rizzo.

In the general election, white liberals and blacks had chosen neither to stay at home nor to passively accept defeat and vote for their party's candidate. Instead they unified behind Longstreth and came close to defeating Rizzo. This event was most noteworthy for the black voters because it represented their first massive defection from the Democratic party to join in alliance with white liberal-reformers. In the ten wards in which more than 90 percent of the registered voters were black, Rizzo won only 23 percent of the vote. Sixty-four percent of the city's registered black voters cast ballots, and Rizzo was rejected by an amazing 77 percent of the voters in predominantly black wards. That Tate had captured approximately 70 percent of the vote in these black wards 4 years earlier indicates that the black vote represented a "sophisticated" defection from the candidate of the Democratic party. If contrasted to Chicago, where Mayor Richard J. Daley consistently won more black votes than any candidate he faced, including white liberal and black challengers, this demonstration of black independence from the Democratic party seems particularly significant.

As mayor, Rizzo continued to foster black unity. In addition to condoning a policy of police brutality against blacks that ultimately led to a federal investigation of the police force, Mayor Rizzo systematically waged war on the city's black leadership. He engineered the removal of one of the city's most prominent black ministers from the school board. He also removed Samuel Evans, former Mayor Tate's most trusted black advisor, from the vice presidency of the Bicentennial Commission (Hamilton, 1973). Even so, in 1975 Rizzo defeated Republican Thomas Foglietta and Charles Bowser, a black who ran as an independent candidate in the mayoral election. With two candidates dividing the anti-Rizzo vote, the election was really a contest for second place. Rizzo won with 57 percent of the vote, Bowser garnered 25 percent, and Foglietta received 18 percent. Most significantly, voters in the city's white reform wards demonstrated their willingness to support a qualified nondivisive black candidate by giving Bowser 41 percent of their vote. Even in the face of certain defeat, black and white leaders who favored a moderate, biracial coalition continued to work together to preserve the trust and norms of mutual support created under Clark and Dilworth as well as in the Longstreth campaign.

ELECTORAL MOBILIZATION AND THE FORMATION OF A DOMINANT BIRACIAL COALITION

The city's home rule charter prohibited more than two consecutive mayoral terms, so Rizzo began a campaign to amend the charter. "Good government" business leaders, including the GPM, liberal activists from the ADA and similar groups, and black reformers organized, financed, and provided the leadership for a coalition to protect the charter.

When Mayor Rizzo followed a strategy of attempting to divide the city along racial lines by calling upon white citizens to "Vote White," the city's civic leadership joined with the black community in unequivocally condemning and repudiating such tactics. After this blatant attempt to foster racial polarization, Rizzo was constantly on the defensive (Philadelphia *Inquirer*, 1978). The election results suggest—and interviews conducted by the author confirm—that the wide spectrum of leaders that condemned Rizzo's polarizing strategy produced an anti-Rizzo coalition broader than any he faced before (or subsequently). Sixty-seven percent of the voters voted against changing the charter. The winning coalition was comprised of blacks, reformers, liberals, and Jews (Featherman and Rosenberg, 1979). Displaying unprecedented unanimity, voters in predominantly black wards cast 96 percent of their ballots against Mayor Rizzo's proposal to change the charter.

Perhaps even more significant than black unanimity was the degree of mobilization in the black community. The voter registration drives in the black community were hugely successful and raised the black proportion of total registered voters by 6 points to 38 percent. The rate of turnout in predominantly black wards was 63 percent. Only 3 years before, when Charles Bowser ran as an independent mayoral candidate, blacks composed 31 percent of the city's registered voters and the rate of turnout in the black wards was 54 percent. Bowser's mayoral candidacy had not succeeded in getting unregistered black voters to register or in getting registered black voters to vote for him. However, Rizzo's blatantly racial appeal did succeed in catalyzing massive black voter registration and turnout against Rizzo.

In the race to fill the vacuum left by the removal of Frank Rizzo from the 1979 mayoral race, Congressman Bill Green, Jr. jumped out to an early lead. Green, who had narrowly lost to Rizzo in the 1971 Democratic primary, did not even wait until Rizzo had lost the charter change before he began recruiting support and raising funds for his campaign chest. He aimed his appeal at the biracial coalition of white reformers and blacks. Green publicly stated that he would strongly consider blacks for major positions in his administration and reiterated his record as an ally of black political advancement.

Within the black community, however, some leaders argued that after the massive registration and turnout of blacks precipitated by the charter referendum, a black mayor could be elected with little or no white support. They convinced Charles Bowser to be their candidate.

Seeking to remobilize the additional 100,000 blacks who registered to vote against the Charter change, Bowser shifted from the moderate tenor of his 1975 campaign and relentlessly attacked Bill Green, whom he tried to equate with the Rizzo gang. Green, however, refused to be provoked into confrontation and spoke only of healing the wounds left from Rizzo's tenure.

Green captured 53 percent of the vote and defeated Bowser (44 percent) in the Democratic primary. Bowser won every black ward and two predominantly white wards, but he was not able to mobilize the degree of support in the black wards that was necessary for victory. Turnout in the thirteen predominantly black wards was only 54 percent, which, although high for a primary election in Philadelphia, was lower than the 63 percent black turnout in the charter referendum.

Green faced Republican David Marston in November. Marston immediately began to try to build support in the black community. He publicly pledged that if elected, he would name a black as the city's managing director (city manager), the second most powerful post in the city government. Marston also initiated a dialogue with Bowser and attempted to win his endorsement.

Arguing that an independent black candidate would have a better chance in the general election against the two white candidates, Marston and Green, than Bowser had in the primary head-to-head with Green, Councilman Lucien Blackwell entered the mayoral race. Green believed that Bowser's criticisms and denunciations had diminished the support Green could expect from blacks, especially against Blackwell and Marston. Such considerations led Green to strike a deal with Bowser, in which, in exchange for his endorsement, Green matched Marston's promise to appoint a black as managing director. Again competition for the pivotal black vote produced a major step forward in the complete incorporation of blacks into the dominant political coalition.

Green emerged victorious with 53 percent of the vote, to Marston's 29 percent and Blackwell's 17 percent. Green waged an especially vigorous campaign in the black community and an analysis of the thirteen wards in which at least 90 percent of the registered voters were black shows that Green and Blackwell evenly split the black vote (Keiser, 1987a). The rate of turnout in predominantly black wards was 55 percent.

Bowser's endorsement was a watershed event. Many of the city's black leaders followed Bowser and endorsed Green over Blackwell, thereby preempting the possibility of a polarizing campaign based on dividing the white vote and mobilizing a black bloc. Because of the history of mutually advantageous cooperation and coalition formation between middle-class white liberals and blacks, lining up behind Green was not perceived by blacks as "selling out." Rather, the strategy yielded a black managing director and brought blacks one step closer to the mayor's office. The man Mayor Green named as managing director was Wilson Goode.

When Green took over the reins of Philadelphia's government the city was in the midst of a fiscal disaster, facing a $167 million deficit and a declining municipal bond rating. To attack this deficit, Green increased taxes and laid off more than 1200 city employees, including more than 700 police officers. The Green administration also stood firm and granted no first-year wage increase to city employees. At the end of the first full fiscal year of the Green administration, the city reported a surplus of $37 million.

While Green's economic courage and technocratic approach won him the admiration of the fiscally minded members of the community, the leaders of the Democratic organization, the unions, and the leaders of the black community all came to view the mayor as someone lacking in the political skills of bargaining and concession making. Green clashed with black leaders over an affirmative action hiring program for black police officers. Although in 1980 only 17 percent of Philadelphia's police force was black (while 39 percent of the population was black), Mayor Green opposed legislation to redress this balance because earlier in his administration he had laid off policemen and did not want now to hire new officers. Yet Councilman Blackwell and others argued that blacks deserved preferential treatment from Green, not only to remedy an unjust system built on past discrimination initiated by then Police Commissioner Rizzo, but also because, as crucial members of the mayor's electoral coalition, blacks had earned such rewards.

Blacks and white liberals on the city council also clashed with Mayor Green over set-aside legislation to aid minority-owned and female-owned firms in winning city contracts on a range of services from construction to consulting. The legislation called for minority-owned businesses to get 15 percent of the city's contracts, with another 10 percent to be reserved for businesses owned by women. Green vetoed this bill, but the city council overrode the Mayor's veto.[2]

Because of the emerging split between Green and his black supporters, there was considerable discussion in the black community about mounting an electoral challenge to Mayor Green. However, on November 2, 1982, Green shocked everyone in Philadelphia by announcing that he would not be a candidate for mayor in 1983. Attention immediately focused on two men: Green's predecessor, Frank Rizzo, who had long been hinting that he would run again, and Green's right-hand man and natural successor, Wilson Goode.

Wilson Goode is part of the moderate, reformist black political leadership group that distinguishes cities like Philadelphia and Atlanta from a city like Chicago, which has not fostered a moderate black political cadre (Keiser, 1987b). Like many in this group, Goode has strong ties to the black clergy, having long been a deacon in his church. He also has worked closely with the business community as the president of a nonprofit housing agency from 1967 to 1978. Goode was also a familiar face to the city's liberal activists, having long been a member of Americans for Democratic Action. In 1978, Governor Milton Shapp was having trouble filling a vacancy on the Public Utilities Commission (PUC), as the state Senate turned down nominee after nominee. Goode's name was suggested to Shapp, and he was confirmed unanimously. At the PUC, Goode gained attention for his skillful handling of the Three Mile Island nuclear facility disaster. From there he went to the most powerful post in Philadelphia government aside from the mayor, the office of managing director.

THE 1983 MAYORAL CAMPAIGN

To the surprise of almost every observer, the campaign between Rizzo and Goode was almost totally free of overt racial divisiveness. Why did Frank Rizzo conduct a racially nonpolarizing campaign in 1983? What had changed since 1978, when Rizzo had mobilized his base of support with a call for them to "Vote White"? Rizzo's campaign had an amicable, nondivisive tenor because that was the most expedient strategy for being elected mayor in the Philadelphia of the 1980s. Given an electorate in which blacks composed 39 percent of the registered voters, a Rizzo victory hinged on three factors: a large turnout of white ethnic blue-collar voters, winning some black votes, and minimizing his losses among white, middle- and upper-class reformers. Blacks and white liberal reformers previously had turned out and voted against Rizzo in heavy numbers because of his racially divisive tactics.

---

[2]Green and the black community leaders also clashed over his refusal to divest the city's pension fund from its investments in companies doing business in South Africa. See "Philadelphia Mayor in Trouble over Minority Aid," *New York Times*, May 17, 1982.

Therefore, to Rizzo and his campaign strategists, the way to diminish the turnout and anti-Rizzo voting of blacks and liberal whites was to avoid the race issue.

Goode understood the political environment in much the same way that Rizzo did. On the one hand, he had seen just how close to defeat Frank Rizzo was in the 1971 Democratic primary, when the combined votes of white liberals and blacks would have outpolled Rizzo (blacks were only 26 percent of the registered voters then). The cost of that failure to unify was a Rizzo victory that lasted 8 years. Conversely, in 1978 Rizzo was stopped by a coalition of registered, mobilized black voters in alliance with the business community and liberal white voters. Goode reached the same conclusion that Rizzo had reached: the road to victory was not to be found in an overtly racial appeal to blacks, which might polarize the electorate, but in a more moderate appeal to white liberals and the business community. Neither the black vote nor the white ethnic, blue-collar vote was big enough to win alone.

Goode's campaign was a position-paper campaign, not a racial crusade. Goode's major campaign themes were the problems of unemployment, the imperatives of creating and maintaining jobs in the city, and the need for the city to attract new firms while preventing the city's present employers from leaving. He also discussed the need to create and refurbish public and private housing and reform of the criminal justice system, often adding that there was no black or white way to deliver such city services. And he criticized Rizzo as an administrator.[3] He reminded voters of the corruption that existed in the Rizzo years, the cronyism in city hall, the huge tax hikes in the second Rizzo term, and the fiscal disaster that the Green administration inherited. When the newspapers did allude to the race factor in the campaign, the discussion was more often about the striking absence of race as an issue (Philadelphia *Daily News*, 1983; *New York Times*, 1983).

Goode was very successful in galvanizing the business community to make a strong effort on his behalf. In fact, the CEO of one of Philadelphia's largest banks and the president of ARCO Chemical both agreed that the support given to Goode by the business community was "the broadest . . . ever seen" (Philadelphia *Inquirer*, 1983a). Among Goode's backers in the business community, which included the Greater Philadelphia Partnership (the new name for the former GPM), two themes were consistently evident. First, the business and banking leadership believed that electing Goode would improve the city's position in the economic competition for new and relocating capital. Second, Goode would "unify the city" and be fair to all neighborhoods as well as to the downtown interests (Philadelphia *Inquirer*, 1983b,c).

Goode also had strong ties to community groups and liberal organizations. As managing director, Goode had demonstrated that he had a genuine desire to improve the conditions of the city's neighborhoods. He had approached representatives of more than thirty neighborhood groups in order to familiarize them with ways that

---

[3]Goode had impressive credentials to discuss government administration. He had earned a master's degree in government administration from the University of Pennsylvania's Wharton School in 1968.

they could influence city hall to improve program and service delivery in their neighborhoods. In meetings throughout the city, Goode explained how the budget was formulated, where the money went, the effects of federal government funding cutbacks, and how citizens could make the city government more accountable to their demands. An agenda that included the issues most commonly raised throughout the city was presented to Mayor Green and the city council (Schwartz, 1982a). Because of Goode's role in this activity, he received strong backing from some of the city's most liberal activists, including Edward Schwartz, director of the Institute for the Study of Civic Values.

Goode won the primary, capturing 53 percent of the vote, while Rizzo received 43 percent. Goode's general election victory would turn out to be a virtual replay of the primary vote. In the primary, black turnout was 69 percent; about 70 percent of registered whites voted. In predominantly black wards, Goode won 91 percent of the vote in the primary and 97 percent in the general election. Goode won about 18 percent of the white vote in the primary and 23 percent in the general election against Republican John Egan, a successful businessman, and independent candidate Thomas Leonard, formerly a Democrat and the city's controller. Rizzo's nondivisive campaign failed to win over liberal, upper-class voters in Chestnut Hill and Center City. In those wards (which Bowser had failed to win in the 1979 primary against Green) Goode captured 70 percent of the vote. In addition, Rizzo won only 44 percent of the vote in West Philadelphia-Overbrook and in the Logan Circle area, both of which were largely white (65 percent of the registered voters), middle-class areas with growing black populations.

THE GOODE RECORD

Evaluating the performance of Goode and his administration is a difficult task. Goode and his supporters argue that he has compiled a record of accomplishments that, if compared with either that of his predecessors or of mayors in other cities, would inspire praise. But, they claim, his performance has been measured— especially by the media—against the lofty expectations people had of him. One frequently mentioned example of this concerns the quality of city services. The Goode administration argues that it has been unfairly blamed for the numerous potholes in the city streets because this condition has existed for at least 30 years and no mayor has been able to address it except in an ad hoc fashion (*Christian Science Monitor*, 1986; Philadelphia *Inquirer*, 1987a). Yet the Goode administration did maintain relatively clean streets and created temporary dump sites until it successfully broke a garbage workers' strike, in which the issue was not the wages of a largely black work force but winning the right for the city to audit the union's books against a powerful union leader who had dictated terms to previous mayors. Moreover, decline in the quality of city services in Philadelphia has more to do with cuts in federal funding than with who sits in the mayor's office (Philadelphia *Inquirer*, 1987b).

When the Philadelphia Eagles professional football team threatened to leave the city for financial reasons, Mayor Goode personally negotiated with the team's ownership and carved out an agreement by which the Eagles, the jobs generated by the team, and the multiple sources of revenue the city collected because of the team did not leave. Goode received heavy criticism because he agreed to have the city pay the costs—and receive partial rental rights—for deluxe corporate sky boxes to be built atop the stadium. But by September 1987, when the Eagles wanted to buy back the skyboxes because of their popularity, Goode appeared to have scored a coup that promised financial gains for the city. This is but one example of the successes that the mayor has had in convincing large businesses to remain in Philadelphia and in attracting new companies to the city because of his personal involvement. The rapidly changing face of Center City Philadelphia—with scaffolding, construction cranes, and new office buildings—is testimony to the city's expanding economy (Summers and Luce, 1987).

Yet it would be totally inaccurate to view the Goode administration simply as a "business administration." Job creation was, and still is, the number-one issue in the black community. As Goode argued,

> Unless I can lay a good, sound economic foundation, no one will benefit from it. If I can build a strong economy here, then the black community benefits most from that, in my view, because they are the most unemployed. (*Philadelphia Magazine*, 1984)

The vast majority of the city's blacks have continued to support Wilson Goode not only because he is the city's first black mayor and not only because he has brought blacks into many positions of real power and responsibility (discussed below), but also because Goode has delivered on his promise by creating 37,000 new jobs (Philadelphia *Inquirer*, 1987a).

In the neighborhoods, the Goode administration has used federal Urban Development Action grants and block grant dollars to supplement private capital and bring to fruition efforts to revitalize neighborhood shopping areas. This investment has created construction jobs as well as permanent service industry jobs, in addition to upgrading the quality of life in the neighborhoods. While these projects have developed throughout the city, the Goode administration, unlike its predecessors, has not ignored the low-income black and Latino sections of North Philadelphia, where private capital has been least willing to invest.

The Goode administration has not ignored the city's poor. The single largest shift in spending in the budget ($2 million in the first year of the program) has been toward programs that provide shelter and provisions for the homeless of the city, a program that deserves its national recognition (U.S. Conference of Mayors, 1987). The city also has made significant improvements in its public housing program by placing tenants on the board of directors of the Housing Authority for the first time, putting managers in every building, and tripling the amount of money spent on rehabilitation of the property. Still, the city's housing efforts, especially in rehabilitating private housing, have been considered a disappointment because of the high expectations observers had; housing, after all, was Goode's area of prior expertise. Although the question of who gets what in black mayoral administrations requires additional case-study data, such as are presented in this book, it is clear that under Wilson Goode issues of concern to the largely black poor receive greater attention than they have under previous white mayors. While certainly there is more that can be done, the Goode administration has not limited political and economic advancement to middle-class professionals.

The problem that has slowed the work of the housing authority and stalled Goode's efforts in a number of areas is the same problem that has overshadowed almost all of the mayor's achievements—the MOVE disaster. MOVE is a radical, back-to-nature group that has existed in Philadelphia for the past decade. In Mayor Rizzo's second term, an armed confrontation between the police and MOVE led to the death of an officer. MOVE had received virtually no sympathy or support from Philadelphians of any stripe, while in the areas where MOVE has settled, it has quickly alienated its neighbors. In May of 1985, after members of the group refused to evacuate a house they were occupying, a Philadelphia police helicopter dropped a bomb on the house. The bomb started a fire that killed eleven MOVE members, including five children, and destroyed sixty-one homes and two city blocks of the surrounding black neighborhood.

This outcome shocked and outraged even the most passionate enemies of MOVE. The mayor convened a blue-ribbon commission to investigate the bombing and decide which city officials were responsible. Rather than being a whitewash, the commission launched a thorough investigation that dragged on even after the resignations of the police commissioner and the managing director. Because of this, the mayor was unable to act to put the disaster behind him and move forward (Philadelphia *Daily News*, 1986).

Meanwhile, the construction firms selected to do the reconstruction of the burned-down homes were generating cost overruns as well as controversy about the quality of their work. After 8 months of such controversy, the construction firms were replaced. A grand jury investigating charges of impropriety against the firms concluded that "much of the blame for the project's unfortunate waste of resources lies with the mayor and the key people on whom he relied. He often exercised bad judgement and frequently exhibited inflexibility" (Philadelphia *Inquirer*, 1987c).

While the MOVE disaster—especially the perception that the mayor was not "in charge" during these events—weakened his claims to be a hands-on administrator, many citizens recognized that the unique situation he faced was not one on which judgments of administrative competence could fairly be made. But the reconstruction fiasco hurt the mayor because it shook the confidence of his former supporters in the white liberal and business communities. It seems that at least one of the contractors involved had a reputation for winning jobs by giving unrealistically low bids and then producing huge cost overruns. Furthermore, though the mayor was apprised of this practice, he insisted on going with minority-owned firms for the reconstruction of this largely black neighborhood, and leaned toward these contractors. Some of the mayor's supporters-turned-critics charge that he allowed racial considerations not only to influence a major executive decision but also to blind him to early indications of incompetence that resulted in more than $1 million in overruns.

Goode's choice of incompetent or corrupt administrators and his failure to remove them quickly again became evident in the scandals surrounding the Inner City Organizing Network (ICON), the recipient of a major share of the city's federal housing funds. ICON Director Charles L. "Boo" Burrus, an associate of the mayor, was charged with theft and misuse of housing money.[4]

Aside from MOVE, the mayor was harshly criticized for his inability to resolve a number of problems inherited from the Green administration. Although Goode took credit for resolving a long-standing impasse that blocked the legislation necessary for establishing cable TV franchises in the city, the politics behind the resolution of this issue indicates some of the constraints that a moderate reformer like Goode faces. Mayor Green believed that the licenses and contracts for cable television service should go to companies making the best offers, on the basis of cost per customer and area of service. But some members of the city council believed that companies that were, or would become, political and financial supporters of individual members of the city council deserved these contracts. The result was a stalemate that angered the citizens who could not get access to cable television services that their neighbors in the suburbs enjoyed. Goode was expected to come in as a strong mayor and force the city council to be a vehicle for "good government." Instead, he balked at confronting the council. Goode chose to satisfy the demands of the citizenry for cable television service by giving the city council control of the awarding of the contracts. But two other issues that Goode promised to resolve—the future plan for trash disposal in the city and construction of a major convention center—languished in the city council because the mayor refused, in his own words, to "do the kind of political trading that goes with that. . . . We simply can't afford to satisfy the insatiable appetite of members of Council if you're going to base votes on political trading" (Philadelphia *Inquirer*, 1987d). While the mayor has offered a number of sound proposals to resolve these issues, he cannot proceed without the approval of the city council. Unless he persuades the council to take action on his legislation or allows the council to address these problems in its own way, Goode will be popularly perceived as a weak leader who is unable to move the city forward.

POLITICAL RESPONSIVENESS
TO MINORITY DEMANDS

In both the Green and Goode mayoral elections, blacks represented the largest voting bloc in the victorious electoral coalition. Green campaigned extensively in

---

[4] Another issue that hurt the mayor, though less severely, arose when Goode could not provide an adequate explanation for his failure to report gifts of clothing (nineteen men's suits) from union officials.

the black wards and identified himself with the struggle for equal opportunity for blacks and an end to racial discrimination. Whether Green was overly cautious about producing a racial backlash or whether he believed that black loyalty could be maintained with liberal rhetoric and little substance, as Mayor Jane Byrne mistakenly believed in Chicago, remains a source of debate. What is beyond debate is that the Green administration made only minor efforts to increase the political and economic power of the city's blacks to levels even approaching parity with the 39 percent of the population blacks represented. Even after the Abscam affair—in which three members of the conservative, Rizzocrat leadership of the city council were videotaped receiving kickbacks in exchange for help on real estate deals and two were forced to resign—altered the nature of the city council and shifted it from domination by the city's conservative forces to the liberal reformers, the mayor did not take the lead on minority issues (Schwartz, 1982b). Although Green's record was without a doubt an improvement over the pattern of rollback of black political achievement evident in the Rizzo years, it compared poorly with the accomplishments of Mayor Goode.

In the area of executive appointments, where the mayor of Philadelphia is given nearly total discretion by the city's charter, Wilson Goode was the only black appointed to Green's four-man cabinet. In Goode's six-person cabinet, there were two black males, one black female, one white male, and two white females. Sixty percent of the agency chiefs appointed by Goode were black, while in the Green administration the comparable figure was 30 percent. In 1987, after a number of top-level reorganizations, 43 percent of these executive appointments were black. As of 1980, the Bureau of the Census reported that blacks represented 39 percent of the city's population, Latinos were just under 4 percent, and 52 percent were white.

The Green administration also did not enthusiastically attack the problem of racial and gender discrimination in the awarding of contracts with the city. After the city council passed set-aside legislation against the mayor's will, the Green administration awarded a total of only $2.4 million to minority- and female-owned firms. In contrast, in 1984 the Goode administration awarded $43 million worth of contracts to such firms (32 percent to female-owned firms), while in 1985 $63 million worth of contracts went to minority-owned firms and $27 million went to female-owned firms. This still represented only 26 percent of the city's aggregate contract expenditures.

With respect to affirmative action in the municipal work force, the record of the Goode administration also is noteworthy. According to Equal Employment Opportunity (EEO) reports filed by the city with the federal government, in the last year of Mayor Green's administration (1982–1983) blacks represented 28 percent of the municipal work force, Latinos 1 percent, and whites 70 percent. By the end of the second year of the Goode mayoralty, blacks held 41 percent of the jobs in the city government, and Latinos held 14 percent. The Goode administration has not been satisfied with simply raising aggregate numbers of minorities in city jobs; it has actively sought to prepare minority applicants for the highest-level jobs by implementing an "Upward Mobility Program." This program places clerical incumbents into special trainee classes and promotional tracks in order to remedy more directly the situation of white male domination of professional-status, better-paying jobs. Figures for 1987 show that the Goode administration had increased the proportion of blacks in the top three EEO job classifications from 24 percent under Mayor Green to 28 percent.

Has the election of Wilson Goode economically benefited the black community? While more remains to be accomplished, the answer to this question is yes. Middle-class blacks have won a greater proportion of city contracts and high-level city jobs; poor blacks have won a greater share of low-skill city jobs. The mayor's efforts have improved the employment outlook in the private sector as well. Goode has improved the quality of life in poor neighborhoods that were largely ignored in the past and his administration has produced a comprehensive, humanitarian response to the homeless.

LATINOS IN PHILADELPHIA

In contrast to some of the other chapters in this volume, discussion of the Latino population of Philadelphia has been conspicuously absent. This is because Latinos have until recently played a very minor role in the city's politics. According to Census Bureau data, in 1970 only about 2 percent of the city's population were Latinos ("Hispanics," in census terminology); by the 1980 census almost 4 percent were Latinos, with nearly three-quarters of these Puerto Rican. Even with the small numbers they represent, however, the competitiveness of the city's politics has forced all politicians seeking citywide offices to court Latino voters.

Wilson Goode has done this assiduously and, under Goode, black empowerment has initiated Latino incorporation. In his initial mayoral campaign, Goode listed liberal lawyer Angel Ortiz on his sample ballot for an at-large seat on the city council. While Ortiz was not elected, he came very close to winning. As mayor, Goode appointed him to the post of commissioner of records, the first Latino to head a city department. Because of the death of a councilman, Ortiz ran in a special election and won, with Goode's support, becoming the first Latino to serve on the city council.

Wilson Goode has received strong electoral support from the Latino community. He received approximately 66 percent of the vote in predominantly Latino precincts in the 1983 Democratic primary against Frank Rizzo and 77 percent of their votes in the general election. Goode's level of support declined in the 1987 Democratic primary, in which he received approximately 70 percent of the Latino vote. The largest part of this decline came in those Latino voting divisions (precincts) that were in state Representative Ralph Acosta's district. Acosta, another prominent Latino politician, had endorsed Goode's opponent, Edward Rendell. In the general election, Ortiz, who was again elected to an at-large seat on the city council, campaigned vigorously for Goode against Republican candidate Frank Rizzo, warning that a Rizzo victory would mean a "return to slavery . . . and racism.'' Goode won about 75 percent of the Latino vote in his narrow victory over Rizzo.

THE FUTURE OF BIRACIAL POLITICS
IN PHILADELPHIA

Following Frank Rizzo's announcement that he was switching to the GOP to challenge Wilson Goode, approximately 50,000 of his most ardent supporters gave up their Democratic registration and became Republicans. This increased the black proportion of registered Democrats, so that for the first time in the city's history, blacks outnumbered whites in the Democratic party. Will Rizzo's switch to the Republican party divide the city and make the Democrats a "black" party? Was the nonracially polarizing tenor of the 1983 mayoral campaign, which so markedly differentiated Philadelphia from Chicago, a fluke? What are the prospects for the continuation of the political leadership of the biracial, reform coalition? Is there a possibility that a biracial organizational (that is, a machine-style and non-reform) alliance could emerge?

It is important to recognize that even with the MOVE incident overshadowing the mayor's accomplishments and sullying his reputation, political divisions have not had racial overtones or implications in Philadelphia. Goode's opponents have not attacked him for favoring blacks in appointments nor have they condemned black politicians in general for the mistakes of the mayor. In the Democratic mayoral primary, Goode won 57 percent of the vote and defeated Edward Rendell, a former District Attorney and unsuccessful gubernatorial candidate. Rendell had previously enjoyed the backing of the biracial reform coalition and had been an ally of Goode. Rendell argued that MOVE and its aftermath "stood as a monument to the mismanagement and incompetence of Wilson Goode." Rendell received the support of white liberals and business executives who had supported Goode in 1983 (Philadelphia *Inquirer*, 1987e) as well as support from both of the city's newspapers, which had endorsed Goode in 1983. In personal interviews, these reform-minded former supporters of Mayor Goode indicated that while they were backing away from a mayor whom they perceived to be incompetent, they had not lost faith in the ethos of biracial, reform coalitions. Some already were looking toward 1991 and the opportunity to vigorously support blacks such as state Secretary of Welfare John White, Schools Superintendent Constance Clayton, or Congressman William Gray, Jr. for the mayoralty.

Yet Rendell was by no means the clear favorite of either the city's liberal activists or the business community. Goode maintained significant support from these groups (Philadelphia *Inquirer*, 1987f,g). A number of liberal neighborhood activists indicated that Goode's commitment to addressing issues of housing, service delivery, and neighborhood economic revitalization was beyond doubt and that they had high expectations for a second Goode term, once the mayor put the crippling MOVE debacle behind him. Leaders of the business community were not as optimistic about the potential for accomplishments by a second Goode administration, in part because they felt that the mayor's image and ability to attract new investment had been irreparably tarnished. Still, the continued support for Mayor Goode from both liberal activists and business leaders against Rendell and even more so against Republican mayoral candidate Frank Rizzo—and the stated intent to support black reformers in future mayoral races—indicated that the incremental incorporation of blacks in a biracial, reform coalition has made, and will continue to make, a difference in the way political alliances are evaluated in Philadelphia. This is why there has been no equivalent to Chicago's "Council Wars," nor has there been a prominent politician who has declared that he would support "anyone but the mayor," as Edward Vrdolyak of Chicago did.

But the persistence of the biracial reform coalition is not the only reason why in Philadelphia, party and race do not coincide. The white ethnic and labor leadership of the Democratic party did not defect from Wilson Goode in 1983 or 1987, even though many of their constituents did. The Democratic party organization, largely because of the unifying leadership of ward leader and former union leader Robert Brady, has also been able to reach accommodations with Mayor Goode and even more so with black leaders in the city council: While rumors had anticipated defections of white Democratic politicians to Rizzo and the Republicans, none materialized. Only one of the city's twenty-eight-member Democratic delegation to the state house and senate defected to the Rizzo team. While credit for Goode's 1987 mayoral victory goes foremost to blacks, who turned out at a rate of about 70 percent and gave Goode 97 percent of their votes, as well as to those living in the city's upper-income reform areas, who gave the mayor 54 percent of their votes, Goode could not have eked out his 18,000-vote victory without the support of Democratic party ward leaders who persuaded their friends, families, and city jobholders to vote for Goode. Unless the Republican party can recruit a candidate who can command the loyalty of white ethnic voters as Rizzo did—which seems unlikely—the Democratic party will maintain its white constituency and a nearly 3-to-1 edge in registration.

Brady and the Democratic ward leaders have pragmatic reasons for re-electing Goode: in a Republican administration, many of them would have much less clout. But more significantly, these white leaders of the Democratic organization believe that in 1991 they may be able to elect a black Democrat who is not a reformer but is amendable to their machine style of politics. In the post-Rizzo era, the city council has shifted from an arena in which Rizzocrats fought the white-reform–black coalition over the issue of political incorporation to one in which a biracial coalition of politicians who favor a machine style of politics is in conflict with a biracial, reform coalition allied with the city's business community. Black leaders such as Councilman Lucien Blackwell and state Representative Dwight Evans are now powerful figures within the Democratic organization that once tried to subordinate them. Issues of patronage, the dispensation of city contracts, the selection of candidates for political offices, and spoils for their supporters are all areas in which they can align with white ward politicians and party leaders. But other black leaders, most notably Congressman William Gray, Jr. and former Councilman John F. White (appointed state secretary of welfare by Governor Casey), remain committed to the good-government tenets they share with the city's white liberal and business communities.

In short, two biracial coalitions now exist in Philadelphia. Mayor Goode has walked the line between both groups and, depending on the issue, has been a champion or a disappointment to either group. In October 1986, even before the campaign had begun, the leaders of these black factions unanimously endorsed Goode for a second term. They stated that they did not want the city "to go the way of Cleveland"—a city where an incumbent black mayor lost to a white challenger. But in 1991, unless a white candidate drives the black leadership together, there may be a contest that pits Blackwell against a black reformer, perhaps John F. White, or Councilman George Burrell, Jr., or Councilwoman Augusta Clark. That a similar split between "reform" and "machine" blacks emerged in Chicago after the election of Mayor Harold Washington, and again after his death (and in New Orleans, after the election of Mayor Morial, although here the contours of the split differ) suggests not only the difficulty in maintaining unity after the threshold election of a first black mayor but also that white voters may play the pivotal and decisive role that black voters have sometimes played in deciding what kind of coalition governs the city (Rivlin, 1986).

PHILADELPHIA'S BIRACIAL COALITION IN COMPARATIVE PERSPECTIVE

For the student of biracial coalition formation, the Philadelphia case yields a number of interesting points of comparison. As in Atlanta, as well as in Baltimore, another city that recently elected a black mayor, in Philadelphia the business community unified in an effort to make their city an attractive climate to which new firms would locate. The Greater Philadelphia Movement was formed by businessmen who personally encountered difficulty in attracting new firms to the city because of its reputation for corruption (Lowe, 1967; Petshek, 1973). These leaders of the business community realized that the prevailing climate of race relations was also an important aspect of the city's image and attractiveness for investors, and this led them to strike an alliance with middle-class black leaders.

But urban coalition formation and policy making cannot be reduced to the products of efforts by city leaders to advantageously position themselves in the national political economy. In Philadelphia, as well as in New York and Los Angeles, the biracial coalition included an organized, vibrant liberal-reform community that, among other issues, was opposed to the political and economic subordination of blacks. Their basis for participation was ideological, having little to do with economic competition among cities. With social and economic dynamics very similar to those of post-Lindsay New York, Philadelphia's biracial coalition suffered a rollback of its power in the Tate–Rizzo era. But the political response of the participants in the biracial coalition was very different in the two cities. In New York, liberal Jews parted ways with their former black allies after the Ocean Hill–Brownsville school crisis and increasingly moved toward an alliance with conservative whites (Rieder, 1985). In Philadelphia, both liberal reformers and the business leadership maintained and further solidified their alliance with black leaders in an 8-year rearguard experience as the opposition, minority coalition. Certainly the fact that the alternative to the biracial coalition was an alliance with Mayor Frank Rizzo helped to maintain the unity of the biracial coalition. But efforts such as the business–black Urban Coalition, the joint defection of blacks, liberal Democrats, and the GPM to the Longstreth candidacy, and the victory of the biracial coalition against the 1978 charter-change referendum have more to do with the political trust that was a product of the Clark–Dilworth era and that has been maintained because of the continued electoral viability of this alliance.

The historical alliance within which this political trust was developed has been facilitated by the weakness of the regular Democratic organization that has allowed the factionalization of the traditional urban Democratic party coalition. Politics in Philadelphia has been less like that of New York and Chicago, where strong Democratic party organizations have persisted, and more like the intraparty factionalism of New Orleans as well as the fluid nonpartisan politics of Atlanta and Los Angeles. In Philadelphia, partisan loyalties have not been strong enough to preclude a biracial reform coalition of traditionally Democratic white liberals and blacks, with broad support from the business community, from engaging in intra- and interparty competition against traditionally Democratic conservative whites.

REFERENCES

Banfield, Edward. 1965. *Big City Politics*. New York: Random House.

Banfield, Edward, and James Q. Wilson. 1963. *City Politics*. New York: Vintage Books.

Christian Science Monitor. July 22, 1986. Goode's Bright Promise Beset by MOVE, Strike.

Daughen, Joseph, and Peter Binzen. 1977. *The Cop Who Would Be King: Mayor Frank Rizzo*. Boston: Little, Brown.

Ekstrom, Charles A. 1973. The Electoral Politics of Reform and Machine: The Political Behavior of Philadelphia's "Black" Wards, 1943–1969. In Miriam Ershkowitz and Joseph Zikmund II, eds., *Black Politics in Philadelphia*. New York: Basic Books.

Featherman, Sandra, and William L. Rosenberg. 1979. *Jews, Blacks and Ethnics: The 1978 "Vote White" Charter Campaign in Philadelphia*. Philadelphia: American Jewish Committee.

Fonzi, Gaeton. July 1963. Cecil Storms In. *Greater Philadelphia Magazine*.

Hamilton, Fred. 1973. *Rizzo*. New York: Viking Press.

Keiser, Richard. 1987a. Amicability or Polarization? Patterns of Political Competition and Leadership Formation in Cities with Black Mayors. Presented at the annual meeting of the Midwest Political Science Association, Chicago.

Keiser, Richard. 1987b. Why Biracial Coalitions Matter: Patterns of Black Leadership and the Election of Black Mayors in Chicago and Philadelphia. Presented at the annual meeting of the American Political Science Association, Chicago.

Lowe, Jeanne. 1967. *Cities in a Race With Time*. New York: Random House.

Mayhew, David. 1986. *Placing Parties in American Politics*. Princeton: Princeton University Press.

New York Times. May 12, 1968a. Philadelphia Poor Pledged $1 million by Business Group.

New York Times. November 24, 1968b. Negro Help Is Planned in Pa. City.

New York Times. April 12, 1983. Race Is a Muted Issue in Philadelphia.

Peterson, Paul E. 1967. City Politics and Community Action: The Implementation of the Community Action Program in Three American Cities. Unpublished Ph.D. dissertation, University of Chicago, chap. 4.

Philadelphia *Bulletin*. January 24, 1965. Parties Court Negroes, Who Hold Key to Power.

Philadelphia *Bulletin*. January 23, 1974. Tate Felt a Rizzo Win Would Save Democratic Control.

Philadelphia *Daily News*. November 9, 1983. Hard Work Supplied Goode's Mandate.

Philadelphia *Daily News*. March 7, 1986. The MOVE Report.

Philadelphia *Inquirer*. September 30, 1978. City's Religious Leaders Censure Racial Rhetoric.

Philadelphia *Inquirer*. October 31, 1983a. Business Leaders Give Less to Goode for This Campaign.

Philadelphia *Inquirer*. May 22, 1983b. Philadelphia Was Also a Winner in the Primary.

Philadelphia *Inquirer*. January 31, 1983c. Business Leaders Give Less to Goode for This Campaign.

Philadelphia *Inquirer*. April 22, 1984. Strong Start, Few Fumbles for the Mayor.

Philadelphia *Inquirer*. November 27, 1986. Goode's Re-election is a Dilemma for Blacks, Also.

Philadelphia *Inquirer*. May 24, 1987a. Goode Pulled Black Vote for a Range of Reasons.

Philadelphia *Inquirer*. October 18, 1987b. City Services Have Been Tied as Much to Federal Aid as Mayoral Leadership.

Philadelphia *Inquirer*. May 12, 1987c. Mayor's Race Dominates the Primary Election.

Philadelphia *Inquirer*. January 4, 1987d. For Goode, a Year of Recovery.

Philadelphia *Inquirer*. April 25, 1987e. Many on Green's Team Help Rendell.

Philadelphia *Inquirer*. April 23, 1987f. "Progressive" Group of 50 Lawyers, Activists Endorses Mayor Goode.

Philadelphia *Inquirer*. November 2, 1987g. Business Community Putting Fewer Bucks Behind Goode in 1987.

Philadelphia Magazine. December 1984. The No-Frills Mayor.

Ransom, Bruce. 1987. Black Independent Electoral Politics in Philadelphia: The Election of Mayor W. Wilson Goode. In Michael Preston, Lenneal Henderson Jr., and Paul Puryear, eds., *The New Black Politics*, 2nd edition. New York: Longman.

Reichley, James. 1959. *The Art of Government: Reform and Organization Politics in Philadelphia*. New York: The Fund for the Republic.

Reynolds, Barbara. 1975. *Jesse Jackson: The Man, the Movement, the Myth*. Chicago: Nelson-Hall.

Rieder, Jonathan. 1985. *Canarsie: The Jews and Italians of Brooklyn against Liberalism*. Cambridge: Harvard University Press.

Rivlin, Gary. February 14, 1986. The Heart of a New Machine. Chicago *Reader*.

Rogers, David. 1971. *The Management of Big Cities*. Beverly Hills: Sage.

Schwartz, Edward. 1982a. *The Neighborhood Agenda*. Philadelphia: Institute for the Study of Civic Values

Schwartz, Edward. September-October, 1982b. The Philadelphia City Council: From AB-SCAM to Activism. *Ways and Means.*

Strange, John Hadley. 1966. The Negro in Philadelphia Politics: 1963–1965. Unpublished Ph.D. dissertation, Princeton University.

Strange, John Hadley. 1969. The Negro and Philadelphia Politics. In Edward Banfield, ed., *Urban Government.* New York: The Free Press.

Strange, John Hadley. 1973. Blacks and Philadelphia Politics. In Miriam Ershkowitz and Joseph Zikmund II, eds., *Black Politics in Philadelphia.* New York: Basic Books.

Summers, Anita, and Thomas Luce. 1987. *Economic Development Within the Philadelphia Metropolitan Area.* Philadelphia: University of Pennsylvania Press.

U.S. Conference of Mayors. May, 1987. *A Status Report on Homeless Families in America's Cities.* Washington, D.C.: U.S. Conference of Mayors.

Weiler, Conrad. 1974. *Philadelphia: Neighborhood, Authority, and the Urban Crisis.* New York: Praeger.

PART III
Barriers

CHAPTER 4

New York: The Great Anomaly

John H. Mollenkopf

Editors' Note

New York is the largest city in the United States. About half of its population is black and Latino. These groups have a long history of sophisticated political participation and at times have formed an alliance with a sizable, politically active, liberal white population. Knowing these facts make it easy to predict that blacks and Latinos are strong partners in Mayor Edward Koch's long-term and popular administration.

Easy, but wrong. As John Mollenkopf shows, blacks and Latinos have been politically much weaker in New York than we would expect. The contrast to other large cities is striking. Los Angeles, Chicago, and Philadelphia have all had black mayors, but in New York neither blacks nor Latinos are even strong members of the governing coalition.

Why have blacks and Latinos been so weak in New York? Read Mollenkopf's explanations as a kind of sourcebook of barriers to minority incorporation. The barriers he describes are not unique to New York, but they have come together with special intensity and in unique combination to block minority political incorporation in that city.

Given the adverse conditions in New York, is there anything that can be done, any strategy that might produce a successful minority-based coalition? Mollenkopf draws lessons from the Chicago experience to recommend ways of strengthening minority politics in New York.

In *Protest Is Not Enough*, Rufus Browning, Dale Marshall, and David Tabb present several straightforward and convincing ideas about political development in ten California cities over the last 20 years. They argue that these city governments did not respond to minority interests in direct proportion to the amount of minority protest. Rather, they did so only when new, more liberal biracial coalitions defeated the conservative white coalitions that had previously wielded power. Where such new coalitions failed to come to power, government continues to resist policies that benefitted minorities. But where new coalitions did succeed, and especially when blacks or Latinos led the way in organizing the challenging coalition, then policies shifted in favor of minority interests. This kind of minority participation, termed political incorporation by Browning, Marshall, and Tabb, stemmed from previous minority activism—both protest and electoral—and from the degree of white support for minority political advancement. Finally, the size of the minority community and its leadership capacity determined the degree of protest and electoral mobilization.

KOCH'S NEW YORK BY WAY OF BROWNING, MARSHALL, AND TABB'S CALIFORNIA

If applied to the political raw material of New York City, this neat theoretical model would predict that a new, liberal coalition should be in power, that blacks and Latinos should enjoy substantial political incorporation, and that policy outputs should as a result favor minority interests. After all, the antecedent conditions that Browning, Marshall, and Tabb say promote such outcomes are present in abundant supply. Blacks and Latinos not only make up over half the city's population, but they have a long history of electoral mobilization and direct protest actions. Even more important, from Browning, Marshall, and Tabb's perspective, New York's white population, particularly its Jews, have been comparatively much more liberal and supportive of civil rights than have the white ethnic populations of other large, old cities. Applied to New York, Browning, Marshall, and Tabb's theory thus predicts the success of a dominant liberal coalition with significant minority partnership. In fact, until recently such a coalition has been hard to find on the local political scene; the dominant coalition is conservative and, some would charge, hostile to minorities. What explains this anomaly?

It is not New York's failure to fulfill the assumptions of Browning, Marshall, and Tabb's model. In the 1980 census, New York's population was 23.9 percent black and 19.9 percent Latino; these numbers may have been substantially undercounted. Today, nearly a decade later, the statistically less reliable current population survey suggests that blacks and Latinos make up just over half of the city's population. Both groups also have a long history of political mobilization. Blacks broke into the ranks of the city's elected officials with Adam Powell's and Benjamin Davis' election to the city council in 1941 and 1943. The first Puerto Rican assemblyman was elected on the Republican and American Labor Party lines in 1938.

The subsequent political development in both groups has been steady, though not continuous. A high point may have been reached in the early 1970s, when the Bronx was represented by a reform-oriented Puerto Rican borough president and Manhattan by a more regular party black borough president. From the 1960s onward, a new generation of leadership, particularly in Brooklyn, produced an increase in the number of black reform victories in such offices as the state assembly. Among the city's prominent black and Latino politicians are Congressman Charles Rangel, Manhattan Borough President David Dinkins, Bronx Borough President Fernando Ferrer, and former borough president and deputy mayor Herman Badillo.

Concerning the white liberalism that Browning, Marshall, and Tabb hold to be essential for the advent of a biracial coalition, the city's votes in state and national elections over the past several decades clearly place its whites on the liberal end of the urban political spectrum. Indeed, Mayor Lindsay's election in 1967 and reelection in 1971 provided a national model of what such a new liberal, biracial coalition could be like in city politics. The Lindsay regime experimented with new forms of political incorporation such as offices of neighborhood government that became models for other cities. It would be reasonable to expect that these experiments would be institutionalized in New York's political development, even after Lindsay's departure, resulting in a more favorable distribution of policy benefits toward minority groups. During the 1980s, however, New York had neither a Lindsay-style biracial governing coalition nor a perpetuation of the spending and distributional priorities that the Lindsay regime sought to put into place.

A replication of Browning, Marshall, and Tabb's measures of minority incorporation clearly shows that the degree of minority political incorporation is weak in New York. At the most crucial level, blacks were not part of the mayor's electoral coalition. Indeed, they were the group most strongly opposed to him in the 1985 election. Nor, despite its reform roots, can the Koch administration be called liberal. Mayor Koch is widely criticized for polarizing racial attitudes, or at any rate for capitalizing on prevailing racial cleavages. Although he denies this characterization and points to his minority appointments, he has given his critics much ammunition, most recently in his harsh attack on Jesse Jackson in the 1988 presidential primary. He has called a committee working for better black–Jewish relations a "cabal" against him. He has also castigated the national Democratic party for losing touch with the white middle class.

Blacks and Latinos are also poorly represented among the larger group of elected officials who, with the Mayor, make the key decisions in New York City government. The most powerful body is the Board of Estimate, composed of the mayor, controller, and city council president (all elected citywide and holding two votes each) and the five borough presidents (each with one vote). After a decade of no minority representation on the Board, one black, David Dinkins, who had long ties to party regulars, was elected (Manhattan borough president) in 1985, and the Bronx regular Democratic organization appointed a Puerto Rican city councilman, Fernando Ferrer, to replace a white borough president forced to resign in 1987 in the city's corruption scandals. Thus minorities have only two of eleven votes on this body. While both minority borough presidents have been effective, neither got his position via independent grass roots mobilization.

While a tradition of reciprocity gives these officials influence on Board decisions affecting their boroughs, the Mayor has had little problem securing Board acquiescence in his policies. The minority members do not constitute a challenge to the Mayor's policy agenda. Moreover, because boroughs that are widely divergent in population cast the same vote on the Board, it has been ruled unconstitutionally malapportioned. A Charter Revision Commission has recommended that the Board's primary powers be abolished, thus eroding the influence of Manhattan's and the Bronx's minority borough presidents and shifting their powers to minority members of the City Council, who are even more dependent on the regular county party organizations.

The less powerful thirty-five member City Council, termed by some "worse than a rubber stamp because it leaves no impression," has better minority representation. It includes seven blacks (20 percent) and three Latinos (8.6 percent), as contrasted with black and Latino proportions of 24 percent and 20 percent in the overall population and 23 percent and 13 percent in the 1985 Democratic mayoral primary electorate. But these minority councilpersons were divided in the 1986 factional maneuvering to organize the Council and seven were on the losing side. In addition, most of the black and Latino members are politically incorporated through the regular Democratic party organizations of their respective boroughs. Only two black council members may be considered reform or insurgent; the other five and the three Latinos are aligned with "the machine." While minority representatives in the state legislature and congress may be considered somewhat more independent, many are also influenced by the regulars. The black and Puerto Rican caucus depends heavily on the Assembly Speaker, who is a major figure in the Brooklyn regular Democratic organization, for its slice of the legislative pie. This dependence largely confines caucus challenges to the realm of rhetoric and symbol.

In sum, minority elected officials are not a powerful and independent force in the overall allocation of public benefits, although they do extract rewards from the white political establishment. In general, this establishment can secure their cooperation at a relatively low price in patronage, contracts, and similar benefits. With the exception of Congressman Charles Rangel, none of the city's minority representatives can be called a highly influential legislative leader. Collectively, blacks and Latinos are either excluded from the dominant coalition (as in the mayoralty or the Board of Estimate) or (as in the Council and Legislature) have been incorporated as a dependent, controlled, and numerically underrepresented minority. This adds up to a surprisingly low score on Browning, Marshall, and Tabb's political incorporation index.

New York City is also anomalous from the perspective of *Protest Is Not Enough* because minority influence actually retrogressed after the early 1970s. While Browning, Marshall, and Tabb concede that the conservative shift in national politics and the elimination of antipoverty programs have threatened minority gains, none of their case-study cities has experienced the kind of political rollback that has occurred in New York. The Lindsay administration needed minority support to retain power. Since then, successful citywide candidates have not felt impelled to make minority support a central part of their coalition, a stance that has had visible results in the distribution of benefits.

The fiscal crisis and federal cutbacks severely reduced funding for many of the community-based programs developed in the late 1960s to incorporate minority interests. In New York City, these cuts reduced subsidized housing development, the community development block-grant program, and the community services block grant. Local resources devoted to such programs were also reduced. Based on their *Setting Municipal Priorities* project, Charles Brecher and Raymond Horton found that social spending lost out to developmental and basic services through the cycle of austerity and recovery between 1975 and 1983 (Brecher and Horton, 1984, pp. 1–11). Mayor Koch also held wage raises for municipal employees, many of whom are black or Latino, below increases in the cost of living during these years. New York therefore illustrates the possibility that the advent of a new dominant coalition is not enough to prevent the subsequent rollback of minority political incorporation.

At a broader level, however, the conservative coalition embodied by the Koch administration has maintained and even expanded some of the patterns established in the Lindsay years. Browning, Marshall, and Tabb use minority public employment, the establishment of police review boards, minority appointments to commissions, and distribution of CDBG funds to minority areas and contractors to indicate policy responsiveness. Although the Koch administration has rejected the establishment of an independent police review board and racial quotas or set-asides, it has added civilians to a departmental review board. Minority public employment has risen to 42 percent overall and more than 50 percent of the new hires. The Mayor prides himself on having appointed blacks or Latinos to 18 percent of his managerial positions, including a black police commissioner and a black and a Latino deputy mayor. Community development funds have been well targeted on poor neighborhoods in New York; the single biggest expenditure has been on operating abandoned *in rem* housing, found largely in the poorest parts of minority neighborhoods.

Although it is hard to derive exactly analogous measurements to those Browning, Marshall, and Tabb use, these numbers suggest that New York, compared with the ten California Cities, would not rank low on policy outcome measures. For example, New York's 42 percent minority public employment rate is above the ten-California-city median, as extrapolated to 1987 (Browning et al., 1984, p. 172, Figure 19). Certainly, the record in managerial hires would compare well with any of the sample cities beside Oakland.

Browning, Marshall, and Tabb allow that such external factors as federal affirmative action policy and local demography contribute to local policy responsiveness, and it may well be that the Koch administration has little choice but to hire minorities when increasing the number of traffic- and sanitation-enforcement agents. Yet his acts go beyond this: even with minority political incorporation as weak, controlled, and divided as it is in New York, the leader of a conservative dominant coalition still seeks to blunt black opposition and woo Latino support by maintaining hiring patterns that benefit these constituencies. In his 1985 re-election campaign, Mayor Koch reportedly spent half his $7 million war chest on field operations in black and Latino neighborhoods. This suggests that the desire to keep a potential opposition disunited may produce some aspects of policy responsiveness that Browning, Marshall, and Tabb attribute to a biracial dominant coalition. New York shows that a conservative dominant coalition can seek to contain the potential for an electoral challenge and manage the tensions arising out of underlying social inequality with the tools of political incorporation invented by the earlier liberal experimenters.

These anomalous conditions raise interesting questions about how to revise and extend the analysis presented in *Protest Is Not Enough*. They can best be explored by asking why, given its paradigmatically liberal image, New York has been so conservative. Comparisons with the political cultures of the western cities and with Mayor Washington's regime in Chicago provide part of the answer.

EAST VERSUS WEST

Four important differences between New York City and the California ten-city sample help to explain New York's anomalous position. First, their political cultures are on opposite sides of the historic divide between machine and reform analyzed by Martin Shefter (Shefter, 1983). Though political scientists and even local observers usually classify New York as a reformed city in which the party is dead, New York still undeniably partakes in an eastern urban political culture characterized, to use Wolfinger's distinction, by machine politics if not by political machines (Wolfinger, 1972). Regular county party organizations, somewhat fuzzily called "the machine" or "the regulars" in local parlance, continue to exert a strong, if not always complete, hold on politics in four of New York's five boroughs. In some ways, these organizations have been in decline (Ware, 1985). District-level clubs, for example, have decayed in number, membership, and vigor. The scandals of 1986 and 1987 caused the Queens County leader to commit suicide and sent the Bronx leader to jail. Brooklyn's former leader has also been convicted. But the county party organizations have also become stronger in some respects since the 1950s. They generally continue to control access to the ballot. More important, they have turned legislative staff operations (both in district offices and in the assembly campaign committee) into the functional equivalent of the old machine, this time funded directly by the state. Some district organizations, such as Assemblyman Anthony Genovese's Thomas Jefferson Democratic Club in Canarsie, have evolved into powerful campaign organizations. From their position on the city's periphery, the regular Democratic organizations thus exercise considerable power in the Board of Estimate and state legislature and can constrain any Manhattan-based reform thrust.

Second, in contrast to such California cities as Berkeley, Oakland, and San

Francisco, that reform thrust, at least in its liberal version, has ebbed over the last two decades. At one time, ideological liberals in New York could overcome the regular influence on citywide office holders and contest it in a number of borough- and subborough-level contests. Since the 1960s, both the "movement liberalism" of the pro-civil-rights and antiwar young professionals and the more traditional liberalism of older, unionized, blue-collar and lower-middle-class Jewish constituencies have atrophied in New York.

On the one hand, the cycle of retrenchment and political conservatism at the national and local levels has made the ideas of ideologically liberal Lindsay-type activists unfashionable. In addition, many of this group have become the incumbent establishment. The Koch administration's roots among reform Democrats are revealed by the many now-pragmatic liberal reformers that it has appointed to high positions. Moreover, many of the insurgents who won election to the assembly and council have slowly been melded into the regular-dominated hierarchy.

The old liberal, unionized, blue-collar or lower-middle-class Jewish constituency that so distinguished New York from other eastern cities also has been squeezed by a chain of events. As Shefter has shown (1986), this process began in the 1950s with the destruction of the American Labor party as the admission price Jews paid to enter the Democratic establishment. In the 1960s, the personal traumas of racial succession in neighborhoods and labor markets pushed them further to the right in ways well described by Rieder (1984). Their demographic strength has also declined relative to other groups. Finally, growing international competition, a declining job base, and racial transition in the labor force have put the crucially important trade unions that articulated this old-left perspective, such as the ILGWU and ACTWU, in an increasingly weaker position.

While it oversimplifies matters to say that New York shifted from liberal to conservative when racial conflict sheared Jews from their alliance with minorities and sent them into alliance with the Catholics, this dictum catches an element of truth. Regular and reform Democrats joined to promote a web of social spending patterns and alliances with service-provider groups (such as the public employee unions) that bind white, often Jewish, professionals in the "helping professions" with a minority rank and file of workers and service recipients. This somewhat tempers the Jewish shift toward more conservative Catholic Democrats. For example, the Jewish president of the teamsters local that represents public employees was an articulate supporter of Jesse Jackson's 1988 campaign in New York. But it is undeniable that the bulk of white liberal opinion supported Mayor Koch in 1985, not his black and reform challengers. Even after the scandals and racial polarization of the 1986–88 period, it remains unclear whether the mayoral candidacy of David Dinkins, a black, will provide a framework to bring Jews and other liberal whites together with blacks and Latinos to create a biracial liberal coalition capable of winning the mayoralty. While many external forces undermined white liberalism in New York, its satisfaction with being part of the establishment and its disinclination to risk that status by joining with outsiders contribute to its weakness as a force for political change.

Third, black and Latino political mobilization have often worked at cross-purposes in New York City (Falcon, 1985). Both groups are also internally divided. While Browning, Marshall, and Tabb note tensions between the groups in the California cities, they conclude that black incorporation strengthened Latino incorporation. No such result has occurred in New York. The relatively similar size of the black and Latino populations contributes to this tension. On its own, the black community is simply not large enough to cause the kind of breakthrough that took place in Chicago, Detroit, or Atlanta. But the division between blacks and Latinos, and indeed among geographic and ethnic factions within these groups, runs far deeper.

Blacks and Latinos do not generally support each other at the polls when given the alternative of supporting a candidate from their own group. An attempt to select a consensus minority challenger to Mayor Koch in the 1985 mayoral primary foundered because the established Harlem leadership refused to support Herman Badillo, even though no strong black candidate would agree to run. Instead, they ran a weak black candidate, in part because Badillo would not bow out of the 1977 mayoral primary in which they thought a black candidate, Percy Sutton, had a chance. Black leaders seem to believe they have an historic and political claim to lead any minority coalition, whereas Puerto Rican leaders think blacks have always put them at the end of the line. Most Puerto Ricans in New York feel that blacks and Latinos are equally discriminated against and two-thirds feel that they should work together. But most also feel that Puerto Rican elected officials are "more interested in their own careers than in serving the community" (Velazquez, 1988, p. 11). Latinos gave their racial identity as white (50 percent) as opposed to black (10 percent) or other (40 percent) in the 1980 census. When added to their religious affiliation with the Catholic Church, which tends to have a conservative institutional perspective and an ideological tendency toward political conservatism, the road toward an effective black–Latino alliance is something of a minefield.

Blacks and Latinos are both heterogeneous groups, divided by issues of ancestry and nativity. Although those of Puerto Rican birth or ancestry are most numerous among Latinos, they are declining relative to other immigrant groups, particularly Dominicans. Among blacks, those of West Indian nativity or ancestry also tend to distinguish themselves politically from the native born. There are also tensions between the traditional black leadership elite, based in Harlem, and a newer generation of leaders based in Brooklyn. These kinds of tensions provide fertile territory for both the Koch administration and the county party organizations to prospect for support.

Finally, it might be argued that the structure of political mobilization in New York works against the coalescence of the reform thrust. In the California cities, white liberals and minority groups had a major incentive to coalesce because they were all outsiders. They also had a variety of organizational vehicles to use to build coalitions. No institutional mechanism currently facilitates cooperation among the disparate elements that have historically powered the reform cycle in New York. Instead, existing political arrangements tend to divide them.

In part, this pattern resembles an effect V.O. Key noted about the South before the rise of the Republican party: one-party political systems tend to produce factionalism and a politics of personalism and invidious distinction (Key, 1949, Chap. 14). It should be remembered that all of the cities Browning, Marshall, and Tabb studied had Republican mayors in the late 1950s. Party competition gave the Democratic party an incentive to mobilize all politically excluded groups. In New York, the tables are turned. Democrats established one-party hegemony a century earlier; the Republican party offered itself only sporadically (in 1932 and 1969) and haltingly as the organizational stimulus for liberal reform. Reformers must therefore contend for power within the factional kaleidoscope of the kind of weakly organized, one-party system penetratingly analyzed by Key in the South of the 1950s.

These four conditions presently impede the re-emergence of Browning, Marshall, and Tabb's new liberal dominant coalition in New York and have favored Mayor Koch's conservative brand of reform government. Yet, ironically, they also lead to some of the policy benefits for which such a coalition might be thought a prerequisite. To reduce the possibility of a multiracial liberal political challenge, the Mayor has relied on minority hiring, appointments, and contracts to community-based social services within his administration's larger retreat from social spending.

The strength of regular organizations in the outer boroughs is particularly important. Many observers seem not to realize that three-quarters of all New Yorkers, including most of the minority population and its fastest-growing concentrations, live outside Manhattan. The ability of the Brooklyn, Queens, and Bronx regular Democratic organizations to cope with demographic trends in their boroughs is crucial to the city's overall political future. In the 1985 election, for example, the Mayor outpolled his black opponent in Bedford-Stuyvesant's 56th Assembly District and all but three of the thirteen majority black ADs in the city. The 56th AD assemblyman, Al Vann, one of the city's leading black independents, polled 79.8 percent of his own district (which is 89 percent black and 11 percent Latino) but fared poorly in the rest of Brooklyn in a race against the incumbent white regular borough president. Minority regulars also defeated insurgent opposition in many of the minority city council districts. Despite real gains in building an independent black political organization in Brooklyn, these results show that regulars continue to command substantial, if not always majority, support for their candidates in black and Latino districts.

The political sponsorship of contracts and funding to community-based organizations has perpetuated the influence of the prevailing political establishment. Regular black and Latino leaders control some of this funding as political patronage. Even where the state or the Koch administration grants funding to community-based organizations "on the merits," these groups need sponsorship from elected officials and know that any overt political challenge to the Mayor would cost them their funds. As a result, established white politicians can compromise a potential resource for independent minority mobilization.

It must be cautioned that the regulars achieve their influence over minority political mobilization by being relatively liberal, at least compared with such organizations in other eastern cities. Rieder's analysis of Canarsie does not give sufficient weight to the fact that the local club, the Thomas Jefferson (TJ) Democrats, leads Canarsie citizens to vote for liberal democrats for state and national office. Former Assembly Speaker Stanley Fink and many other powerful city officials came out of this club. The state supplemental budget bill carried by the Speaker is a major source of nourishment to New York's black and Latino legislators. TJ Club leaders worked against the school boycott against integration that more radically conservative community activists wanted. Canarsie thus illustrates how the web of measures enacted to secure or reinforce the allegiance of minority elected officials has the side effect of inoculating some white ethnic areas against the worst forms of backlash mobilization.

The other three conditions—the decline of white liberalism, the division among minorities, and the absence of a mechanism for dialogue and for coalition formation among them—are interrelated. There are tensions between natives and immigrants, between different ethnicities, and between the traditional black and Latino minorities and more recently arrived groups. Although they still make up only about 6 percent of the city's population, the fastest-growing racial minorities are neither black nor Latino but Chinese, Korean, and Indian. Such potential ingredients of a new liberal dominant coalition as young white professionals, black and Latino service workers, and older unionized ethnics have a hard time talking to each other. It is difficult to see how these divisions can be overcome, but a comparison with Chicago offers some instructive lessons.

KOCH'S NEW YORK BY WAY OF WASHINGTON'S CHICAGO

Black insurgents in Chicago succeeded in a number of areas where their New York peers have not. According to informed observers, the Washington victory was preceded by racial polarization, the alienation of black leadership from the regular Democratic organization, a consensus-based candidate recruitment process, and an upsurge in minority turnout. Candidate recruitment and voter turnout particularly contrast with New York: Barker describes how in Chicago black leaders used a survey to unearth the names of ninety possibilities that the Chicago Black United Communities then reduced to twenty. These names were then submitted to a vote at a meeting attended by a thousand grass-roots leaders who overwhelmingly endorsed Washington (Barker, 1983). This contrasts starkly with the narrow, closed-door deliberations of the Coalition for a Just New York in the 1985 election.

The grass-roots surge was also crucial: Preston reports that registration was up 29.5 percent in black wards, that the lowest general election turnout in a black ward was 73 percent, and that Washington won 73 percent of the black vote in the primary and 97 percent in the general election (Preston, 1983). By contrast, in New York, as we have seen, the black mayoral candidate in 1985 got only 41 percent of the black vote and increased registration for the 1984 Jackson presidential candidacy did not raise black turnout above historical lows in the 1985 mayoral primary. Furthermore, Washington won over 50 percent of the Latino votes in the general election and around 20 percent in the primary. In 1985, New York's black candidate gathered only 12 percent of the Latino primary vote and Mayor Koch got 70 percent.

Peterson has suggested that the political resources that blacks gradually accumulated within the Cook County regular Democratic party organization and the division among white regulars made Washington's victory possible (Peterson, 1983). Brooklyn, the "Chicago" of New York's five boroughs, experienced a similar split between white regulars in the wake of Meade Esposito's retirement as county leader. In 1985, black independent Al Vann, backed by an organization that had wrested a number of state legislative seats from the regulars challenged the incumbent white borough president, as did a white from one faction of the regulars. In this race, however, Vann polled only 60 percent of Brooklyn's black votes and 28 percent of the Latino votes, and he lost decisively to incumbent borough president and county leader Howard Golden.

This comparison suggests that while such objective factors as the greater relative preponderance of blacks account for Chicago's strong political incorporation relative to New York's weakness, subjective or organizationally controllable factors are also important. Before 1989, independent liberal politics in New York simply did not produce a candidate for mayor who strongly mobilized black voters, much less the biracial alliance necessary to install a new dominant coalition.

One hopeful note for such a coalition was Jesse Jackson's presidential primary races in 1984 and 1988, and his victory in the city in 1988 suggests that such a coalition is still conceivable, despite the barriers. The 1984 race produced a ground swell of black registration and turnout, but did not mobilize Latinos. In 1988, however, Jackson strongly improved his standing with Latinos (garnering 61 percent of their votes) and also attracted 15 percent of the white vote to win a narrow plurality of 43.5 percent in the city. This included 9 percent of the Jewish vote despite Mayor Koch's assertion that Jews would have to be crazy to vote for Jackson (*New York Times*, 1988, p. D25). Jackson's victory provided a basis for the elements of a biracial liberal coalition to work together. Whether such a coalition can carry David Dinkins into the mayor's office in 1989 remains an open question.

Washington's victories in Chicago hold an important lesson for New Yorkers. An independent dialogue among the potential elements of the reform coalition must be undertaken as a first step in jointly mobilizing them. In Chicago, Washington's forces used a dense network of community-based organizations (within a racial boundary) to mount an independent political challenge. Similar networks exist and might be mobilized in New York. A stronger process of forming multiracial slates among liberal reform challengers, which Browning, Marshall, and Tabb rightly hold to be a key sign of the strength of minority mobilization, could also have a major impact in New York.

IN CONCLUSION: TOWARD
THE 1989 MAYORAL RACE

Since 1986, three conditions have changed sufficiently to undermine, and perhaps alter, the stability of New York City's conservative dominant political condition. First, the city's corruption scandal led to the suicide of one borough president, the conviction of another, and the resignation of three commissioners and numerous other senior appointees from the Koch administration. These events caused Mayor Koch's approval rating to plummet, opening the way for well-known, well-financed candidates to challenge the mayor in the 1989 Democratic primary. The charter revision commission's proposal to abolish the Board of Estimate has also helped create a moment of unusual political openness and uncertainty.

Second, the 1988 Jackson campaign and the subsequent mayoral campaign of Manhattan borough president David Dinkins have united a previously divided black leadership. The 1988 Jackson victory showed that a coalition of blacks, Latinos, and white liberals, with an organizational base in public sector trade unions and reform political clubs, could win a 43.5 percent plurality in a Democratic primary. Black leaders were subsequently able to recruit a consensus candidate, David Dinkins, to challenge the mayor in 1989. Having gotten his political start in Harlem clubhouse politics, Dinkins drew broad support from whites in his 1985 race and used the borough presidency to establish his independence from the mayor. In contrast to 1985, black leaders from Brooklyn, the Bronx, and Queens united behind his candidacy. In contrast to 1984 and 1985, most Latino leaders also supported Jackson in 1988 and Dinkins in 1989. Latino voters also shifted toward Jackson and away from Koch, setting the stage for stronger black-Latino cooperation. By weakening the hold of the Bronx and Queens county party organizations over aspiring black and Latino politicians, the scandals contributed strongly to this development.

Finally, a series of polarizing events have reawakened white concern over race relations. The fatal mob attack on three blacks in Howard Beach, the black teenagers' "wilding" assault on a white woman jogger in Central Park, and the murder of a black in the conservative Italian neighborhood of Bensonhurst, have sharply worsened racial tensions. A significant portion of white public opinion evidently supports a more conciliatory leadership stance than Mayor Koch has sometimes shown.

What can be said about the implications for minority political incorporation? Minority political incorporation might actually be decreased if Dinkins were defeated and the Board of Estimate's powers abolished, shifting power to the council's white, regular leadership. But another scenario is also possible. With support from almost all black voters, most Latino voters and 30 percent of white voters, David Dinkins was able to defeat Mayor Koch in the September Democratic mayoral primary. By October 1989, public opinion polls suggested that Dinkins would be able to defeat a popular former federal prosecutor, Rudolph Giuliani, running on the Republican and Liberal lines in the general election. To do so, Dinkins must win considerably more white votes than any other black mayoral candidate (besides Tom Bradley) in a first race for the office. This will be a revealing test of prospects for biracial politics in New York City.

REFERENCES

Barker, Twiley. 1983. Political Mobilization of Black Chicago: Drafting a Candidate. *PS* 16 (Summer): 482–485.

Brecher, Charles, and Raymond Horton, eds. 1984. *Setting Municipal Priorities: American Cities and the New York Experience.* New York: New York University Press.

Browning, Rufus, Dale Rogers Marshall, and David Tabb. 1984. *Protest Is Not Enough.* Berkeley: University of California Press.

Falcon, Angelo. 1985. *Black and Latino Politics in New York City: Race and Ethnicity in a Changing Urban Context.* New York: Institute for Puerto Rican Policy.

Key, V. O., Jr. 1949. *Southern Politics in State and Nation.* New York: Vintage.

New York Times. 1988. New York Times/CBS Exit Poll, Thursday, April 21, D25.

Peterson, Paul. 1983. Washington's Election in Chicago: The Other Half of the Story. *PS* 16 (Fall): 712–716.

Preston, Michael. 1983. The Election of Harold Washington: Black Voting Patterns in the 1983 Chicago Mayoral Race. *PS* 16 (Summer): 486–488.

Shefter, Martin. 1983. Regional Receptivity to Reform. *Political Science Quarterly* 98:3 (Fall): 459–483.

Shefter, Martin. 1986. Political Incorporation and the Extrusion of the Left: Party Politics and Social Forces in New York City. *Studies in American Political Development* 1:50–90

Velazquez, Nydia. 1988. Puerto Rican Voter Registration in New York City: A Comparison of Attitudes Between Registered and Non-Registered Puerto Ricans (Migration Division, Department of Labor and Human Resources, Commonwealth of Puerto Rico).

Ware, Alan. 1985. *The Breakdown of Democratic Party Organization, 1940–1980.* New York: Oxford University Press.

Wolfinger, Raymond. 1972. Why Political Machines Have Not Withered Away and Other Revisionist Thoughts. *Journal of Politics* 34:2 (May): 365–398.

CHAPTER 5

Harold Washington and the Politics of Reform in Chicago: 1983–1987

Robert T. Starks and Michael B. Preston

Editors' Note

As John Mollenkopf suggests in Chapter 4, the successful movement to elect Harold Washington mayor of Chicago in 1983 offers guidelines for minority mobilization and incorporation in New York and other cities where people of color are divided and unable to realize the full potential of their primary political resource— population. "The man, the moment, and the movement," as Robert Starks and Michael Preston show, must be brought together to overcome a long-entrenched regime. Read this chapter as a sourcebook of strategies, leadership characteristics and recruitment, opportunities, and organization for the development of multiracial coalitions in the face of intense opposition.

In its particulars, of course, Chicago is unique, but in the general structure of the obstacles facing the movement to elect a black mayor and of the movement itself, it is not. We see similar elements and dynamics brought to fruition in otherwise very diverse cities where minority mayors have been elected, including Philadelphia, Los Angeles, Oakland, and Berkeley.

The long struggle to elect a black mayor in Chicago, then to consolidate the power of his administration over a divided city government, had hardly been brought to a successful conclusion when Harold Washington died. The pain of his passing is heightened by the subsequent division and uncertain prospects of his coalition.

In 1983, Harold Washington was elected as the first black mayor in Chicago's history. His election was a significant event in American politics, not only because he was black but also because he vowed to destroy the political machine that had existed in Chicago for over 25 years. His pledge to reform city government met with hostile resistance from machine politicians. Both his election and 3-year battle with the machine-dominated City Council were also frequently in the news. It took over 3 years before Harold Washington and his allies were able to gain some measure of control over the council and other institutions of city government. Harold Washington's attempts at reform proved an old axiom in politics: People don't voluntarily give up power, it must be taken from them!

Harold Washington had a new vision for Chicago. He pledged to open city government up to all and not just a select few. He also vowed to end the corruption and patronage that had long dominated Chicago politics. In short, he wanted Chicago to become a "world class city" and this became a major theme of most of his speeches as he traveled around the nation and the world. He and his city became linked, and he came to be viewed by many people as a "world class mayor in a world class city," as he described Chicago in one of his last speeches to an academic audience before his death:

> Chicago suffers from an archaic and outdated reputation as the city of Al Capone and the political machine of Daley. All of that is the Chicago of yesterday. Today, Chicago is a *world class city*! It is the city of banking and finance; of medicine and healing; of technology, research and development; of great learning and great universities; of enormous renaissance—we are presently engaged in a $2 billion central area redevelopment program; and lastly and most importantly, we are a city of multi-cultural and multi-ethnic greatness! We have represented in our city people from every corner of the earth all living together and working together for a better Chicago. (APSA, 1987)

Harold Washington ended his speech with these words:

> For those of you who will write, analyze and teach about today's Chicago as political scientists and political historians, it is my sincere hope that you will focus upon the progressive world class character of Chicago and not its real or imagined historical shortcomings. *We have changed Chicago and it will never be the same again!* (APSA, 1987)

There is ample evidence to suggest that had Harold Washington lived, the progressive agenda he had developed for Chicago might have become a reality. The developments after his death, however, leave open the question of Chicago's political future. And an even more compelling question for the black community is whether the new black political leadership will be able to sustain the kind of enthusiastic support that Harold Washington enjoyed from the overwhelming majority of black voters. The Washington administration represented a dramatic break with the past and sought to replace "machine politics" with a more "progressive politics" of the future.

Harold Washington forged pride in the city among all of its citizens because of his insistence upon upgrading the delivery of services in all areas of the city and his policies of openness and fairness. His administration was a breath of fresh air in an otherwise closed and institutionally corrupt political environment. Washington's style can be characterized as one which exemplified strength, aggressiveness, fairness, openness and the delivery of quality municipal services on an equal basis throughout the city. The details of his style and policies will be discussed later in this chapter. First, however, we need to present a model which we believe helps explain why and how Harold Washington could be elected in a city which had been for over 25 years dominated by a political machine.

THE CHICAGO MODEL OF BLACK POLITICS: FROM MOTIVATION TO MOBILIZATION

It is clear that the 1983 election of Harold Washington, which has been properly characterized as a crusade, defied the traditional behavioral approaches to black politics. Most of the traditional theories are inadequate to explain his election. The traditional approaches, according to Hanes Walton, "have generated theories and strategies based on a single, deterministic factor . . . bound to be of limited use because they have caught only a portion of black political reality, and many, . . . have mistaken the shadow for reality" (Walton, 1985, pp. 7–8).

Walton is careful to point out that "Black political behavior is a variety of political patterns, experiences, and activities." He stresses its dissimilarity to ethnic politics: "Black political behavior is not ethnic political behavior. Despite the similarities, it is different" (Walton, 1985, p. 8). In brief, Walton argues that if scholars are to understand black political participation and politics, they must be aware of the limitations placed on black political behavior by systemic, structural, and contextual variables found in each city (Walton, 1985, pp. 18–19). Walton's approach is closely related to our attempt to explain the election of Harold Washington in Chicago in 1983. Clearly, one has to understand how the policies of the machine (systemic variables) and the structure of the electoral system were used by machine leaders to control black representation and thereby reduce their effectiveness. As black protest against the negative public policies of the machine grew, political actors and individuals were motivated to seek not only a change in policies but a change in the leadership itself.

The Chicago model developed to help explain Harold Washington's election contains several important elements:

- Motivation (of political actors)
- Political mobilization (of the core groups and their allies)
- Goals and candidate identification
- Agenda setting (for the government)
- Policy formation and policy outcomes which grow out of the agenda
- Evaluation

Of all these elements, the least understood and the most important is political motivation.

Political Motivation of political actors is perhaps the most understated and underexamined of all the variables in politics. It is, however, for the Chicago model, the most important one. Motivation gives birth to action which animates the rest of the variables in the model. Without the motivation, no serious and sustaining action is possible. Political action without political motivation is, in the words of Leon Trotsky: "Steam without a piston box." Political motivation lays the basis for the organization, goals, and direction of political action.

> Without a guiding organization, the energy of the masses would dissipate like steam, not enclosed in a piston-box. But, nevertheless, what moves things is not the piston or the box, but the steam. (Trotsky, 1969, pp. 16–17)

Motivation is arrived at after analysis, mass education, and a thorough assessment of group interest. Group interests are assessed in tangible and nontangible terms, material and nonmaterial terms, as well as psychic terms. It is this group assessment process that gives birth to political motivation.

Mere representation was not the major motivation for mobilization. The major motivation among Chicago black political actors was the desire to exercise political power and political control over the political system in order to change it, rather than to gain representation in a system in which major structural and operational changes were precluded. Black Chicagoans have had representation in city government and both political parties for most of this century. It was recognized that representation was not enough. The political assessment of black representation in both city government and the Democratic party led to the conclusion that limited gains had been achieved through representation but much more could be achieved if the reins of political power could be grasped by blacks as leaders of a multiracial coalition. Only in this way could government and party agendas be restructured so that black interests were protected and realized.

The dilemma that black political actors faced was one of building the broad-base citywide coalition that was needed to achieve electoral victory; this required mobilization of the members of groups outside of the black community, which in turn required building a coalition that allows room for people who may or may not share the exact same motivation as the black community. The potential coalition members, then, had to be shown an agenda and an agenda-setting process that was inclusive and allowed room for them to satisfy their motivational drive.

Clearly, potential allies and potential coalition members fully understood that their motivational drive was different from that of blacks, but their experience in coalitions with blacks has never been one of exclusion. Blacks who lead political coalitions to which whites are recruited are usually overly cautious in an effort to maintain the coalition (Carmichael and Hamilton, 1967, pp. 77–84). Furthermore, since whites fully control the private sector, white political actors, especially the "power elite," feel little real threat from a black-led reform coalition when it has clearly articulated an agenda that stays within the bounds of liberal democracy. In fact, such a coalition faces the danger of co-optation by the "power elite" within the private sector (Browning et al., 1984, pp. 46–74).

Policy formation and policy outcomes must be guarded in a watchdog manner to balance the demands of the coalition and the "power elite." Constant evaluation of the model and the interplay of the processes that occur within will help to assure maintenance of elements that lead to the motivation that put the model in motion in the first place.

While blacks were represented in the Democratic party machine and thus had achieved a modest level of political incorporation, this did not for the most part lead to responsiveness (Preston, 1982, pp. 102–105). The finding that representation alone may produce little change in city government supports the same conclusion by Browning, Marshall, and Tabb based on the ten Northern California cities studied (Browning, Marshall, and Tabb, 1984). However, the Chicago experience adds the knowledge that even what seemed to be a substantial black representation in the Democratic party machine could be sharply limited in its impact on policy. Browning et al. observed that "dominant coalitions that explicitly include minorities always took at least moderately liberal positions" (Browning, Marshall, and Tabb, 1984, p. 27). The Daley organization was so strong that it was able to co-opt numbers of blacks without having to make significant policy concessions to them. Machine responsiveness to the black community came more from external pressure by the community than from internal political forces.

Political Motivation and Mobilization

Harold Washington's rise to political power did not happen overnight. He was the son of a minister and lawyer who served as a Democratic Party precinct captain and taught Harold well in the arts of politics. While in law school at Northwestern University, he served as assistant Democratic precinct captain of his precinct along with his father and continued as precinct captain after his father's death in 1954. This precinct work gave him access to his government job as assistant city prosecutor from 1954 to 1958. From 1960 to 1964, he worked for the State of Illinois as an arbitrator for the Illinois Industrial Commission and set up a private law practice (Moritz, 1984, pp. 43–45).

From 1965 to 1977, he served in the Illinois House as a regular Democrat. Washington distinguished himself in the Illinois House as one of the prime movers in organizing the first black caucus. He emphasized social reform in areas such as welfare rights, fair employment legislation, human rights, and housing. He was most proud of his 1969 sponsorship of the Dr. King birthday bill which was signed into law in 1973, making Illinois the first state to legislate a King holiday.

By 1977, Harold Washington was lionized in the black independent community as an independent Democrat with progressive credentials. This was evidenced by his participation in the 1971 to 1975 movement to break away from the Daley machine (Preston, 1982, pp. 88–117). Although Mayor Daley was reelected in 1971 and 1975, there was a noticeable decrease in the number of black voters supporting him in those elections. Some considered Washington for mayor as early as 1974, but he did not actually run for mayor until the 1977 special mayoral election. This election followed the death of Mayor Daley in 1976 and the appointment of a machine-picked acting mayor, Michael Bilandic, over a black, Alderman Wilson Frost. Frost, according to the rules, should have been first in the line of succession since he was President Pro-tem of the city Council. Although Washington lost decisively to Bilandic in 1977 (he won only 11 percent of the vote), he showed that he was a good campaigner and could get support outside the black community.

In the fall of 1978, Washington's mentor, Congressman Metcalfe, died 1 month before the November election. Metcalfe's death precipitated a power struggle in which the machine named then Alderman Bennett M. Stewart to run for Congress at that point. While Washington and others did not like the choice, Washington opted to wait until 1980, when he handily defeated Stewart.

THE DECLINE OF BYRNE AND THE RISE OF HAROLD WASHINGTON: 1979–1983

The 1979 defeat of Michael Bilandic for mayor by Jane Byrne sent shock waves throughout the machine and the nation. It was especially significant when it became clear that black voters had helped elect Byrne. However, it also became immediately clear to black voters after the election that Mayor Byrne had no intention of honoring the promises that she had made to black voters. These broken promises presaged open political warfare between the Mayor and the black community that lasted throughout her tenure (Preston, 1982, pp. 171–174).

The abuses handed out to the black community by the Byrne Administration multiplied with each year. Byrne reneged on her promise to appoint a black police superintendent; she allowed a transit workers' strike to go on for a week by refusing to negotiate with union leaders who were black, while the majority of black people depended upon public transportation for travel to work and play; she refused to appoint a black school superintendent initially and appointed a subordinate of the highest-ranking black to the post; she attempted to stack the school board with hostile white board members and a school board president that the black community opposed. Her handling of the teachers' and firefighters' strikes, allowing them to go on for a long time, had a particularly negative impact on the black community. Both strikes had to be settled by the Reverend Jesse Jackson and the black leadership (Preston, 1982, pp. 171–174). All these blunders were committed in her first year in office. The following years were even worse.

Several additional events in 1981 and 1982 were critical to the eventual political demise of Jane Byrne and the rise of Harold Washington.

1981: The Remap Fight

The battle over reapportionment in 1981 was important because it was the first instance in which a black population politicized the process of reapportionment at all three levels (city, state, and federal) on a mass basis. The politicization proved to be an excellent mass education tool to drive home the need for increased black representation and the need for a black mayor. Determined to fight for reapportionment, equity, and parity, black community leaders prepared for a protracted battle that would eventually take the form of voter registration, political education, rallies, independent remapping efforts, lobbying and lawsuits (Starks, 1982, p. 54).

Mayor Byrne recruited former Alderman (31st) Thomas P. Keane to create a

> map similar to the one that he had designed in 1970 that retrograded black and Hispanic voting power. Thomas Keane's new creation reduced the nineteen majority black wards to seventeen by extending the ward boundaries of the fifteenth and thirty-seventh wards and adding enough whites to these wards, thereby making them the majority. In addition, the 1980 Keane map "impotized" the Hispanic vote by dispensing their voting power into several adjoining predominantly white wards on both the northwest and the southwest sides of the city. (Travis, 1986, pp. 539–540)

Despite the lobbying and rallying of the Coalition, made up of Operation PUSH, CBUC, NAACP, and the Urban League, the Byrne-controlled city council passed the Keane map and subsequently forced the coalition to request the support of the Justice Department in a lawsuit. The same pattern followed in the cases of the state and congressional reapportionments (Starks, 1982, pp. 53–63). From 1981 through 1985, the federal courts heard the reapportionment cases at each level. In each case the black community won as a result of mass politicization, organizing, and determination. Congressman Harold Washington was one of chief plaintiffs in the remap cases.

In fact, it was the final settlement of the redistricting lawsuit in 1985 that give Mayor Washington his majority in the city council. And it was the two black wards 37 and 15 and two Latino wards 26 and 31 in particular, which were redrawn after the 1985 settlement that resulted in the election of the two black and two Latino aldermen in the spring of 1986, enabling Mayor Washington to finally control the city council.

The reapportionment fights in Chicago's black community in 1981–1982, plus the early battle to reduce the number of signatures required by independent candidates to get on the Democratic party ballot in a mayoral primary, were crucial structural-legal victories. These two victories, won in the courts, removed significant structural barriers to a successful black candidacy for mayor. The reapportionment victory enabled the black community to keep those legislative seats that they had won over the years and realize significant increases at two legislative levels. All of these victories proved to be most vital to the Washington election scheme in 1983 and necessary to Harold Washington's political survival when he became mayor. His ability to control the city council and push his legislative agenda came only after the federal court made its final favorable ruling in 1985 and after a special election for the four newly redistricted wards in which he was able to get his people elected.

Last, the political education gained from the reapportionment fights set the stage for the mayoral campaign because they demonstrated the significance of determination, cooperation, organizing, and the use of applied technology such as computers. Black Chicagoans became the first American minority group to combine all of these aspects by investigative research, initiating the fight in the legislative bodies and the courts, and by actually producing alternative maps in each case. The skills and most of the same people were used in the 1983 election campaign. In a real sense, the reapportionment battles served as a dress rehearsal for 1983.

1982: Voter Registration

While the reapportionment battle was in progress, many of the same groups and people who had initiated it were busy convincing the rest of the black community that the only real solution to all of these many-faceted political problems was the election of a black mayor. Lu Palmer, Chairman of CBUC in August of 1981, called together a citywide convention to examine these political questions at Malcolm X College. It was at this community convention that he came up with the rallying cry that became the motto of the crusade: "We Shall See in '83." The major accomplishments of the convention were the following:

1. The call for the election of a black mayor in 1983 and initiation of a process within the black community that would identify a consensus candidate.
2. The pledge to raise sufficient funds to finance the mayoral campaign.
3. The immediate launching of a voter registration campaign to register 200,000 people.
4. The institution of political education classes that would train 2000 workers for the campaign.
5. The pledge to increase black representation in the City Council and the state legislature.

On July 7, 1982, Lu Palmer's organization, CBUC, announced the results of its survey which listed the top ten people that the black community wanted to be possible candidates for mayor. Congressman Harold Washington's name was at the top of the list. Washington was contacted and asked if he would run. His reply was one of hesitation. He said, "There has to be a war chest of at least $250,000 to $500,000 and you (Coalition) have to go to prove that you can get a number of people registered, at least fifty thousand" (Starks, 1982, p. 547). The cry for a black mayor grew louder with each day. Two voter registration groups were organized to meet the Washington demand—The People's Movement for Voter Registration, and POWER (People Organized for Welfare and Employment Rights). These two groups eventually registered more the 100,000 new voters.

The call for a boycott of ChicagoFest (the annual summer lakefront festival) along with the arrests of political activists Lu Palmer, Dorothy Tillman, and Marion Stamps at a city council meeting set a chain of events in motion that stimulated the massive voter registration (Travis, 1986, p. 547). The following Saturday, at the regular Saturday morning meeting of Operation PUSH, community leaders and allied public officials (including Congressman Harold Washington) announced the boycott. The boycott was successful because most blacks did not attend the ChicagoFest and the two top entertainers, Stevie Wonder and Aretha Franklin, canceled their performances at the request of the Reverend Jesse Jackson. While Washington participated in the picketing of the ChicagoFest and savored the voter registration activity that it had stimulated, he was pleased to learn that black businessmen, led by Mr. Edward Gardner, Chairman of Seft Sheen, Inc. (manufacturer of black hair care products), had decided to finance the voter registration efforts. Voter registration activities continued full speed throughout September under the banner "Come Alive on October 5." October 5th was the last day for registration before the November elections.

Congressman Washington repeatedly said in his speeches that Byrne would be challenged in the 1983 election but stopped short of committing himself. After being reelected to the Congress on November 3 by more than 95 percent of the voters, he was not to give his answer concerning running until November 10 (Travis, 1986, p. 564). On November 10, at a press conference, the announcement that Harold Washington was running for mayor was made:

> The emotionally-charged press conference started with a prayer by the Reverend John Port of Christ United Methodist Church, "Lord we thank you, for the man, the moment, and the movement have come together." (Travis, 1986, p. 564)

The important thing here is that what had started out as a protest movement against the betrayal of Byrne and past machine leaders ended in not just a call for more representation: that had already been achieved; what was missing was the type of leadership that would be responsive to black concerns. White machine leadership had failed at this important task and now black leadership was being demanded. Thus, the crusade for a black mayor led to the drafting of Harold Washington as the candidate.

THE CHICAGO MAYORAL ELECTIONS
OF 1983 AND 1987

The motivation for Harold Washington to enter the 1983 Chicago mayoral election was based on a lifelong involvement on Chicago politics. He understood the history of black political involvement in machine politics better than most because he was a member of the regular democratic organization for most of his career until he broke with them in the mid-seventies. The past negative policies of the machine toward the black community and the betrayal of the community by Jane Byrne caused black political leaders to seek alternatives to machine rule. Washington was an active part of the groups calling for change. He was well aware of the need for new leadership but understood, better than most, the odds against achieving it. He nevertheless entered the race for mayor and changed the landscape of Chicago politics in a very dramatic way.

Much has been written about the 1983 primary and general election in Chicago because of its historic dimensions (Preston, 1987, pp. 139–171; Preston, 1984, pp. 39–52; Green, 1984; Kleppner, 1985). Our purpose here is not to provide a detailed discussion of either the 1983 or 1987 elections but rather to briefly summarize these findings by comparing the election of 1983 with that of 1987. Our summary discusses how Harold Washington was able to generate overwhelming black support, at the same time combining that support with a coalition of liberal whites and Latino voters to achieve victory.

The 1983 primary was a contest between incumbent Mayor Jane Byrne, Richard M. Daley, the son of the former mayor and current State's attorney, and Harold Washington. Byrne and Daley split the white vote while Washington received overwhelming support from the black community, plus some Latino and a few white lakefront liberal votes. Washington received 424,146 votes to 380,840 for Jane Byrne and 339,227 for Richard Daley (Preston, 1987, pp. 166–171).

Harold Washington was now the official Democratic party standard bearer. however, most of the white Cook County Democratic party ward committeemen and the chairman of the party, Edward Vrodlyak, then Alderman of the tenth ward, chose to support the Republican party candidate, Bernard Epton, in the general election. Washington won the election 668,176 to 619,926 for Epton (Preston, 1987, pp. 166–171). Most whites voted for Epton, while blacks, some white liberals, and some Latinos voted for Washington.

Race was the dominant factor in the campaign. The racist tone in the Bernard Epton campaign became so loud on Palm Sunday, March 27, when Congressman Harold Washington and former Vice President Walter Mondale visited the St. Pascal's church on the Northwest side, that the national media became attentive. The congressman and the vice president were greeted by Epton demonstrators shouting, "Go home! Tax cheater! Carpet Bagger! Epton! Epton!" The door that Mondale and Washington had to enter to get inside the church was freshly sprayed with the words: "Nigger, nigger die!" Mondale and Washington left shortly after they had entered in deference to those who wanted to worship in peace.

Several important things need be noted about the 1983 mayoral primary and general elections. First, the key to Harold Washington's victory in the primary and general elections was black registration and mobilization. For example, in 1979, voter registration in Chicago stood at 1,423,476. By 1983, it had grown to 1,594,253, and the largest increase in voter registration had taken place in black wards—up 29 percent (Preston, 1984, p. 47). Second, black voter turnout was up substantially from past elections, with four black wards giving Washington 98 percent to 99.3 percent of their vote (Preston, 1984, p. 49). The high black voter turnout also included low-income black voters. Third, Washington put together a

TABLE 5.1. MAYORAL VOTE 1983 AND 1987

	Turnout (%)	Votes for Washington	Votes for Washington opponents	Percentage for Washington
1983 Democratic Primary				
Black wards[a]	74.8	204,070	38,683	84.1
White wards[b]	82.3	2,194	183,389	1.2
Lakefront[c]	75.2	30,319	108,865	21.8
Citywide	77.0	424,146	738,048	36.5
1983 General Election				
Black wards	82.0	280,199	2,985	98.9
White wards	87.6	11,123	195,243	5.4
Lakefront	78.8	63,520	88,083	41.9
Citywide	82.1	668,176	623,682	51.7
1987 Democratic Primary				
Black wards	74.8	239,836	2,816	98.8
White wards	82.7	9,878	168,649	5.5
Lakefront	67.8	53,921	62,748	46.2
Citywide	74.6	575,020	508,446	53.1
1987 General Election				
Black wards	76.6	251,992	2,995	98.9
White wards	80.4	8,406	172,908	4.6
Lakefront	67.5	52,285	74,204	41.3
Citywide	74.1	600,290	524,622	53.4

[a]Black wards are the ten wards where black residents compose 95 percent or more of the voting age population (the 3rd, 6th, 8th, 16th, 17th, 20th, 21st, 28th, and 34th).
[b]White wards are the six wards where white residents comprise 95 percent or more of the voting age population (the 13th, 23rd, 36th, 38th, 41st, and 45th).
[c]Lakefront refers to the six wards along the city's north lakefront (the 42nd, 43rd, 44th, 46th, 48th, and 45th).
Washington opponents refers to the following candidates: 1983 Primary: Jane M. Byrne, Richard M. Daley, Sheila Jones, Frank R. Ranallo, William R. Markowski; 1983 General Election: Bernard E. Epton, Ed Warren; 1987 Primary: Jane Byrne, Sheila Jones; 1987 general election: Edward R. Vrdolyak, Donald H. Haider, and Thomas Hynes.
All information comes from the Chicago Board of Election commissioners, except for Hynes' vote totals, which were furnished by the News Election Service. Data analyzed by the *Chicago Reporter*. (Source: John Schrag, The Chicago Reporter, May 1987, p. 8.)

TABLE 5.2. 1987 CHICAGO MAYORAL PRIMARY ELECTION HISPANIC VOTE IN THE 1987 PRIMARY

	Percentage of 129 precincts[a]	Percentage of Puerto Rican votes[b]	Percentage of Mexican votes
Byrne	48.0	30.6	59.9
Washington	45.1	62.2	36.5

[a]There were 129 precincts in 13 wards that had a majority (more than 50 percent) of Latino registered voters.
[b]There were 112,347 registered voters, one-third in nine wards and two-thirds in four wards. These four wards are the 22nd, 25th, 26th, and 31st. The 22nd and 25th are predominately Mexican and the 26th and 31st are predominately Puerto Rican. (Source: *John Schrag,* The Chicago Reporter, *April 1987.*)

coalition of liberal whites along the lakefront and received an average of 20 percent of their votes. He received only 12,798 Latino votes in the primary but received 43,082 votes in the 1983 general election—more than 50 percent (Preston, 1984, p. 49).

The 1987 election was much less dramatic than the 1983 election. However, the racism of the campaign was just as intense while not as overt. The 1983 election was historic because it was the first. In 1987, Washington again beat Byrne in the primary, this time in a one-on-one battle, and defeated his archenemy Edward R. Vrdolyak in the general election. The results of these two elections can be seen in Tables 5.1 and 5.2. In the next section, we show how the 1983 election differed from that of 1987.

How the 1983 Election Differed from 1987

Some factors existing in 1987 that were not present in 1983 were as follows:

1. The Washington electoral coalition in 1987 was undoubtedly stronger and had a much more multiethnic character than the coalition of 1983.
2. The 1987 primary found Washington in a one-on-one battle with Jane Byrne. While the Cook County Democratic party did not endorse a mayoral candidate in this election, the majority of the white committeemen were clearly and solidly supporting Mrs. Byrne. The Washington win of 53.1 percent against Byrne's 46.6 percent clearly demonstrated that he had used his tenure of 4 years to build a multiethnic coalition that was strong enough to overcome his opponent.[1]
3. In the Primary of 1983, much of his victory could be attributed to the fact that he was the lone black candidate with a solidly black constituency running against two strong white candidates, the incumbent, Mayor Jane Byrne, who had the endorsement of the party, and the son of a former mayor, Richard M. Daley. The split white vote contributed greatly to the Washington victory.
4. While the primary was a one-on-one contest, the General election in 1987 was another three-way battle in which Washington's arch nemesis, Edward R. Vrdolyak, resigned from the city council and ran on the Solidarity party ballot, splitting the white vote with Northwestern University Professor of Business Donald H. Haider, running on the Republican ticket.[2]
5. Another key difference in 1987 was Washington's increased voting strength in Latino wards, particularly those with a large number of Puerto Rican voters. Washington received fewer votes in the 129 precincts than did Byrne,

---

[1] The 20 percent difference of the vote in the primary was a total of 2520 votes that went to Ms. Sheila Jones, the LaRouche candidate.

[2] The Solidarity party was the creation of the 1986 Democratic party nominee for Governor, Adlai Stevenson, who chose to create a new party and run on that ballot rather than run with the LaRouche running mates Fairchild and Hart, who had won the Democratic party primary nominations for lieutenant governor and state treasurer, respectively. After the Stevenson defeat on the Solidarity party ticket for governor, it was abandoned and allowed to lay fallow until Mr. Vrdolyak chose to use it as a vehicle for his mayoral ambitions. Thomas Hynes, the Cook County assessor, created the Chicago First Party but quit the race weeks before the April 7 mayoral election.

earning only 45.1 percent to Byrne's 48 percent. Byrne won handily in precincts that were more than 50 percent Mexican, but Washington easily captured precincts that were more than 50 percent Puerto Rican (Ojeda, 1987; Table 5. 2).

6. City clerk candidate Gloria Chevere, a Puerto Rican personally chosen by Harold Washington as his running mate, swept the Puerto Rican precincts, but she evenly split the Latino vote with incumbent Walter Kozubowski in the Mexican precincts.

7. About 70 percent of the registered voters in the 129 precincts turned out to vote in 1987.

8. In 1983, Washington received 10 percent of the Latino vote of the 200,000 eligible to vote throughout the city.

9. Of the 129 Latino precincts in the 1987 General Election, Washington received 53.1 percent of the vote, Edward R. Vrdolyak of the Solidarity party 37.6 percent, and Donald H. Haider 2.9 percent. However, Puerto Rican voters gave Washington 74 percent of their vote, while Mexican voters gave him 41.4 percent (Starks, 1987).

10. Washington's victory in 1987 was successful in bringing about a solid 26–24 majority of Aldermen that supported the mayor and thereby assured a much less hostile legislative body and smoother sailing for the mayor's agenda. (Source: Ojeda, April 1987).

The mayor ran on a fairly comprehensive platform for 1987. It included more neighborhood revitalization, continued development of the central business district, riverfront development, the development of industrial parks that would result in the creation of more jobs, school reform, health care and human services improvements, and a more aggressive infrastructure repair and upgrading program. Let us now look briefly at the Washington legacy.

THE WASHINGTON LEGACY: POLICY SUCCESSES AND FAILURES

Reform was a consistent theme throughout the Washington campaign of 1983 and became the central theme of his administration. In addition, he made the themes of "openness" and "fairness" trademarks of his administration.

Harold Washington's political career is a demonstration of his commitment to the principles of liberal democracy. Albert Szymanski describes the politics of liberal democracy as an "advocacy of relatively minor and slow changes in the direction of equalitarianism" (Szymanski, 1978, p. 30). Washington's tenure as mayor reveals an essential belief in the centrality of government as an instrument of potential good. Liberal democrats seek change as a means of furthering the welfare of the individual; they seek this change through process, method, stability, equality, and order. While government is the instrument, the goal is promotion of the common good.

However, as Bowles and Gintis point out in their critique of modern capitalist society, *Democracy and Capitalism*, the liberal ''democratic capitalist society'' is such that social change is difficult because of the institutional and structural barriers that frustrate the desire for an equal society (Bowles and Gintis, 1986, p. 16). Washington fully understood these limitations and sought to work within them. Further, he was fully aware of the tendency within liberal capitalist democracies for the ''economically dominant class to rule through democratic institutions.'' The many battles that he had with the business community are proof of this tendency. Nowhere was that more evident than in the Cook County Democratic party and the business community. The members of each of these institutions rejected him initially and attempted to perpetuate their rule through the democratic institutions which they dominated.

Reform

Reform is usually defined as a process of political change within the framework of a constitution, and without questioning the legitimacy of the sovereign power. The new result of continuous reform may be a change of constitution (whether in fact or in law), but the essential feature is the absence of challenge to the perceived political process (Scruton, 1969, p. 22). Reform has also been defined as taking from others (by restructuring organizations, policies and programs) those things one wants for oneself (Preston, 1984, pp. 3–9), a definition that was not lost on machine politicians. They understood that Washington's plans would take away their privileges and power; therefore, it was not surprising that during his first term, they were the primary opponents of reform.

Washington was forceful and often boastful of his reform agenda, which he wore as a badge of honor. Because it was totally compatible with the notion of liberal democracy, it was embraced with enthusiasm, although he was fully aware that it meant different things to different sectors of society. While it meant long overdue inclusion to blacks, it meant an open challenge to ethnic and economic domination to whites; and to the white middle-class liberals (often referred to as lakefront liberals) it meant good government free of institutional corruption and patronage, except in those cases where they were the immediate beneficiaries.

In an attempt to fulfill this campaign promise, Washington began his tenure by signing a federal court agreement to adhere strictly to the limitations on political hiring as defined by the Shakman Decree. Michael Shakman ''filed suit in 1969. He argued that he had lost his campaign to be a delegate to the 1970 state Constitutional Convention because city workers had been coerced into hustling votes for his opponent, who was slated by the regular Democratic Organization'' (Joravsky, 1984, pp. 6–8). As a result of the 1969 lawsuit, the City of Chicago agreed in 1972 to stop forcing employees to engage in political work as a condition of employment. The decree signed by the mayor in 1983 further restricted his powers by exempting only 790 positions from the total of 42,000. Even though Washington voluntarily signed this decree, as a demonstration of his dedication to reform and in keeping with his liberal democratic character of gradual change, he was slow in filling these positions. His slowness in filling these positions angered black community leaders. An analysis of their concerns showed that

- fifteen months after he took his oath of office, Mayor Harold Washington had moved his own selections into only 18 percent of the highest ranking and most sensitive positions in his administration.
- . . . The jobs range from the Commissioners of the City's 21 departments and their deputies, to selected clerks, aides and secretaries who handle sensitive city business.
- . . . 60 percent of the positions in question were held by persons hired during the administration of Mayor Jane Byrne, Washington's predecessor.
- . . . Another 15 percent were filled by persons appointed during the tenure of Mayor Richard J. Daley, who died in December, 1976.
- . . . 6 percent of the posts were held by persons appointed from January, 1977 to April 1979, during Mayor Michael A. Bilandic's two year tenure. (Joravsky, 1984, p. 8)

The constraints were real because under the terms of the decree, all hiring and firing was monitored by federal court Judge Nicholas J. Bua. The federal court decree relegates about 98 percent of the work force to the level of non-policy-making employees. This meant that Washington could not fire them unless he proved they had been derelict in their duties. The decree exempted about 900 policy-making jobs, supposedly enabling Washington to fire key advisors. But there was a catch. Exempt employees could appeal to federal courts if they were fired (Joravsky, 1985, p. 3). Even by mid-1985, by the mayor's own admission, he had only filled 200 of the 900 exempt positions. While the Shakman decree was a formidable structural constraint, the caution with which Washington dealt with it was in keeping with his liberal democratic-reformist vision.

The other structural constraint that became a real obstacle to his first three years in office was his inability to control the city council. The Cook County Democratic party's rejection of his candidacy after winning the Democratic nomination for Mayor was carried over into the city council. When he moved to reorganize the city council in 1983 after winning the general election, he was blocked by Alderman Edward R. Vrdolyak and his group of twenty-nine white aldermen. These white Democratic aldermen blocked his legislative agenda, held up confirmation of his appointments to boards and commissions, and otherwise undermined and frustrated his entire reform agenda. This obstacle was not removed until the special aldermanic election in the spring of 1986. The election was ordered by the federal court as a result of the settlement of the city reapportionment case. All four of the Washington-sponsored candidates won in their respective wards and added four additional allies to his group of council supporters. With the defection of Alderman Vrdolyak to the Republican party after the mayoral election in 1987, and the subsequent election of George Dunne as the President of the Cook County Board, the mayor was able to count on Dunne's alderman (Burton Natarus, forty-second ward) as a Washington ally. However, until that election, the council was split 25 to 25, and it was only the Mayor's parliamentary power to break a tie vote that enabled him to pass his legislation. Washington received high marks from most of his critics for the manner in which he was able to work through this period.

In keeping with his promise of openness, Washington signed an executive order for freedom of information as one of the first acts after being sworn into office. Shortly thereafter, he established a Freedom of Information Office in city hall and institutionalized it in all departments and city agencies. The openness of the Washington administration was a welcome change in Chicago government. Fairness was also a major hallmark of his administration. The major demonstration of fairness was his policy of equalizing city services across the city.

Most of these changes were loudly applauded by the Lakefront liberals. As early as 1984, the *Chicago Reporter* observed:

- Washington has cut the payroll and trimmed the budget
- The Washington administration has overseen a boom in downtown development that may be jeopardized by the council fights.
- The city has pumped more Federal Community development funds into poor neighborhoods despite funding cutbacks . . .
- Washington has nearly doubled city monies awarded to minority-owned businesses . . .
- The mayor has made changes long endorsed by good government groups—a revised budget with a line items account of federally funded programs and extensive public budget hearings. (Joravsky, 1984, pp. 6–8)

Extensive public budget hearings were in keeping with his policy of openness, an unheard-of practice before his administration.

Furthermore, he was proud of stating that his government was free of institutional corruption. It was true that in spite of the involvement of "Raymond the Mole" with some aldermen and an ex-political aide, Mr. Clarence McClain, his administration was considered by most Chicagoans as a welcome change from the institutional corruption, and the demonstrated efficiency in government that wiped out a huge debt that he inherited (and restored the city to double-A bond rating) earned him high marks as a serious reformer.

Political Accomplishments

His major political accomplishment was dethroning and forcing his political nemesis out of the party. Mr. Vrdolyak, the former alderman of the tenth ward, was the chairman of the Cook County Democratic party in 1983 and supported Jane Byrne in the primary and the Republican candidate Bernard Epton in the general election. Vrdolyak led the fight against Washington in the city council and worked vigorously to undermine his administration. In 1987, he resigned from the city council and sponsored his brother for his seat and ran for mayor on the Solidarity party ballot. After losing the election, he declared himself a Republican and announced his candidacy for the Cook County clerk of the circuit court. Thus, less than two months before Harold Washington died in November 1987, he was proud to declare that he had run Mr. Vrdolyak out of the Democratic party to the Republican party, where he should have been all of the time.

Furthermore, Washington helped build the foundation for the first multiethnic progressive coalition in the city's history. By his adherence to liberal democratic principles, despite their limitations, and his commitment to reform fairness and openness, he was able to change citizens' thinking about their city. He was able to demonstrate tangible change in the conduct of city government. He also became one of the Democratic party's major critics of Reagan's urban policy and a major policy innovator in urban organizations.

Finally, he expanded the duties of the mayor by establishing close links between his office and progressive agenda items, nuclear free zones, the Commission of Latino Affairs, Commission on Women's Affairs, Municipal Sanctions Against Businesses that are Connected to South Africa, and environmental concerns. In addition, he vastly increased the political confidence and efficacy of black citizens.

The 1987 election platform for the Washington campaign can be summarized as (1) major core redevelopment; (2) industrial parks and job development; (3) development of affordable housing; (4) education reform; and (5) better police and municipal services.

Failures

Just as there were successes, Washington also had some failures. First, he made consistently poor appointments to the Chicago Housing Authority (CHA) and it was poorly administered. Second, he never developed a policy for the homeless, even though he considered it a major problem in Chicago and elsewhere. Third, he was not able to reduce high unemployment, especially acute among blacks and Puerto Ricans in Chicago. And while it is clear that unemployment is more a national than a local problem and that it calls for a federal response, people still look to the mayor for some relief. One of Washington's final failures, especially from the black community's standpoint, is that he did not leave a strong successor. It should be pointed out, however, that few leaders ever consider this as one their responsibilities. Washington believed that he would be mayor for the next 10 to 20 years and was not about to set up a young challenger for his job.

CONCLUSION

The election of Harold Washington as mayor of the city of Chicago in 1983 and 1987 can be viewed as the culmination of black dissatisfaction with the Chicago Democratic machine that had been building up for years. The Byrne years were simply the final episode in a long and continuous battle against the negative policies of machine leaders. There are several important things to be learned from the Washington campaign and the legacy he left before he died.

Black representation into the democratic machine had existed for over 25 years, but that representation had led only to very limited responsiveness. Indeed, most of the responsiveness that did occur was not because of action by the machine leadership (black or white) but because of external pressure from the federal government, lawsuits, and community activists. A few low-level jobs were provided to black clients of the organizations, but the machine fought the most critical black demands for better and more integrated schools and an end to police brutality and did not support fair housing, to name just a few of the issues of concern to the black community. In short, while incorporation occurred, the political machine posed organizational and political barriers to black interests and demands.

Second, political movements like the one that ended in Harold Washington's election are based on past dissatisfaction with the dominant regime. Indeed, one of the most important lessons about this movement is understanding what motivated Harold Washington to get involved in a process that asks so much but promises so little. No doubt, he was partially motivated by his long history of involvement in Chicago politics, his ambition, and the kind of support offered by other political actors. Yet is also clear that he believed that the only way blacks would get their concerns addressed was by taking over political power in the city. And he understood that the only way a black politician could do that was by developing a coalition with liberal whites and Latinos. The overwhelming support of blacks plus support from Latinos and liberal whites enabled him to be elected in both 1983 and 1987. His election led to the political incorporation of liberal whites and Latinos into the governing coalition. Liberal whites were interested in reform and so was he; Latinos wanted representation and jobs and he tried to provide some of both. The result was the development of a coalition that sought to be much more inclusive than the old regime.

Third, Washington's reform agenda and his emphasis on a more equitable service delivery system was a refreshing change from the past. While members of the coalition were not always happy with the pace of change, he was able, after much resistance from the old guard, to start instituting his more progressive program for the city.

Fourth, political movements are fragile enterprises. They can be sustained only by strong political leadership and cohesive support of the coalition. Where leadership is weak, coalitions break apart, and this can lead to the demise of the movement and a loss of political power. Indeed, weak leadership is the current situation in Chicago.

The new Mayor, Eugene Sawyer, a black who was appointed after Washington's death, was supported for office by the very people Washington fought so hard to defeat. He was opposed by a substantial number of people in the black community, and his appointment has split the black community into several factions. His lack of aggressiveness and leadership has been questioned by all groups. He has publicly said that he will push the Washington agenda, but there are serious concerns about his inclinations and ability to do so. Tim Evans, Sawyer's challenger, had the support of some blacks and Latinos.

In the recent election to fill Washington's 2-year term, Richard M. Daley defeated Sawyer to win the Democratic primary. In doing so, he won most of the Latino and white liberal vote. Evans opted not to run in the primary and did not support Sawyer. He ran in the general election as an independent candidate. Sawyer's black supporters did not support Evans, and he also had limited appeal to the two other coalition members—liberal whites and Latinos. Daley won the 1989 general election by receiving almost all of the white vote, and a majority of the Latino vote.

Finally, it is clear that weak political leadership can destroy a movement and the coalition that enabled it to exist. What is not clear is what the short- and long-term consequences of the lost of political power will mean for black Chicago in the future. How this scenario will play itself out will depend a great deal on whether the Daley regime provides the kind of leadership that takes into consideration the concerns, needs, and desires of black constituents. If the new leadership fails, we may see more protest and political mobilization by blacks again in the near future.

REFERENCES

American Political Science Association Annual Convention. September 4, 1987. Hilton Towers Hotel, Chicago.

Browning, Rufus P., Dale Rogers Marshall, and David H. Tabb. 1984. *Protest Is Not Enough*. Berkeley: University of California Press.

Carmichael, Stokely, and Charles V. Carmichael. 1967. *Black Power: The Politics of Liberation in America*. New York: Vintage Books.

Joravsky, Ben. August 1984. Mayor Show to Fill Top City Jobs: Blames Shakman Decree. *The Chicago Reporter*.

Joravsky, Ben. April 1985. Midterm Report: Washington Reform Progress Burdened by Errors, Politics. *The Chicago Reporter*.

Kleppner, Paul. 1985. *Chicago Divided: The Making of a Black Mayor*. DeKalb: Northern Illinois University.

Moritz, Charles, ed. February 1984. Washington, Harold. *Current Biography*. New York: H. Wilson Publications.

Ojeda, Julio. April 1987. Close Look at Primary. *The Chicago Reporter*.

Ojeda, Julio. May 1987. Hispanic Split Vote Again. *The Chicago Reporter*.

Preston, Michael B. 1984. *The Politics of Bureaucratic Reform*. Champaign: University of Illinois Press.

Preston, Michael B. 1982. Black Politics in the Post-Daley Era. In *After Daley: Chicago Politics in Transition*. Champaign: University of Illinois Press.

Preston, Michael B. 1984. The Resurgence of Black Voting in Chicago: 1955–1983. In *The Making of the Mayor; Chicago 1983*. Grand Rapids: William B. Eerdmans Publishing Company.

Preston, Michael B., Lenneal J. Henderson, and Paul L. Puryear. 1987. *The New Black Politics; The Search for Political Power*. New York: Longman.

Scruton, Roger. 1969. *A Dictionary of Political Thought*. New York: Basic Books.

Starks, Robert T. April 23–25, 1987. Harold Washington and the 1987 Primary and General Election. Delivered at 1987 Meeting of the National Conference of Black Political Scientists. Atlanta.

Szymanski, Albert. 1978. *The Capitalist State and the Politics of Class*. Cambridge: Winthrop Publishers.

Travis, Dempsey. 1986. Part 5. The Harold Washington Years. *An Autobiography of Black Politics*. Chicago: Urban Research Press.

Trotsky, Leon. 1969. *History of the Russian Revolution*. London. 1:16–17.

Walton, Hanes, Jr. 1985. *Invisible Politics: Black Political Behavior*. Albany: State University of New York Press.

CHAPTER 6

Boston: The Unfinished Agenda

Toni-Michelle C. Travis

Editors' Note

Black political leaders in Boston, although occasionally elected to city council or school board positions, have been excluded from the stronger incorporation that comes with participation in a dominant coalition. With a black population of 22 percent in 1980, why hasn't it been possible for blacks to become part of a strong, biracial, liberal coalition? Some points should be kept in mind.

1. Boston is a city of historically strong ethnic identities—first Yankee, then Irish.
2. As in other older northern cities, machine-style politics has played a significant role.
3. Twenty-two percent black, although substantial, is still a small proportion, compared with other cities described in this book (see Table 12.1), and the Latino population of Boston was only 6.4 percent in 1980. A winning multiracial coalition there would have required unusually high levels of support from whites.
4. Biracial or multiracial coalitions in difficult settings require leadership with special commitments, skills, and resources, from both races. Did that leadership emerge in Boston?

In January 1986 Bruce Bolling, a member of the Boston City Council, became the first black president in the council's 170-year history. Bolling's presidency marks the culmination of the slow but steadily growing empowerment of blacks in Boston politics. While blacks have always been present in Boston politics, they have been more often observers than participants because the Yankees and the Irish have dominated the political stage. In order to understand the role of blacks in Boston it is necessary to have some background knowledge of how Yankee paternalism retarded black political development and how Irish displacement of the Yankees resulted in the exclusion of blacks from Democratic party politics.

RACE RELATIONS UNDER YANKEE AND IRISH RULE

Boston politics has its roots in the historical relationships among the Yankees, the Irish, and the blacks. Under Yankee domination colonial and pre–Civil War blacks experienced racial harmony in an atmosphere where they could enjoy civil and political rights. Wealthy Yankee traders viewed free blacks paternalistically, as a low-income class of people (Lupo, 1977, p. 124). Since Yankees were members of the political and cultural elite, they did not perceive blacks as an economic threat to their position. Consequently blacks could freely operate businesses, buy property, and run for office (Horton, 1979).

As slavery became an increasingly important issue in the 1850s, free blacks and Yankee abolitionists formed integrated organizations to end slavery. Abolitionist organizations provided an opportunity for free blacks to learn organizational and political skills. Yet, blacks often found that their efforts to become leaders were thwarted by white patrons who expected blacks to work only as obedient followers. A notable case among many was the conflict between white abolitionist William Lloyd Garrison and Frederick Douglass, a former slave, over the crucial issue of the future role of blacks in electoral politics (Quarles, 1969). Frederick Douglass broke with Garrison, who felt that blacks should not be encouraged to vote in a political system where the Constitution protected the rights of slaveholders (Horton, 1979, p. 86). Douglass adamantly advocated electoral participation and pulled some black abolitionists from Garrison's ranks. Douglass felt that participation in the electoral process was a necessary step in the political development of blacks. To affirm his convictions Douglass ran for office on the Liberal ticket in New York State.

Discrimination against blacks has always been present in Boston, but it has rarely been a public issue. Yankees accepted the Protestant blacks who could be molded in their image. Blacks were seen as children to be guided by Protestant values of hard work and civic duty. This nineteenth-century paternalistic relationship benefited blacks, while it caused no competition with the Yankees for jobs, housing, or political benefits. Middle-class blacks who were members of the State House or the Common Council (now City Council) and who led successful careers in pharmacy, medicine, and law inculcated Yankee values, especially an integrationist philosophy of race relations. Middle-class blacks were the community leaders who promoted the NAACP integrationist approach to racial problems. This race relations model called for prominent black and white community leaders to convene to discuss racial issues. Black leaders considered this to be an acceptable procedure in a racial climate where there was no overt discrimination. Under Yankee rule blacks were free to buy property, operate businesses, and in general attend public cultural and civic events. The few racial incidents that did occur were considered isolated and were usually attributed to less urban southern newcomers. Racial incidents were considered an individual, not a group, problem.

The era of integration and the Yankee dominance began to decline in 1884 when the Irish elected their first mayor. Yankees noted the growing size of the potential Irish electorate and tried to delay the shift to Irish rule by changing electoral laws to favor their dwindling numbers. These maneuvers, however, amounted to mere holding actions (Eisinger, 1980). Yankees were able to maintain only intermittent control over the mayor's office in 1899, 1907, and 1925 before Irish control was complete. Reluctantly, the Yankees retreated from municipal to state-level politics.

As the Irish rose to power they imposed their cultural values on municipal government (Wilson and Banfield, 1964). Strong family and community ties centered on the Catholic parish, which became a center for social activities and the organizational base for political activities. These community ties had a psychological and a geographic basis as Boston became a city composed of distinct neighborhoods (Lukas, 1986). The males in these tightly knit families quickly saw politics as a possible route for upward mobility through patronage benefits. Consequently, early in the twentieth century, politics strongly appealed to the Irish immigrants who desperately sought the economic security that municipal employment offered.

With the Irish in control of city government, blacks were excluded from electoral politics. Blacks could run as Republicans, but that party was no longer viable in Boston, only in suburban towns. The Irish did not need the black vote to win municipal elections because Irish Democrats held a clear majority of the electorate, while blacks accounted for less than 3 percent of the population in 1900 (Daniels, 1969, p. 458). Since the Irish were securely in power, they ran the Democratic party as a club which clearly made blacks outsiders. Furthermore, low-income blacks and Irish clashed as they competed for jobs and housing, which created hostility and did not foster integrated political activity (Thernstrom, 1973). Blacks found that the Irish control of the ballot box extended to all municipal jobs, which were retained exclusively for Irish Democrats.

Although Boston Democrats were not seeking black followers, they realized that Franklin D. Roosevelt's 1932 victory was causing blacks to desert the Republican party at the national level. Locally, Michael Curley, a major political force in municipal and state politics from 1930 to 1950, viewed blacks as a political resource that he could use. Curley therefore encouraged black participation through broker-style politics. Through gatekeepers such as the Taylor brothers, the black vote was delivered to Curley in exchange for political appointments. Broker politics, however, benefited only a few middle-class blacks, while it discouraged mass mobilization of the black electorate.

Through the 1950s black political participation was dominated by the Taylors and older Boston residents, the black bourgeoisie who assumed that the political interests of blacks would be best served by cautious, accommodationist efforts through integrated organizations such as the Urban League and National Association for the Advancement for Colored People (Hill, 1952). Although the community had a network of churches, clubs, and fraternal organizations, bourgeois community leaders who thought of themselves as Bostonians preferred to operate on Yankee values, which stressed attaining goals through individual effort and community leadership by the better-educated classes. Blacks adopted this Yankee practice of emphasizing class differences to the extent that class distinctions based on ascriptive rather than economic criteria were emphasized within the small black community (Hill, 1952). Consequently, the black community never produced a core of leaders who focused on a collective, racially based effort to build all-black institutions other than churches. The acceptance of class distinctions, along with the idea of participating in only integrated civic organizations, was so ingrained among blacks that it prevented unity across class lines.

POLITICAL AWAKENING AMONG BLACKS

While the Irish solidified their political power through steady population growth and consistent voting turnout, the black community was undergoing internal changes. From 1900 to 1940 the black population expanded at a rate of less than 1 percent per decade, growing from 2.1 percent in 1900 to only 2.6 percent in 1930. The growth was insignificant politically, but not socially; the in-migration changed the composition of the black community because newcomers consisted of southern blacks, black Canadians, West Indians, and Cape Verde Portuguese (Travis, 1983, pp. 120, 220).

In 1940 the steady stream of northern migrants pushed the population figures up to 3.1 percent and 5.0 percent in the post–World War II year of 1950. The greatest growth occurred between 1960 and 1970 as blacks reached a high of 16 percent in the decade when racial violence over busing gripped Boston.

The population increase in the black community caused friction among the less educated and acculturated southern migrants, who were primarily from the Tidewater areas of Virginia (Pleck, 1979), and the old black Bostonians who placed a high value on light skin color, social graces, and bourgeois respectability. Class tensions were exacerbated as cultural diversity increased among blacks. West Indian migrants also met disdain from northern blacks. West Indians were singled out because of their accent, affiliation with the Episcopal Church, and fierce racial pride, which often led to political protest. West Indians also highly valued getting an education and saving money in order to buy a home. The Cape Verdean Portuguese do not always identify themselves as black and were also not acceptable on the grounds of accent, income, and lower-class values.

A large black community by the 1950s produced a concentration of blacks and visibility. Black newcomers needed housing, but incomes were so low that affordable housing meant seeking rental accommodations in old housing stock in the South End or Roxbury. Clusters of blacks living in poorer housing quickly led to clear patterns of segregated schools (Clay, 1985).

In the 1950s Boston blacks were politically complacent because they felt that their civil and political rights were secure, compared with the rights of blacks in southern cities, where the civil rights movement was fighting for voting rights and access to public facilities. Discrimination in Boston was subtle, but it surfaced when blacks tried to join unions, to obtain supervisory positions in municipal jobs, or to secure loans for residential or commercial property (Thernstrom, 1973). The subtlety of discriminatory practices caused blacks not to see political empowerment as a critical factor until the 1970s when the school busing issue crystallized racial differences. At that point blacks began to develop all-black community organizations to promote political mobilization and black candidates for municipal and state office (King, 1981).

The court-ordered desegregation that resulted in school busing in 1974 propelled blacks to a new stage of political development in which they asserted themselves as political leaders instead of the followers of liberal whites. Community leaders, who were usually not part of the black bourgeoisie, galvanized blacks into forming politically oriented organizations. These young activists, who were often of West Indian descent, created organizations focusing on single issues such as education, urban renewal, black union membership, and black representation on the school committee and city council. These groups sought inclusion in the policy-making process through protest activities, rejecting the tradition of negotiation and accommodation of the bourgeois-dominated Urban League and NAACP. Political mobilization became a priority, including voter registration, get-out-the-vote campaigns, and the promotion of black candidates for office. Through the community-based efforts of these organizations, political activity among blacks greatly increased (King, 1981). When the black activists realized how entrenched machine Irish politicians were in city hall, on the city council, and on the school committee, they knew political victories were not going to be easy. In order to become a part of the policy-making process, blacks needed multiple representation and sufficient numbers to help form a liberal coalition. This was a difficult task in a city where blacks constituted only 9.1 percent of the population in 1960 and only 16.3 percent by 1970 (Thernstrom, 1973, p. 179). Activists decided that black candidates had to be advanced in every election even if they had little chance of victory.

Population changes were beginning to have a positive political impact for blacks. Although the black population was still less than 25 percent of the total population, the percentage of blacks was increasing while the total number of whites was decreasing. For the period 1970–1980, the black population increased by 21 percent; the white population declined by 25 percent (Jennings, 1984, p. 224).

Veteran community activists such as Ruth Batson and Mel King, who had played key roles in trying to reach peaceful solutions to the school busing crises,

---

[1]The U.S. Census, 1870–1970, is cited in Thernstrom, p. 179. Census data for Boston are a problem because the census racial categories do not remain consistent from one census to the next. It is not clear where Latinos, Cape Verdeans, and West Indians are counted for some census reports.

were among the first to seek seats on the school committee. Batson ran unsuccessfully in 1959. Mel King continued to run for the school committee with the support of his campaign manager, school counselor John O'Bryant. King never did achieve a seat in his 1961, 1963, or 1965 attempts. However, his persistence in seeking an elective office proved to be a symbol of black demands for incorporation. King's organizational base set the stage for the 1977 election of John O'Bryant to the school committee.

As blacks were shifting from protest to electoral strategies, Tom Atkins, executive director of the NAACP, won a major victory by securing a seat on the city council in 1967 (O'Brien, 1982). Since Atkins was from Indiana he was not a part of the factions that had long divided the black community. Atkins' NAACP role also provided name recognition in a campaign that stressed citywide issues in an effort to attract blacks, liberal whites, and other minority votes (King, 1981, p. 83).

Atkins served two terms on the city council, running in at-large races in 1967 and 1969. In 1967 Atkins was one of the forty-five candidates in the nonpartisan preliminary election for one of nine council seats. With the support of blacks and liberals, Atkins placed fifteenth in the preliminary election, where the top eighteen candidates qualified for the general election. Atkins went on to place seventh out of all the candidates (interview with Robert Hannan).[2]

The 1967 and 1969 city councils were dominated by the Democratic politicians, who had no interest in allowing blacks or any minority groups into the policy-making process. The only non-Irish members were Frederick C. Langone from the Italian North End and John L. Saltonstall, Jr., of the well-known Yankee family. Atkins and Saltonstall were the only liberal Democrats, so there was no hope of creating a liberal coalition.

Atkins' second term began in 1969. The number of Italian Americans increased to two, but the implacable antibusing advocate Louise Day Hicks of South Boston also joined the Council. Once again, Atkins was not able to significantly affect policy decisions.

Atkins' successful races for city council indicated that he had sufficient appeal among white and minority voters to continue on the city council beyond 1971. Atkins, however, decided to run for mayor in 1971 against Democratic party faithfuls Kevin White and Louise Day Hicks. In losing that race, he ended his electoral career. Subsequently, Atkins was appointed the first black secretary for communities and development under Governor Francis Sargent.

The election of Tom Atkins proved that a black could attract white voters, even in racially polarized Boston (Travis, 1983, p. 244). Atkins appealed to white voters because he represented the old style of race relations symbolized by the NAACP, which spoke for the nonmilitant segment of the black community. Unlike protest-style candidates, Atkins was acceptable to a percentage of the few remaining liberal Yankees and the new urban white middle-class professionals.

---

[2] Telephone interviews were conducted in April and May 1986 with Robert Hannan, Chief of Research, Boston City Council; Attorney Fletcher Wiley; Sharon Wilmore of Councilman Yancey's staff; and Robert Jones and Joseph Kaigler of Councilman Bolling's staff.

Atkins and Kevin White were elected in the same year. White, however, remained in the mayor's office until 1983, solidifying his power into a machine patterned after Richard J. Daley's Chicago model. Atkins' two terms on the city council did not constitute strong incorporation. After Atkins' term ended, blacks lost ground politically. Between 1971 and 1981, only John O'Bryant was elected to public office, to the school committee in 1977.

KEVIN WHITE'S ADMINISTRATION

As blacks became more active in seeking office they found that they still faced a formidable political system controlled by Irish-Americans. The question facing voters in 1967 was who was the least racist among the mayoral candidates. Kevin White, rather than the South Boston militant Louise Day Hicks, the mother of the antibusing movement, received the support of the black community. White courted the votes of the black community and won office on the platform that he was the moderate candidate who could bring the black and white communities together by reducing racial tensions. However, once in office he made only symbolic gestures to the black community, which asked for inclusion in municipal decision making and increased services.

White did not see the need for increased police protection in Roxbury, for additional low-income housing, or for black input on school issues, and most of his city hall appointments of blacks were merely symbolic. Black Deputy Mayor Clarence "Jeep" Jones soon learned that his task was to contain the problems of the black community, while he served as a broker between white downtown business interests and black Roxbury.

As an experienced politician with ambitions for national office, White realized that he could continue to win the black vote without including blacks in most policy-making decisions. White's election results showed that he could appeal to a broader section of the population than his rivals Louise Day Hicks and Joseph Timility because they were more closely identified with South Boston. As a graduate of Tabor Academy and Williams College and a former West Roxbury resident, White appeared to be a cut above his Irish political opponents. However, once in office White began to use his clout to build a machine that hindered black political expansion.

White was able to use the black vote and ignore black demands for services because the black population in 1970 was only 16.3 percent. White could clearly stay in office by pulling a majority of the white votes and some black votes, especially in the preliminary election when he had to face a field of challengers. In the General election the black vote was not crucial, but it gave him a wider margin of victory.

An additional factor giving White power was the lack of mobilization in the black community. Tom Atkins' city council victories had not resulted in any sustained mobilization or established any ongoing institutions to promote black participation. Consequently, Kevin White did not have to give serious consideration to black demands when blacks could not command a high and consistently solid voter turnout. The highest voter turnout for a preliminary election between 1967 and 1979 was 55.4 percent for Ward 12 in 1967, while the city turnout rate was 56.4 percent. In all preliminary and general elections between 1967 and 1979, the predominantly black wards, 9, 12, and 14, had a lower turnout than the city as a whole (Jennings, 1984, pp. 228–229).

Since Mayor White excluded blacks from city hall policy decisions, blacks took their problems to blacks who represented Boston in the state house. As a result of redistricting in 1971, blacks had improved their chances for gaining more than just the one seat Roxbury usually controlled.

Redistricting brought four blacks, Doris Bunte, Bill Owens, Royal Bolling, Jr., and Mel King into the state house. This cluster of black legislators formed the Massachusetts Black Caucus, a new institution which played a role in municipal politics. Caucus members constantly criticized Mayor White for his inadequate delivery of police, fire, and sanitation services to black areas. The caucus successfully maintained visibility and kept pressure on White's administration by holding hearings on the controversial issue of police–community relations (King, 1981, p. 215).

State house representatives gave a needed push to black mobilization. Blacks could now point to two electoral accomplishments: Atkins' two terms on an at-large city council and the election of blacks to the state house. The situation indicated that blacks needed to increase black voter registration and turnout, as well as develop strategies for coalition building with liberal white and nonblack voters to achieve black incorporation.

FROM PROTEST TO ELECTORAL POLITICS

Mel King used his visible position in the state house to bring together a new breed of political activists interested in developing electoral strategies. Their targets were the school committee, dominated by South Boston antibusing advocates, and the city council. This time King did not run. Instead, John O'Bryant, a black counselor who was well known throughout the school system, was selected in an appeal to white voters; O'Bryant was not considered a militant, as King was often labeled. O'Bryant's 1977 campaign also overcame the organizational problems of previous King campaigns. It was based on the strategy that all blacks should use bullet voting, casting ballots only for O'Bryant. O'Bryant won by finishing fourth in a race for five seats. He drew 43.9 percent of his total from the black community. He was also able to top the ticket in nine of Boston's twenty-two wards (It's All in the Numbers, 1977). O'Bryant did well in the liberal white areas of Back Bay and Beacon Hill, while he pulled needed white votes from the North End, West End, Savin Hill, Dorchester, Codman Square, Mattapan, and Brighton (Travis, 1983, pp. 301–302). Not only was O'Bryant's 1977 win a victory for the black community, but it was also a defeat for the anti-busing forces because Louise Day Hicks and Pixie Pallidino lost.

O'Bryant's school committee victory marks a definite turning point for black empowerment. His presence on the school committee had a direct bearing on the selection of Robert Wood as superintendent of the school system. The choice of Wood was significant because he was a respected educator who had served as the president of the University of Massachusetts at Amherst and he came from outside of the patronage-ridden school system.

O'Bryant is currently the senior black member of the school committee, which was reorganized from a five- to a thirteen-member committee in 1983. Blacks have now reached a high of four out of the thirteen seats. Now blacks have to develop new strategies for coalition building and achieving policy objectives within this new structure.

The O'Bryant school committee victory was followed by increased efforts on the part of Mel King, along with other black activists and Latinos, to create a Black Political Task Force to review the positions of candidates for local offices. The task force would then endorse acceptable candidates and urge black voters to campaign and vote only for the endorsed candidates. After the establishment of the task force, mobilization of the black community became more manageable because it provided a structure for screening candidates who would support policies favorable to the black community and for promoting voter registration.

RAYMOND FLYNN'S ADMINISTRATION

The White era ended with decreased racial strife, but without achieving racial harmony. White's successor, Raymond Flynn, a native of South Boston, raised a number of questions regarding the future role of blacks in municipal decision making. To win office Flynn shifted his position on a number of issues. No longer was he a militant opponent of busing; his stance was now moderate. His speeches stressed serving all of Boston not just his old South Boston neighborhood. Flynn was in the difficult position of running a city which needed economic revitalization in terms of new jobs and neighborhood redevelopment without exacerbating racial tensions.

Flynn's first administration stressed citywide economic development. But by 1986 neighborhoods such as the South End, Charlestown, and Chinatown as well as Roxbury were dissatisfied with Flynn's performance (Radin, 1986, p. 67). The mayor's approach to development involved community participation, which invariably caused delays in decision making and implementation of housing and transit projects. Delays would in turn attract negative press coverage for Flynn.

The difficult task of establishing his priorities and trying to meet neighborhood demands after the White administration plagued Flynn. Flynn raised the level of expectations among irate residents who expected immediate results. City Councilor Bruce C. Bolling offered an assessment of Mayor Flynn:

In some respects, Flynn has a holier-than-thou attitude.

He says, "I understand the poor, I understand the oppressed . . . I'm their champion, and I'm going to do what needs to be done for them because I'm the mayor." (Radin, 1986, p. 70)

Although Flynn's objective was to bring about development and cooperation among communities, he was often criticized for his "skittish, well-intentioned, and inconsistent" administration (Radin, 1986, p. 70).

In the midst of these community relations problems, four black professionals developed the idea of a separate district for blacks called Mandela. The issue was presented to the voters on the 1986 ballot. The proponents of Mandela, who were not natives of Boston, concluded from their experiences that Boston blacks lacked the economic and political power to improve their status (Kenny, 1987, p. 14). Consequently, they felt that blacks should secede and establish Mandela, which would be composed of the heart of Boston's black neighborhoods.

The failure to establish Mandela showed the reluctance of a cross section of Boston residents to accept this unorthodox approach to black empowerment. Corporate leaders clearly did not see Mandela to be in their best interests, and a number of white residents and some black leaders opposed the proposition (Kenny, 1987, p. 14). The issue also served to highlight the fragmented state of black leadership (Kaufman, 1988, p. 1).

Mandela would have radically altered the geography of Boston. It would have comprised 25 percent of Boston's land, but 90 percent of its minority population (Kenny, 1987, p. 14). This is not a viable economic unit, given that most blacks are confined to low-paying jobs in a dual labor market. The Boston neighborhoods that compose the proposed Mandela are besieged by high teenage and adult unemployment, along with the concomitant problems of poverty, female-headed households, divorce, mental illness, and a dependency on welfare (Clay, 1985, p. 7). Geographically, Mandela consisted of an area of Boston that was excluded from the downtown transformation of the New Boston. These neighborhoods did not benefit in the shift from a large-scale manufacturing and wholesale trade economy to services such as communications, money management, or business and professional services. Consequently, a separate, incorporated black-run community was not economically feasible (Radin, 1987).

Mandela was more than just another political strategy. It was an indication that economically based racial problems still shaped policy priorities. The issue of separation pointed to the continuing divisions in the black community that prevented concerted community leadership among ministers and elected officials, who split over the issues of separatism. The battle lines within the black community remain clear between natives and nonnatives and between the old black bourgeoisie and the new black middle class. The black community still lacks not only leadership, but also a sufficiently strong institutional base to bring about policy changes in downtown Boston politics.

POLITICAL INCORPORATION

A number of factors have brought Boston blacks to the point where they now have representatives on the school committee, in city council, and in the state house. Irish politicians have dominated all aspects of Boston politics for so long that black representation on the city council alone was not going to bring about policy changes. Atkins' election to the city council was only a step toward incorporation. When O'Bryant won his seat on the school committee in 1977, he was the lone black. However, O'Bryant had the support of black state house representatives who were bringing increasing pressure on Mayor White to address the problems of the black community. In 1977 racial tensions stemming from the school busing order were the overriding concern. Beneath the surface was the larger issue of the future role of blacks in all policy-making areas. The school crisis clearly served to crystallize black–Irish tensions and to bring to light the extensive control the Irish had over school appointments and promotions.

Electing black candidates to office has brought about changes in school committee policy and municipal administration, but not empowerment for blacks, who must systematically seek to attain longevity in electoral positions. Previously successful black officeholders have made strategic errors that were costly to the individuals and to the community. Capable blacks have made the mistake of voluntarily leaving their elected positions to seek a higher office in an uncertain political climate. For example, two-term city council member Tom Atkins ran unsuccessfully for mayor against Kevin White in 1971. Atkins subsequently left Boston to work for the NAACP in New York. Mel King had a 10-year record in the state house representing the South End that ended because he ran unsuccessfully for mayor and for a U.S. House seat. He currently is not in office. Bill Owens, the first black elected to the state senate, switched from the Democratic to the Republican party only to lose his state house seat. In each case the black community lost experienced politicians who could have guided the community in building political institutions.

Black officeholders could benefit from a strategy employed by Mel King. In 1983 King stressed coalition building as a member of the Rainbow Coalition. King's campaign successfully built a multiracial coalition of Latinos, Asians, blacks, feminists, and gay rights activists which could be used as a model in future Boston campaigns (Green, 1983–1984, pp. 2–3).

The Black Political Task Force played a major role in socializing and educating the black voter. Differing from previous black political organizations, the task force did not disband between elections but remained in operation. The task force also took on the role of planning voting strategy for elections, a key factor in mobilizing the black community. Along with bullet voting, the task force stressed the importance of voter turnout in preliminary elections, which is the stage where most black candidates were eliminated. In addition, the task force endorsed quality candidates, regardless of race. This encouraged racial cooperation among blacks, whites, and the increasing number of Asians and Latinos in Boston.

Political power is built by experienced politicians who have a broad political base. The Black Political Task Force has played a role in the political process since 1978, but it has not institutionally expanded beyond its role of screening and endorsing acceptable candidates for office. Screening and endorsement are of value, but they do not address the larger issue of how to train young leaders to build biracial coalitions and to establish permanent institutions for future campaigns.

Flynn's administration has sought to achieve racial harmony as it addresses the political demands of ethnic neighborhoods. Blacks have found Flynn more receptive than White to hiring blacks for municipal positions. In 1988 alone, as of October, Flynn had appointed five blacks or Latinos to head city departments (Appointee to Boston Post Once Felt Racism's Pain, 1988). Throughout municipal agencies Flynn has encouraged affirmative action hiring. One of the most successful agencies has been the Boston Water and Sewer Commission, which went from a hiring rate of 6 percent for nonwhites in January 1988 to 20 percent in October (Kaufman, 1988).

In this more open political climate blacks should take the initiative to establish black-run economic enterprises and to develop public-private partnerships. The mayor might play a new role in community relations by acting as an intermediary between Boston bankers, with their ties to the developers, and those black activists who are trying to insure that blacks obtain jobs in New Boston.

To achieve political and economic progress the black community must first address its internal problems. Fragmentation remains a continuing problem. The bourgeois-based NAACP and the Urban League have yet to join forces with grass-roots organizations and the clergy to tackle the pressing community problems of obtaining adequate housing, health care, and services for elderly and low-income residents. The problems of the black community are so rooted in economic inequality that a united effort is needed for blacks to improve their status (Clay, 1985, pp. 17–74).

Mobilizing the black vote has been a long, frustrating process for community activists. For many years Mel King was the symbolic leader of the black community because he was a perennial candidate for political office. In the 1979 mayoral race, the press labeled King a spoiler, not a serious contender. Without Kevin White in the 1983 race, King made a creditable showing against Ray Flynn. King was able to pull votes in the black wards, among the nonwhite population, which is now almost 38 percent, and among liberal whites who are concerned about the future economic development of downtown Boston and the neighborhoods (Lupo, 1986).

King's campaigns for office served a socializing function for the black community. Although King did not become mayor, his campaign forced Ray Flynn to take a position on issues of concern to blacks. King's bid for mayor raised the level of accountability for Flynn who was expected to do more than Kevin White.

The yearly ritual of Mel King running for office increased the visibility of black candidates. John O'Bryant continued to run successfully for a seat on the school committee. Over time his position changed from being the only black to just one of a minority of blacks. The addition of other blacks opened the possibilities of building coalitions that could initiate policy changes.

Another indirect beneficiary of King's efforts was Bruce Bolling, Jr. As a member of the city council Bolling was eligible for the chairmanship. Although his goal was merely council membership, Bolling benefited from the board's dissatisfaction with Joseph Tierney, who had been chairman for five terms. Through political maneuverings and compromises Bruce Bolling, Jr. became council president in 1986. Bolling's service as president for 2 years sent a signal to the black community that blacks could become part of biracial coalitions and obtain offices previously closed to them.

The electoral process remains a feasible way to achieve inclusion. Although political incorporation for blacks is far from complete, it is under way in Boston. Black candidates should continue to run for local office, but the strategy must be to mobilize the 38 percent minority population into a voting bloc. The black churches and community organizations need to sponsor political workshops to develop leaders who can run campaigns, organize voter registration drives, and produce fund raisers. Each election must be viewed strategically if blacks are seeking more than mere visibility. To attain incorporation into power circles that control the policy process, blacks must unify across class lines, develop new leaders, groom candidates for office, and aim for strategic offices which control patronage and policy making.

REFERENCES

Appointee to Boston Post Once Felt Racism's Pain. 1988. *The New York Times*, October 25.

Clay, Phillip L., ed. 1985. *The Emerging Black Community in Boston*. Report of the Institute for the Study of Black Culture. Boston: University of Massachusetts at Boston.

Daniels, John. 1969. *In Freedom's Birthplace*. New York: Arno Press and The New York Times.

Eisinger, Peter K. 1980. *The Politics of Displacement*. New York: Academic Press.

Green, James. 1983–1984. The Making of Mel King's Rainbow Coalition: Political Changes in Boston, 1963–1983. *Radical America* 17 (6); 18 (1).

Harris, Devonya N. 1988. Agency Hiring Record Is Sign of Commitment. *Bay State Banner*, October 13.

Hill, Adelaide Cromwell. 1952. *The Negro Upper Class in Boston—Its Development and Present Social Structure*. Unpublished Ph.D. dissertation, Radcliffe College.

Horton, James Oliver, and Lois E. Horton. 1979. *Black Bostonians*. New York: Holmes Meier Publishers.

It's All in the Numbers. 1977. *Bay State Banner*, November 17.

Kaufman, Jonathan. 1988. Leaders Get Low Performance Rating. *Boston Globe*, June 14.

Kenny, Charles. 1987. The Aftershock of a Radical Notion. *Boston Globe Magazine*, April 12, 19.

King, Mel. 1981. *Chain of Change*. Boston: South End Press.

Jennings, James. 1984. Blacks and Progressive Politics. In Rod Bush, ed., *The New Black Vote*. San Francisco: Synthesis Publications.

Lukas, J. Anthony. 1986. *Common Ground*. New York: Vintage Books.

Lupo, Alan. 1986. Succession and Its Politics. *Boston Globe*, October 19.

O'Brien, Greg. 1982. Dialogue: Tom Atkins. *Boston Magazine*, June.

Pleck, Elizabeth H. 1979. *Black Migration and Poverty*. New York: Academic Press.

Quarles, Benjamin. 1969. *Black Abolitionists*. New York: Oxford University Press.

Radin, Charles A. 1986. Districts to Flynn: Lend Us an Ear. *Boston Globe*, October 12.

Thernstrom, Stephen. 1973. *The Other Bostonians: Poverty and Progress in the American Metropolis, 1880–1970*. Cambridge, Mass.: Harvard University Press.

Travis, Toni-Michelle C. 1983. Racial and Class Consciousness Among Black Political Activists in Boston. Unpublished Ph.D. dissertation, University of Chicago.

Wilson, James A., and Edward C. Banfield. 1964. Public-regardingness as a Value Premise in Voting Behavior. *American Political Science Review* 68, (4) (December).

PART IV
Class and Leadership in the South

CHAPTER 7

Race and Regime in Atlanta

Clarence N. Stone

Editors' Note

Blacks constitute 66 percent of the population of Atlanta and a majority of the city council. Former ambassador to the United Nations Andrew Young, a black, is completing his second term as mayor. Atlanta seems to represent the ultimate in black political mobilization and access. What more could be hoped for?

Plenty, according to Clarence Stone. He argues that even in Atlanta black political power is severely limited by white economic power. The ownership of land and major businesses, the control of financial institutions and investment, all dominated by whites, sharply constrain the willingness and ability of black officials to deal with problems of poverty, minority neighborhoods, and the condition of the black underclass. Stone emphasizes that the nature of the urban regime depends not just on access and incorporation but also on the terms by which incorporation is achieved and maintained and the ability of other powerholders to control the agenda of city government.

Stone's interpretation of Atlanta raises questions about the other cities described in this volume. How do the other cities look with respect to the standards Stone applies? Is Atlanta different, or is Stone applying a different set of values to city government than other authors? Are the same constraints likely to apply in other cities? Should city governments try to deal with the condition of an underclass? Would black officeholders try to do so if they were not constrained by white economic power? Is it the economic interest of a power structure that limits the agenda of black or Latino regimes, or the fact that the power structure is white?

Blacks hold governmental power in Atlanta. They have a two-to-one majority on the city council, and Andrew Young is completing his second term as the city's second black mayor. Moreover, blacks are a substantial presence in the civic life of Atlanta. They have held the presidency of the Chamber of Commerce and are to be found among the members of every important board and commission in the public life of the community. The political incorporation of blacks in Atlanta is strong enough for Mayor Young to have raised the possibility of city–county consolidation. Even with such a move, blacks presumably would remain at the center of public life in Atlanta.

How such a seemingly strong form of political incorporation came about is in part a familiar story. Key facts in the city's political history are widely known:

1. In 1946, Georgia's white primary was invalidated. A voter-registration drive in the black community brought 20,000 new voters onto the rolls, making the black community more than a quarter of the city's electorate (Bacote, 1955).
2. Atlanta's mayor at the time, William B. Hartsfield, recognized the potential for including Atlanta's black community as junior partners in a coalition built around the mutually reinforcing themes of economic growth and racial moderation. He and his successor, Ivan Allen, Jr., profited electorally from that coalition over the next 20 years (see Jennings and Zeigler, 1966).
3. Atlanta's black community entered a new and more assertive phase in 1960 as direct-action protests signalled the end of the era of quiet accommodation between established black and white leaders (Walker, 1963a).
4. The 1970 census reports showed that Atlanta's population balance had tilted to a black majority, and in 1973 Maynard Jackson was elected as Atlanta's first black mayor. Jackson was reelected by a comfortable margin in 1977, and he has been followed by Atlanta's second black mayor, Andrew Young. Mayor Young was reelected in a landslide in 1985.

Blacks have thus been part of the governing coalition in Atlanta for 40 years, and in that time, their electoral power has steadily enhanced their role within that coalition. As electoral power has grown, the earlier period of mainly symbolic benefits has given way to a situation in which blacks have experienced tangible gains in municipal employment and in the receipt of city contracts (Eisinger, 1980).

Electoral mobilization was a key element in black incorporation, and incorporation as a voting majority was central to the ability of the black community to achieve significant policy responsiveness. Clearly elections matter, and majority voting pays real dividends in governmental decisions.

What more is there to say? A great deal, it turns out. Incorporation is a complex phenomenon, shaped by many factors. The ideology of the governing coalition is one factor. A liberal ideology, containing the principle of equality and favoring the redistribution of advantages to promote that principle, paves the way for minorities to be brought into the governing circle (Browning et al., 1984). Ideological opposition to such redistribution is a barrier, and may lead to a struggle between ins and outs over possession of governing power.

But ideology is not the only factor at work. The initial incorporation of blacks into Atlanta's governing coalition occurred under a mayor who held many of the segregationist views prevalent in the Deep South of that time (Martin, 1978, p. 49), but Atlanta's Mayor Hartsfield was first and foremost a pragmatist. He also had strong ties to members of Atlanta's business elite—he was, for example, a former schoolmate and lifelong friend of Coca Cola's Robert Woodruff. Hartsfield's guiding concern was business progress. He professed deep faith in the enlightened self-interest of top business leaders to act in ways that would promote the city's well-being. Hartsfield looked to the business elite for cues about what was acceptable and unacceptable.

While many of Atlanta's prominent businessmen themselves held traditional southern views on race, they also were pragmatic. They aspired to see Atlanta grow and become the dominant city in the Southeast and reach the rank of being nationally prominent. Hence they cared about Atlanta's image in the larger world. The last thing they wanted was for Atlanta to be seen as a backwater defender of an old way of life.

The conventional wisdom of the time held that the white working class was the backbone of segregationist resistance to social change and that the educated white middle class, including Atlanta's business elite, was, while not especially liberal on racial matters, at least amenable to a policy of moderation. Certainly throughout the 1950s and 1960s Atlanta's white electorate divided along class lines, as predicted by this conventional wisdom (Walker, 1963b; Jennings and Zeigler, 1966). But education and social class were not necessarily in themselves the key factors. One active participant in the Hartsfield coalition observed:

> I've found that one of the best ways to anticipate how a man will vote is to ask him where he was born and grew up. If he comes from South Georgia or somewhere else in the Black Belt you can bet he will be against us, but if he's from the Piedmont area or grew up in Atlanta or outside the South, chances are he's with us. (Quoted in Walker, 1963c, p. 46)

Traditional southern views on race and an overriding commitment to black subordination, V. O. Key (1949) argued, were politically rooted in the old plantation areas of the Deep South—what is known as the Black Belt. According to Key, what sustained the Jim Crow system was not the racial attitudes of nonaffluent and uneducated whites. Instead, it was the political power and leadership of propertied elites in the rural and small-town South, particularly in the Black Belt. They were committed to a form of social control that centered in the racial subordination of blacks (see also Bartley, 1983).

Atlanta's business elite operated on a much different basis. In their change-oriented drive to promote Atlanta, they came into conflict with the tradition-minded in Atlanta, who were less educated and less affluent—and who perhaps felt somewhat threatened by change. In the post-World War II period, the Atlanta business elite also came into conflict with stand-patters in statewide politics, and these included individuals who were educated property holders—this was an elite based economically and socially in the agrarian South.

As mayor, Hartsfield had the foresight to see the possibility of a change-oriented coalition around the twin themes of economic growth and racial moderation. Atlanta's electorally mobilized black community provided the numbers for swinging the balance of city voting power toward the forces of change. The state struggle was a different and more complicated matter.

Significantly, when black college students began their sit-ins protesting segregation in Atlanta in 1960, the reaction of the mayor and the governor were diametrically opposed. Hartsfield characterized the statement of the protesting students as "the legal aspirations of young people throughout the nation and the entire world" (*Atlanta Journal*, March 9, 1960). He immediately sought a negotiated settlement. The governor, Ernest Vandiver, characterized the student statement as "anti-American propaganda" and as a "left-wing statement . . . calculated to breed dissatisfaction, discontent, discord, and evil" (*Atlanta Journal*, March 9, 1960). In the face of a threatened student march to the state capitol grounds in Atlanta, Governor Vandiver deployed state highway patrolmen, who were armed with nightsticks, tear gas, and fire hoses—a preview of the coming reaction in Alabama (Walker, 1963c, p. 88).

A predisposition about the political incorporation of racial minorities is therefore complicated. In the case of Atlanta, the predisposition to favor incorporation was based not on pure political ideology so much as on a pragmatic commitment to change. Whether or not the political incorporation of minorities occurs, what kind of incorporation takes place, and when it occurs are matters influenced by the particulars of the community setting.

As an illustration of how setting matters, consider the Atlanta situation. By the time World War II ended, Atlanta had become a "good government" city, with nonpartisan elections, extensive civil service coverage, and minimal patronage. Hartsfield used a public relations firm to guide his campaigns, and he was sensitive to mass media coverage. No precinct network was available to mobilize voters; electoral mobilization was based on group appeals. Without a quantity of jobs, contracts, inside tips, and the like to distribute, Hartsfield had little choice but to make broad group appeals. This need to make broad group appeals may very well have enhanced city hall's willingness to embrace policies of change.

With the "good government" reform context in mind, we can see that the incorporation of blacks into Atlanta's governing coalition is most readily explained by a somewhat unique conjunction of factors. Incorporation is indeed a complex phenomenon. In postwar Atlanta, a key element was the congruence of black interests and white business interests around the policies of change. To be sure, there were conflicting interests between these two segments of the community as well, but Mayor Hartsfield was able to see the congruence and was skillful in mediating the conflicts that otherwise would have made coalition difficult.

It is also important to realize what was not present in Atlanta. As a "good government" city, Atlanta lacked ward-based patronage politics. Within the black community, the absence of machine-style politics made it easy for the black middle class to assume political leadership, and do so on the basis of group appeals. The presence of the Atlanta University complex and a sizable black business class (Alexander, 1951) provided the black community with a body of organizational skills and resources that facilitated organization around group claims. The role of black business and professional people also facilitated communication with the white business elite. Furthermore, black business and professional leaders were not demanding a class-based redistribution of benefits. They were simply asking that doors closed on a racial basis be opened.

The congruence of black interests, especially black middle-class interests, with those of the white business elite has yet another dimension. Atlanta provides a vivid example of the interplay between electoral and economic power (see Jones, 1978). As a city that has come to have a black majority, that has had a significant black middle class of business and professional people all along, and that has also had all along a white business elite broadly active in political and civic affairs, Atlanta represents a case well worth examining.

In particular, Atlanta illustrates the worth of a political economy perspective. Consider Stephen Elkin's (1985) concept of an urban regime. A regime, Elkin explains, turns on the need to bridge the division of labor between state and market, to reconcile the principle of popular control with the community's need for private investment in business activity. In Atlanta, with its black electoral majority and its still preponderant white control of economic institutions, the dual character of an urban political economy is plainly visible, and black political incorporation occurs in that context. Congruence of interest in Atlanta rests on the fact that blacks have numbers and substantial voting power but limited economic resources. The business elite controls enormous economic resources, but lacks numbers. That blacks could supply needed numbers paved their way into incorporation initially, and as those numbers reached an electoral majority, they took on added weight.

Black political incorporation therefore has been no static phenomenon. Instead, incorporation has entailed a series of adjustments in the regime, adjustments influenced by several factors. Not only has black voting strength increased over time, but the national climate for black political mobilization has undergone important changes. Furthermore, the Atlanta business community is no passive partner in devising arrangements through which economic power and voting strength are reconciled. That interests are congruent is no guarantee that a coalition is forthcoming. Divisive forces are also at work, and tendencies toward political fragmentation are never to be overlooked. Atlanta's business elite has understood that point and built bridges to overcome the racial divide. They have seen the need for accommodations between the economic sector of community life and the political-electoral sector. They have also realized that there is nothing automatic about achieving accommodation and nothing certain about the terms on which it is achieved. Much is at issue. Thus, while any urban regime is constrained by the necessity of achieving accommodation between popular control of elected office and private control of investment, community actors can envisage a variety of arrangements through which that accommodation is made. Accommodation is necessary, but the specific terms of accommodation are matters of choice and judgment. Often they rest largely on informal arrangements and understandings.

The character of an urban regime is influenced by more than the fact that blacks or other minorities are incorporated or not. As the Atlanta experience illustrates, the terms by which incorporation is achieved and maintained matter greatly. Furthermore, the case of Atlanta illustrates that as communities change, their urban regimes change. Neither the composition of a governing coalition nor the relationship among its members is static.

PHASE ONE: WEAK INCORPORATION

As argued in the last section, incorporation is shaped by the political character of both the group achieving incorporation and the coalition into which it is being incorporated. The coalition into which Atlanta's black community sought incorporation with its 1946 voter registration drive had its roots in the city's experience with the Great Depression. During that time, patronage-based organization ceased to be a major factor in the city's politics. Beginning nearly a quarter of a century of service as Atlanta's mayor, William B. Hartsfield was elected in 1936 with business support as a reform mayor, promising to replace spoils politics with efficient government. With insufficient revenue to cover the city's debts when he took office, Mayor Hartsfield turned to the city's business community for help and to the banks in particular for loans. Hartsfield thus had an especially close tie with Atlanta's downtown businesses and financial institutions from the beginning. He ran on a business-backed platform of reform, received business support during the mayoral campaign and afterwards, and he depended on business-extended credit to meet city financial obligations and carry out his personal program of reform.

Without a patronage base through which to mobilize mass support, Hartsfield needed to maintain a good-government image, and he saw the city's daily newspapers as vital in projecting a favorable image. He also realized that the newspapers were an integral part of the business community, even holding membership in the downtown business association. Hartsfield tended to check out policy decisions with business leaders, and he was open to their initiatives. He also appointed major business figures to important posts such as the Board of the Atlanta Housing Authority (which also served as the city's redevelopment agency beginning in the 1950s).

Black voter mobilization in the 1940s therefore occurred in a context of a close and ongoing alliance between city hall and main street. Hartsfield saw how black electoral support could be added to that alliance without disrupting the alliance. Blacks were incorporated, but as clearly subordinate members of the governing coalition. In 1952, a Plan of Improvement was put through in order to add a large amount of new land and population to the city, a step that was in part an effort to counterbalance increased electoral participation by blacks. The inclusion of Atlanta's black community in the city's governing coalition thus proved to be a weak form of incorporation in which even their use of electoral power was closely watched.

The reasons for black subordination within the governing coalition are several, but two seem especially significant. First, there was a multifaceted process of co-optation. White business leaders made large donations to black organizations and placed substantial deposits in black financial institutions (Walker, 1963a). Churches and other nonprofit organizations that undertook projects such as the building of subsidized housing found white business elites to be invaluable as allies, not only as a sources of credit and expertise but also for their prestige and connections. In addition, city hall and the Atlanta Housing Authority were sources of particular benefits to blacks. As the city launched redevelopment, black real estate companies and builders were provided with major business opportunities in land acquisition and in relocating and rehousing those displaced. The colleges in the Atlanta University system also benefitted materially from white patrons, and they also were provided with land acquisition opportunities under the city's redevelopment program (Stone, 1976). The go-along-to-get-along system is known too well to require elaboration. The point is that strategically important and co-optable black organizations and institutions were brought into the system of insider cooperation and negotiation, but they came in largely as clients of white patrons. The result was that the moderate Urban League was an effective link; the more militant (by pre-1960 standards) NAACP was not. The benefits of going along were fully understood in both the black community and the white business and civic network. However, there were costs as well. In the 1950s, despite opposition from black neighborhood leaders, Atlanta's governing coalition inaugurated a redevelopment program that displaced at least one-seventh of the city's population.

To understand why co-optation was possible and costs were borne, we need to see those practices in the larger racial context. That brings us to the second element underlying the subordinate role of blacks in the governing coalition. White business leaders controlled more than material benefits. Initial black incorporation into the governing coalition occurred in a political climate and political circumstances that are quite important. *Brown v. Board of Education* had not yet put national authority behind the disestablishment of the Jim Crow system. The United States Congress had proved unwilling to enact antilynching legislation, much less stronger civil rights measures. Georgia's county unit system exaggerated the voting influence of the state's more tradition-bound elements, and racial demagoguery was rampant (Key, 1949). In that racial context, white business leaders stood out as a moderating influence, and they had enough clout in state affairs to be recognized as an element capable of holding in check violence-prone whites.

Hence, in 1961, with the state government prepared for a campaign of massive resistance to even token school desegregation, the business elite, under the leadership of Atlanta banker and lawyer John A. Sibley, pressed for a shift in state policy (Hornsby, 1982). Reluctantly, the governor and the legislature yielded to the argument that the state's economic future required acceptance of social change. As a major source of campaign funds for the state's small-county "court house gangs," Atlanta business leaders had additional leverage that could be used to counteract traditionalism (Key, 1949, p. 123).

In the years following World War II, Atlanta's business elite, with their overriding concern about economic growth and their sensitivity to national image, served as a check on the most volatile elements among traditional whites. At that time, before strong civil rights legislation had been enacted, black voting strength was inconsequential in Georgia politics, tilted as it was so heavily toward rural domination. The economic power of an urban business elite, however, was transferable to some degree into political influence, and it could be used to moderate what V. O. Key (1949) called the "rule of the rustics."

EFFORTS TO STRENGTHEN INCORPORATION

As the 1950s gave way to the 1960s, Atlanta's system of quiet, behind-the-scenes negotiations fell into disrepute in the city's black community. Following the Supreme Court's *Brown* decision ending constitutional protection for racial subordination, a new generation of civil rights activists emerged, and they were willing to challenge both the leaders and tactics of the past. The 1960 sit-ins represented more than an effort to end the exclusion of blacks from Atlanta's public accommodations. They represented an effort to end the white-patron, black-client relationship and enable blacks to be assertive in making a wide array of claims.

Eventually that assertiveness spilled over into the electoral arena as Atlanta moved toward becoming a city with a black majority. In 1969, the black community successfully supported a white mayoral candidate, Sam Massell, in opposition to the candidate backed by the white business community and endorsed by the outgoing mayor, Ivan Allen. Four years later, Maynard Jackson was elected Atlanta's first black mayor. Jackson's assumption of office also coincided with the institution of a new city charter in which the executive power of the mayor was strengthened, two-thirds of the city council were elected by district, and major steps were taken to incorporate neighborhoods into the city's planning process.

Seemingly, a peaceful revolution had occurred. New leadership and new bases of leadership within the black community had emerged. Neighborhood groups had also developed into significant actors in the city's politics, and the new city charter provided access for their participation. The city council enacted a citizen-participation ordinance, dividing the city up into Neighborhood Planning Units and calling for advisory committees to represent each. Mayor Jackson restructured the Planning department to create a Division of Neighborhood Planning and designated twelve staff members as neighborhood planners to work with the citizen advisory committees.

Atlanta's ballot box "revolution" was not the whole story, however. A number of crosscurrents were at work. Once Sam Massell was in office, for example, he sought to realign his political base by working closely with the business community on its policy agenda, in particular the launching of the rapid transit system (MARTA). While unable to ignore a large black constituency, Massell sought to mobilize a white base of support. To try to tilt the population balance, he backed an unsuccessful measure in the state legislature to enlarge the city limits and bring in an additional 50,000 people. He also shifted rhetoric. He cautioned about the long-term consequences of white flight and urged blacks to "think" white and to reflect the general views of all portions of the city, not just a distinctly black viewpoint (Stone, 1976; p. 183). In his unsuccessful bid for reelection in 1973, he campaigned on a "Save Atlanta" theme and attacked Maynard Jackson for being race-minded. He charged Jackson, the incumbent vice mayor, with having "always taken the black position," and added that he couldn't recall anything that Jackson had favored "that wasn't initiated by a racial viewpoint" (*Atlanta Constitution*, October 9, 1973). Bear in mind that at this time, though blacks were a slight majority of the city population, differences in age composition gave whites a slight edge in registered voters. Attacking Jackson for "reverse discrimination" while linking the prospect of black control with city decline, Massell heightened race consciousness. Nevertheless, Jackson won the election.

Maynard Jackson came into office in an atmosphere highly charged with racial feeling. While Massell had lost the election, the concerns he had raised about city hall favoritism toward black interests and about white flight were kept alive by the city's newspapers. Jackson's efforts to see that the city government and its contractors increased their minority hiring thus met with considerable criticism and resistance. Responsiveness to neighborhood groups, particularly in opposing expressway proposals, also generated concern among white business elites.

Before he had been in the mayoralty a full year, Jackson received a letter from the president of Central Atlanta Progress, the association of major downtown businesses, citing the danger of business disinvestment in downtown Atlanta, complaining about the lack of business access to the mayor and telling the mayor he was perceived as being antiwhite (Jones, 1978, pp. 111–112). Criticism of the mayor was also voiced in a business forum on the future of the city and given big play in the newspapers. Jackson avoided confrontation by beginning a series of "Pound Cake Summit" meetings, in which he conferred with business leaders every two or three weeks to discuss issues of concern. By the time his second term of office was over, central business district revitalization once again dominated the city's development agenda, and the number of neighborhood planners had dwindled. When Andrew Young assumed office, he somewhat reluctantly kept a single planner assigned to the neighborhoods—apparently as a symbolic gesture— and committed himself strongly to a development program backed by Central Atlanta Progress. Young stated openly that he could not "govern without the confidence of the business community" (*Atlanta Constitution*, July 24, 1983). While affirmative-action guarantees and joint-venture contracts continue to be occasional friction points, the white business community has ceased to oppose them in principle. A large measure of cooperation and good will between city hall and Central Atlanta Progress marks the emergence of a revamped but apparently stable urban regime, as in the past devoted mainly to promoting economic development especially in Atlanta's central business district.

This account is of necessity much abbreviated, but it bears out the soundness of the comments made by Mack Jones several years ago, when he observed that black officeholders were devoted mainly to "guaranteeing for blacks a more equitable share of existing governmental benefits and services within existing priorities" (1978, p. 99). Still, Atlanta's politics are not conflict free. Members of an unsteady, and now it seems dwindling, city council bloc, which fluctuates from an occasional majority to a minuscule two or three, oppose particular development projects; but without a helping hand from the city administration, they have no program of their own and they make no systematic oversight effort. And, while Atlanta's neighborhoods are not politically quiescent, they have become a fragmented and somewhat dispirited force.

Thus, despite a variety of efforts extending from the 1950s to the present, no one has been able to keep neighborhood development and housing improvements on the city's policy agenda or undertake a searching examination of how widely the benefits of downtown development are distributed. There is an acknowledged split within the black community between haves and have-nots, but no concrete program to bridge that gap (Clendinen, 1986). Atlanta's urban regime is therefore built around accommodations between the black middle class and white business elites. However, there is more to the Atlanta arrangements than officeholder attentiveness to the need for business investment. Let's look more closely at the specifics of Atlanta's contemporary urban regime.

ATLANTA'S CONTEMPORARY URBAN REGIME

It would be too simple to say that the present arrangements in Atlanta prevail because they are what is economically best for the city. In the first place, the present arrangements came about through a process of conflict and negotiation. Black political leaders, dating back to the 1960s, have struggled to garner a significant share of the city's jobs and contracts (Stone, 1976, pp. 142–143). As we have seen, white business leaders have resisted those demands, at one point in effect threatening disinvestment. The present allocation of affirmative-action benefits is by no means guaranteed for the future. Decreasing judicial support for minority set-asides could weaken the bargaining position of black officeholders, perhaps in the process making more difficult their task of politically mobilizing the black middle class.

In the second place, there is a continuing concern in the black community that the benefits of Atlanta's economic growth are not widely enough shared. While this concern is not embodied in a specific program, it is a recurring issue. The white business community for its part is in search of ways to buffer investment activity, even that subsidized by the city, from social-justice demands.

Evolving over time, the strategy of the white business elite has had several facets. As it became increasingly evident that the city would have a black electoral majority, an effort was made to bring the black middle class into the mainstream of civic life of the Atlanta business community. There was, after all, a long history of negotiation and accommodation between the white business elite and the black middle class. In the late 1960s, two new organizations—Leadership Atlanta and Action Forum— were formed to provide means through which black and white business people could be brought together to consider various civic issues and seek common ground. Concurrently the chamber of commerce moved to integrate blacks into its membership and activities. At the same time, while black demands for affirmative action were being resisted, the white business community did not reject those demands totally. Subsequently it came to accept the idea that city employment and city contracts would carry affirmative-action guarantees. However, the white business community has sought to promote development and the public subsidy of development in ways that are insulated from city hall control. Examples of the kind of arrangements the business community has promoted that reduce city hall control over development activities include nonprofit corporations formed under private auspices (Park Central to oversee redevelopment east of the central business district, Underground Festival Development Corporation to bring into being the city's proposed new entertainment district, Atlanta Economic Development Corporation to oversee generally the facilitating of economic development); state rather than city subsidy (the building of an enormous convention facility in downtown Atlanta—the Georgia World Congress Center); and the issuance of tax-free development bonds by an independent authority (Atlanta Downtown Development Authority).

One of the current policies being promoted is, in effect, a privatization of the city's revenue capacity. State legislation allows for the creation within cities of special tax districts through which increased revenue from development in that district can be earmarked for infrastructure expenditures in that district. The business community is urging that the city's posh Buckhead area, currently a site for intense development activity, be designated as such a district. Additional legislation provides for the creation of special service districts through which *the property holders* in such a district can agree to levy a special tax on themselves in order to pay for increased services, such as extra policing, within that district.

Over time, the white business elite has thus made use of the carrot and the stick. It has sought to integrate the black middle class into the network of civic and business associations (formal and informal) that has throughout the postwar years been central in the political life in Atlanta. At the same time, it has been critical of various city efforts to assure a black share in the economic life of the community, but still willing to go along in practice with a number of measures guaranteeing city jobs and contracts for blacks. All the while, business has lobbied for procedures whereby economic activity would be insulated from city hall control. Blacks therefore have achieved a strong form of political incorporation, but their control is over an increasingly limited sphere of economic activity—even though much of that activity is publicly subsidized.

The current urban regime seems to be stable but not static. Neighborhood development and housing improvements occupy no major position on the city's policy agenda and show no signs of gaining such a position. Neighborhood activists have been forced to rely mainly on litigation in what may be losing efforts to stop proposed expressway projects. Benefit from the city's "supply-side" development strategy has accrued to the black middle class, but there is not much evidence the lower class has gained. Atlanta is second only to Newark, New Jersey, among American cities in its poverty rate.

CONCLUSION

The present state of affairs in Atlanta is very much a reflection of prevailing political arrangements. However, it is significant that the city election of 1973 and the initial actions under the new city charter in 1974 seemed to point to a different scenario. Why was the black middle class incorporated but working class and neighborhood groups not? One answer is that the white business elite worked hard to bring about that outcome. But the issue is more complicated than that. Various nonbusiness groups have weaknesses and liabilities they have not been able to overcome.

Neighborhoods are not easy to work with as development partners. They are not usually organized in ways and equipped with resources that enable them to achieve highly visible successes. The same disadvantages are apparently true for other nonbusiness groups as well. For example, when city hall disregarded the wishes of the white business elite in selling a West End site to a black church association (the National Baptist Convention) for redevelopment, the association was unable on its own to put together a successful project. While they had financial capacity, they lacked the kind of organizational and technical experience needed for development projects. By contrast, the business community pulls city hall in the direction of its agenda because business is able to fill an action vacuum with its highly useful policy expertise and its practical experience in development projects.

Other forces also pull the city's black middle-class political leadership toward tight alliance with the white business elite. The black middle class and the white business elite have accumulated a long history of successful and productive back-stage negotiations. It is an alliance that works. It has members who have learned the lessons of bargaining and accommodation. One activist in city politics emphasizes the city's "mercantile ethic" and is reported to have said that a room full of black and white leaders in Atlanta "is nothing but a roomful of people trying to cut a deal" (*Atlanta Constitution*, August 11, 1987).

Wanting to cut a deal is, however, not enough to forge a cohesive coalition. Distrust, particularly across racial lines, is to be expected among individuals who are unaccustomed to interacting with one another and have had little opportunity to build a compact of mutual support (on the importance of repeated transactions and the chance to develop norms of mutual support, see Hardin, 1982; Axelrod, 1984). But Atlanta provides a situation in which interaction across racial lines is a deep and constantly renewed tradition. Newcomers learn from old hands, and organizations such as Action Forum are structured to maintain that tradition. Although the habit of trust does not come easily, the leaders in Atlanta's governing coalition realize that; and they take deliberate steps to preserve the city's tradition of biracial cooperation. This tradition makes possible an accommodation between the city's economic sector and its political-electoral sector. Tight cross-sector cooperation gives the regime a powerful capacity for governing the community.

Yet, despite the presence of a biracial governing coalition, Atlanta is no paragon of democratic practice. The city's version of biracial cooperation leaves out a variety of interests. Neighborhood organizations, historic preservationists, and a range of groups interested in maintaining a supply of affordable housing are outside the governing coalition. They are not part of the community of mutual accommodation. Development policy takes little heed of their concerns. Within the black community, not only are neighborhood concerns neglected, but class tension is significant. Mayor Andrew Young's personal appeal and his position as a principal in the civil rights movement of the 1960s attenuates the conflict, but the issue keeps bobbing to the surface. And Young himself comes under sporadic criticism for a system in which the same few black contractors garner a large share of the city's construction contracts (*Atlanta Constitution*, August 14, 1987; September 6, 1987). Significantly, the city's program of expanded opportunities for minorities calls for primary emphasis on the development of minority business enterprises. Jobs for the working class are not a direct target, and no systematic monitoring of job creation is in evidence.

What lessons do we draw from the Atlanta experience? We have long looked on democratic politics as the process that equalizes opportunities and redresses imbalances. The evolution of Atlanta's urban regime suggests a different conclusion. To a considerable extent, democratic politics mirrors resource inequalities. When the white primary was declared illegal, Atlanta's black middle class, with its rich network of organizations and its substantial store of civic skills, was able to bring off an immediate and substantial voter mobilization. That voting power was converted into policy gains for blacks as a group. But as the Jim Crow system was disassembled, class differences within the black community became more salient. The skills and resources of the black middle class enable its members to take advantage of opportunities that come from a place in the city's governing coalition. The black lower class lacks comparable opportunities.

Numbers alone amount to little. The Atlanta experience also suggests that loosely organized voting carries small weight. Consider the overall picture. Atlanta is a city with weak unions. They are not a central part of the civic and political life of the community, and job creation takes a backseat in policy deliberations. Many neighborhoods are organized, but interneighborhood cooperation across class and racial lines is limited. Furthermore, neighborhoods practice primarily an adversarial form of politics—each mobilizes best around its own immediate crisis; and that seems weak ground from which to try to gain a position in the city's governing coalition. As Atlanta's politics is now organized, neither specifically working class nor neighborhood organizations are essential in mobilizing an electoral majority. Nor do they control other resources essential in community activities. Consequently these groups have no irresistible claim on membership in the city's governing regime, and policy is not responsive to the kinds of interests they represent.

Atlanta offers a sobering lesson. Instead of electoral power serving to equalize resource capabilities, we see that a substantial store of resources is essential in order to make a telling use of the vote. Groups cannot simply make demands on city government; they must be in a position to enhance a city's capacity to govern. At the very least they must be able to deliver a dependable *and needed* block of votes. All groups face that test of whether they can contribute something essential to a community's capacity to govern: economic resources, mobilization of electoral majorities, promotion of civic cooperation, and engagement in the building of durable alliances. Atlanta's black middle class has the resources to pass that test; its lower class does not. Even in a formally democratic system where racial exclusion has been successfully combatted, it is difficult to have an inclusive governing coalition. That is a challenge that remains before us.

REFERENCES

Alexander, Robert J. 1951. Negro Business in Atlanta. *Southern Economic Journal* 17 (April): 451–464.

Axelrod, Robert. 1984. *The Evolution of Cooperation*. New York: Basic Books.

Bacote, C. A. 1955. The Negro in Atlanta Politics. *Phylon* 16(4): 333–350.

Bartley, Numan V. 1983. *The Creation of Modern Georgia*. Athens: University of Georgia Press.

Browning, Rufus P., Dale Rogers Marshall, and David H. Tabb. 1984. *Protest Is Not Enough*. Berkeley: University of California Press.

Clendinen, Dudley. 1986. In Black Atlanta, Affluence and Sophistication Are for the Few. *New York Times* (January 20): 10.

Eisinger, Peter K. 1980. *The Politics of Displacement*. New York: Academic Press.

Elkin, Stephen L. 1985. Twentieth Century Urban Regimes. *Journal of Urban Affairs* 7 (Spring): 11–28.

Hardin, Russell. 1982. *Collective Action*. Baltimore: Johns Hopkins University Press.

Hornsby, Alton, Jr. 1982. A City Too Busy to Hate. In Elizabeth Jacoway and David R. Colburn, eds., *Southern Businessmen and Desegregation*. Baton Rouge: Louisiana State University Press.

Jennings, M. Kent, and Harmon Zeigler. 1966. Class, Party, and Race in Four Types of Elections: The Case of Atlanta. *Journal of Politics* 28 (May): 391–407.

Jones, Mack H. 1978. Black Political Empowerment in Atlanta: Myth and Reality. *Annals of the American Academy of Political and Social Science* 439 (September): 90–117.

Key, V. O., Jr. 1949. *Southern Politics in State and Nation.* New York: Alfred A. Knopf.

Martin, Harold H. 1978. *William Berry Hartsfield: Mayor of Atlanta.* Athens: University of Georgia Press.

Stone, Clarence N. 1976. *Economic Growth and Neighborhood Discontent.* Chapel Hill, N.C.: University of North Carolina Press.

Walker, Jack L. 1963a. Protest and Negotiation: A Case Study of Negro Leadership in Atlanta, Georgia. *Midwest Journal of Political Science* 7 (May): 99–124.

Walker, Jack L. 1963b. Negro Voting in Atlanta, 1953–1961. *Phylon* 24 (Winter): 379–387.

Walker, Jack L. 1963c. Protest and Negotiation: A Study of Negro Political Leaders in a Southern City. Unpublished Ph.D. dissertation, State University of Iowa.

CHAPTER 8

The Evolution and Impact of Biracial Coalitions and Black Mayors in Birmingham and New Orleans

Huey L. Perry

Editors' Note

How much difference do leaders make? How do their styles and strategies shape black and black-white politics? This chapter documents the astonishing change from white and more or less racist regimes in two cities of the Deep South to regimes in which blacks play leading roles. But the chapter demonstrates also that black leadership may unfold in quite different ways in spite of regional and developmental similarities. As Huey Perry shows, Richard Arrington, mayor of Birmingham, Alabama, is a consensus builder who established cooperative relations with business and gained control over city council elections. In contrast, Ernest Morial, mayor of New Orleans from 1977 to 1985, was unsuccessful in controlling council elections, and had a more confrontational style.

Perry credits both Arrington and Morial with progressive moves for blacks in executive appointments, municipal employment, and minority business programs. Have their different styles led to significantly different policy outcomes? When two black candidates for mayor run against each other, as in New Orleans, what difference does it make for the structure and policy commitments of their competing coalitions?

Finally, how do these cities compare with other southern cities with large black populations and black mayors? The reader might ask whether black successes have been greater in these two cities than in Atlanta (Chapter 7), or whether the marked difference in the assessment of black regimes in Chapters 7 and 8 reflects different evaluational criteria of the authors.

Birmingham, Alabama, and New Orleans, Louisiana, have both had black mayors long enough to assess their impact—Birmingham since 1979 (Richard Arrington), New Orleans since 1977 (Ernest Morial, followed by Sidney Barthelemy in 1985). In both cities developing biracial coalitions exerted significant influence in city politics during the late 1960s and early 1970s. By the mid-1970s these coalitions composed the governing coalition in the two cities. These coalitions were responsible for the election of Arrington and Morial. The biracial coalitions that elected these mayors evolved in different ways, with different consequences for the programs and policies of the two city governments and for their black populations.

This chapter analyzes the development of black politics and biracial coalitions in the two cities. The overall trend is the rapid strengthening of black political organizations and the steady rise of black politicians since the 1960s. Within that common trend, the particular focus is on the impact of different mayoral styles and strategies on the evolution of coalition politics and on the policies and actions of city governments, especially the allocation of benefits to blacks. Impact is assessed with respect to appointments to executive positions, municipal employment, and minority business participation programs.

Significant black political participation in both Birmingham and New Orleans, as is the case with most localities in the South, is a post–World War II development. In both cities the push for blacks' inclusion in the political process was organized by black political organizations. In Birmingham the organization principally involved was the Jefferson County Progressive Democratic Council (JCPDC). JCPDC was formed in 1935 to work for the end of white supremacy in Alabama at a time when blacks were excluded from the political process. The leaders of JCPDC filed a lawsuit in federal court, successfully contesting the exclusion of blacks from participation in the Democratic party in Alabama. The lawsuit, the formation of a state black political party (the National Democratic Party of Alabama), and pressure from the national Democratic party resulted in blacks winning the right to participate in politics in Birmingham and in the rest of Alabama within the structure of the Democratic party.

Blacks in Birmingham in the 1950s and early 1960s encountered substantial resistance from whites to their desire to participate in the political process. Whites' resistance to blacks' demands for political rights was more severe in Birmingham than in any southern city of comparable size (Strong, 1972, p. 443; Perry, 1983, pp. 206–207). However, the number of black voters began to increase appreciably during the early 1960s, and as their numbers increased, blacks, in coalition with middle-class whites, began to exert a greater impact on electoral outcomes. The growing black vote in Birmingham played an increasingly important role within the structure of the biracial coalition in electing seriatim the city's first racially moderate white mayor, first racially liberal white mayor, and first black mayor (see Table 8.1).

The growing black vote also played an important role in electing over several city elections a more racially progressive city council, a process which eventually resulted in the election of a black majority to the council. Black voters over the last two decades also have played a significant role in passing bond measures that have allowed the city to dramatically improve its infrastructure and educational system and to increase other public amenities, such as libraries, important to the quality of life; black voters have benefitted as recipients of these resources through the governmental allocation process. These developments comprise what Browning, Marshall, and Tabb refer to as political incorporation, which is "the extent to which" minorities "have achieved not only representation but positions of influence in local policy making" (1984, p. 12).

The emergence of the biracial coalition has played a critical role in shaping political life and policy outcomes in Birmingham. The coalition first emerged in the election of 1962 with a successful effort to change the form of government from the commission form to the mayor-council form. The basis of the coalition was the development of a consensus among blacks, a small number of liberal whites, and members of the business community that Police Commissioner Eugene "Bull" Connor had become a liability to the city. They decided that since he had approximately two years remaining in office, the best way to get rid of him was to change the form of government (Perry, 1983; p. 207). The next major point in the development of the coalition was the mayoral election in 1967, in which the biracial coalition was responsible for the election of George Seibels, the city's first moderate mayor. The coalition consisted of a large number of blacks, a somewhat smaller number of liberal and moderate whites, and a small number of people from the business community.

The third major point in the development of the coalition involved the mayoral election of 1975 when blacks and liberal whites helped to elect David Vann the city's first liberal mayor. At this point the coalition consisted of a significant black minority and a white majority. The 1975 election represented the greatest racial mixture of the coalition. The fourth major point in the development of the coalition consisted of the election of Richard Arrington as the first black mayor in 1979. The composition of the biracial coalition that elected Arrington in 1979 and re-elected him in 1983 is different from the composition of the coalition that elected Vann. The composition of the Arrington coalition is a large black majority with a small but significant proportion of liberal whites and businesspersons.

After several years of increased black voting and officeholding (Table 8.1), a split emerged in the Jefferson County Progressive Democratic Council and another organization was formed—the biracial Citizens Action Coalition. The split was basically generational. Younger black leaders grew uncomfortable with the leadership style of the older black leaders. Arrington provided the central leadership in the formation of the Coalition in 1983. The Coalition soon became the ascendant political organization in the city. It presently is the single most important organizational forum in Birmingham for the discussion of political issues in reference to blacks, the development of the black political agenda, the recruitment of blacks to public office, and the election of both blacks and whites to public office.

In New Orleans the organization most prominently associated with the emergence of black political participation was the Orleans Parish Progressive Voters League (OPPVL). OPPVL was formed in 1949 to push for increased black political participation in Orleans Parish. OPPVL was successful in helping to increase black political participation in New Orleans. As was the case with JCPDC in Birmingham, the influence of OPPVL eventually began to wane and its role as the organizational arena for black politics in the city was successfully challenged by another black political organization.

Like blacks in Birmingham, a growing number of black voters in New Orleans in coalition with middle-class whites played an increasingly important role in the election of the city's first racially moderate white mayor, first racially liberal white mayor, and first black mayor (see Table 8.1). Also, as in Birmingham, the growing black vote in New Orleans was central to the election of a more racially progressive city council and eventually a black majority council.

A key dissimilarity in the strength of the governing biracial coalitions in Birmingham and New Orleans has to do with their ability to pass bond issues and other revenue-enhancing proposals. Whereas in Birmingham blacks as part of the biracial coalition have played a consistently pivotal role in passing bond issues that have improved municipal services, in New Orleans, revenue-enhancing proposals have generally been rejected by the voters. In New Orleans the biracial coalition that made Morial the first black mayor in the city's history in 1977 and re-elected him in 1982 repeatedly broke down on revenue-enhancing proposals. Morial's successor and the second black mayor in New Orleans, Sidney Barthelemy, also has failed in his efforts to convince voters to pass revenue-enhancing proposals. This difference has important implications for the quality of life enjoyed by residents of the two cities, a subject about which more will be said shortly.

TABLE 8.1. PERCENTAGE BLACK OF TOTAL VOTER REGISTRATION AND POLITICAL INCORPORATION IN BIRMINGHAM AND NEW ORLEANS

	Birmingham		New Orleans	
Key Elections	**Year**	**% Black Voters**	**Year**	**% Black Voters**
	1960	10		
Racially moderate mayor	1967	36	1946	**
			1960	17
Racially liberal mayor	1975	40	1969	30
Black mayor (first time)	1979	45	1977	42
Black mayor (second term)	1983	51	1982	46
Black mayor (second generation)	*		1986	51

*Not applicable.
**Percentage black of total voter registration is not available for 1946.

Another difference in the politics of the two cities concerns city council elections. In Birmingham, Mayor Arrington, working through the Citizens Action Coalition, virtually controls who gets elected to the city council. Arrington's control over city council elections resulted in a majority black council being elected in the 1987 elections and a black council president being chosen by the council, both occurring for the first time in the city's history. In New Orleans the experience in terms of mayoral control over city council elections has been just the opposite from that of Birmingham, despite the fact that in the 1987 elections the city also elected the first majority black city council and the first black was chosen president of the council. Former Mayor Morial was unsuccessful in his efforts to control elections to the city council.

DIFFERENCE IN MAYORAL STYLE

The differences between the accomplishments of the mayors' leadership in the two cities are of such magnitude that an explanation is warranted. One possible explanation is the difference in personal style between Morial and Arrington. Morial's style during his 8-year mayoral tenure was confrontational—a style developed during his tenure as a civil rights activist. Arrington's style is that of a consensus builder. Arrington has cooperative relationships with the business community, whereas Morial did not. Arrington makes whites feel comfortable with a black political leadership majority in Birmingham, whereas Morial made whites feel increasingly threatened with majority black political leadership in New Orleans.

Throughout his mayoral tenure but particularly in his current term, Arrington has demonstrated a genuine willingness to cooperate with the business community and indeed to make the business community a part of the governing coalition. An important symbolic manifestation of this approach is that Arrington has held monthly breakfast meetings with business leaders throughout his second term. Moreover, Arrington has made economic development the key policy objective of his second term. The principal beneficiary of this policy initiative has been business interests. Even when the city's leading banks failed to give Arrington his highest priority request, a Minority Enterprise Sector and Business Initiative Cooperation program, Arrington refused to terminate accounts the city had with some of those banks.

This difference in personal style influences the ability of a black mayor to establish a political power base. To the extent that a consensus builder like Arrington can win the trust of whites generally and the business community in particular and still exert influence over blacks, he can exert tremendous influence over who gets elected to the city council and thus over the success or failure of his policy and programmatic initiatives. Arrington controls not only the routes to office, particularly to the city council, but also the substantive agenda of city government, perhaps more than any other contemporary big-city mayor.

The difference in mayoral leadership between Arrington and Morial is primarily one of style rather than issues. The overriding issue facing both cities during Arrington's and Morial's administrations was basically the same: how to maintain city services in the face of dramatically reduced support from the federal government and a declining tax base. However, Morial had an additional problem that Arrington does not have: that is, Morial's policy and programmatic initiatives were constantly opposed by the second most powerful black in city government, then City Council President Sidney Barthelemy, who is the current mayor. Barthelemy's opposition to Morial's policy and programmatic initiatives weakened the support of the black community for Morial's policies and programs and made it easier for other interests to oppose Morial's initiatives.

THE IMPACT OF INCREASED BLACK POLITICAL INCORPORATION ON GOVERNMENTAL POLICIES AND ACTIONS

Political incorporation generally has resulted in blacks in both cities receiving a greater proportion of favorable policies and benefits allocated by city government. This section assesses the impact of political incorporation on the allocation of policies and benefits to blacks in three categories of public sector activity.

Executive Appointments

This category includes appointments by the mayor to his top personal executive staff and heads of departments of city government. Previous research has shown that increased black political participation and influence in both Birmingham and New Orleans have resulted in a significant increase in black representation in these key executive positions. In Birmingham black representation in key executive positions increased from zero in 1975, before the election of David Vann, the city's first racially liberal white mayor, to 44 percent of the mayor's top personal executive staff positions (four out of nine positions) and one department head during Vann's administration (Perry, 1983, p. 212). Throughout his 7-year mayoral tenure, 50 percent of Arrington's fourteen-member top personal executive staff has been black. In New Orleans, the percentage of black department heads increased from zero in 1969 before the election of Moon Landrieu, the city's first racially liberal white mayor, to 42 percent (five out of thirteen) during Landrieu's mayoralty. During Morial's mayoralty, the number of black department heads increased to seven out of thirteen, or 58 percent.

The appointment of blacks to executive positions in city government is important for several reasons. First, although these positions are few, they provide additional financially rewarding and prestigious employment opportunities for blacks. Second, executive positions are generally policy-making positions; therefore, blacks who hold these positions are able to make or influence policies that advance blacks' interests. Third, because these appointments have historically gone to whites, the appointment of blacks to these positions represents an important symbolic benefit. Finally, service in these key positions provides a small number of blacks with valuable experience, which should make them especially attractive for service in future mayoral administrations or as candidates if they should seek elective office. The experience that black urban government executives are currently receiving in running city government should have positive significance for future urban governance.

Municipal Employment

The capacity of increased black political participation to produce a fairer share of municipal employment has received much attention in the scholarly literature on black politics. Earlier research has confirmed the strength of that relationship in New Orleans (Perry, 1987, pp. 243–244). Between 1960 and 1985, the last year of the mayoral administration of Morial, the black proportion of the New Orleans municipal work force increased from a small percentage to 53 percent. The bulk of that increase occurred during the 8-year mayoralty of Landrieu. By the last year of the Landrieu administration, blacks had come to compose 40 percent of the city's municipal work force. Thus, Morial was able to increase the black proportion of the city's municipal work force 13 percentage points beyond what Landrieu had accomplished. Significantly, the substantial increase in the black proportion of the New Orleans municipal work force was attributable to the biracial coalition governing the city during this period.

   Prior research on Birmingham based on 1975 city employment data raised a serious question about the capacity of increased black political participation to generate an equitable proportion of municipal employment for blacks (Perry, 1983). That study found that from 1960 to 1975 the proportion of blacks in the municipal work force increased from less than 1 percent to 9 percent (pp. 210–211). However, as Table 8.2 shows, blacks made much greater progress between 1975 and 1985. In 1985 blacks composed 37 percent of the city's total municipal work force, which

TABLE 8.2. FULL-TIME EMPLOYEES OF THE CITY OF BIRMINGHAM BY RACE, 1985

	Black		White		Other	
Occupational classification	No.	%	No.	%	No.	%
Officials/administrators	11	15.9	58	84.1	0	0.0
Professionals	97	21.7	346	77.2	5	1.1
Technicians	62	20.2	245	79.8	0	0.0
Protective services	186	19.2	782	80.7	1	0.1
Paraprofessionals	52	46.4	57	50.9	3	2.7
Office/clerical	173	47.3	193	52.7	0	0.0
Skilled craft workers	43	20.8	163	78.7	1	0.5
Service/maintenance	651	65.7	339	34.2	1	0.1
Totals	1275	36.8	2183	62.9	11	0.3

represents more than a fourfold increase in the black proportion of the city's municipal work force in 1975.

Table 8.2 also shows that blacks have succeeded in integrating the city's work force at all occupational levels. Although the large black proportions in the service-maintenance and office-clerical categories (66 percent and 47 percent, respectively) are expected (given that these are generally low-skill, low-wage positions), these proportions are important because the jobs in these categories are significant sources of employment for low-income blacks. This is an important consideration because an increasing criticism of black politics is that the benefits that have been produced by increased black political incorporation have gone to members of the black middle class who possessed the requisite education, occupational, and social skills necessary to take advantage of the new opportunities for blacks created by increased black political participation. There is considerable validity to this criticism. The irony of the situation is that the increased black political participation and influence in cities in the 1970s and 1980s is in large part a result of the entry of a significantly larger proportion of the black lower class into electoral politics, whose political awakening was often stimulated by the prospect of electing a viable black candidate to a high-level political office. By increasing employment opportunities for blacks in the office-clerical and especially the service-maintenance categories, black politics in Birmingham has produced significant benefits for members of the black working class.

In addition to strong representation of blacks in the maintenance and office-clerical categories, blacks, as Table 8.2 shows, are also well represented in the middle-level occupational categories, which generally consist of jobs that require more skills and pay better than the service-maintenance and office-clerical categories. These categories include skilled craft workers, paraprofessionals, protective services, and technicians. Blacks compose 21 percent of skilled craft workers, 46 percent of paraprofessionals, 19 percent of protective services, and 20 percent of technicians. Blacks are also well represented in the two high-skill, high-wage categories: professionals (22 percent) and officials-administrators (16 percent). While blacks in Birmingham have clearly not achieved an equitable proportion of municipal employment commensurate with their approximately 55 percent of the city's population, they have made significant progress in increasing their representation in municipal employment.

In New Orleans, a racially liberal white mayor was able to achieve very rapid growth in black employment in city government, whereas the rate of increase in Birmingham under a black mayor was much slower. A major factor in the slower progress achieved in Birmingham was the rigid countywide civil service system, which has in past years denied Birmingham's mayor any appreciable influence in the hiring of all city employees, except the mayor's top personal staff over which he has complete control. For each civil service vacancy in city government the Jefferson County Personnel Board certifies three candidates of which the mayor or his designee (usually a department head if the position is a sub-department head position) must select one to fill the position.

Black leaders discovered early that blacks have difficulty in meeting the certification standards of the personnel board (which includes passing a written and an oral examination). They learned that the county civil service system blocked their goal of increasing black municipal employment even when their political influence may have made city officials sympathetic to increasing the numbers of blacks in the city's employ. To get the personnel board to certify more black candidates for employment with city government, black leaders and their supporters brought public pressure on the board, filed lawsuits against the board to make its certification process more job-relevant, and increased black and liberal white representation on the sixteen-member Citizen Supervisory Committee, which appoints the personnel board's three members. The latter strategy eventually succeeded in getting a liberal majority on the board, including a black as chairman.

Minority Business Participation Programs

Black municipal officials can use the authority of city government's control over contracts for services and products to award city contracts to black companies and to provide technical assistance for those companies. This important possibility, until recently, had been ignored in the black politics literature (see Perry, 1987, pp. 245–246). Because ethnic politics earlier in the twentieth century widely used this practice and because the applicability of the ethnic model of politically based upward mobility to blacks has been frequently questioned, this omission is conspicuous.

Increased black political incorporation in both Birmingham and New Orleans has not significantly increased the dollar amount of municipal contracts awarded to black companies. In Birmingham the minority business participation program was begun by a city ordinance in 1977. Arrington acknowledges that his major disappointment has been his failure to advance the black business community. This sentiment is echoed by Arrington's chief of staff: "The city's minority assistance program has not helped black businesses much. Blacks have not moved into the mainstream of the business sector. In every other way, blacks in Birmingham have been successful."[1] Arrington had hoped that his minority business participation program would have been successful in creating a strong black business sector to complement blacks' outstanding success in the public sector. This has not occurred.

Similarly, the New Orleans business participation program has not been successful. New Orleans authorized its minority business participation program in late 1983; however, the implementation of the program did not begin until 1985. By the end of Morial's term in 1986, the city's minority business participation program was widely regarded as a failure (see Perry, 1987). The failure of the black political leadership in both Birmingham and New Orleans to significantly increase the number of municipal contracts awarded to black businesses constitutes a limitation

---

[1] Personal interview with Dr. Edward LaMonte, Executive Secretary to Dr. Richard Arrington, Mayor of Birmingham, Alabama.

of black political participation as a vehicle for producing private sector benefits for blacks.

THE SOCIAL AND ECONOMIC IMPACT OF THE INCREASED ALLOCATION OF GOVERNMENTAL BENEFITS TO BLACKS

The benefits that blacks have received from their increased political power in Birmingham and New Orleans have been both symbolic and substantive. Some observers seem to feel that symbolic benefits are not important. Symbolic benefits that confer an aura of legitimacy, respect, and equal standing to a previously disadvantaged, discriminated against, and subordinate group are very important (see Barker, 1987). Increased black political participation and especially increased black officeholding have moved the black populace toward that type of enhanced group social standing, which concomitantly has elevated blacks' self-esteem. A derivative of the symbolic benefits that ensue from blacks' holding important governmental position is that it becomes easier for other blacks to move into important positions of public responsibility. Mayor Arrington's chief of staff describes the working of this phenomenon as regards the symbolic importance of Arrington in Birmingham: "Arrington provides a personal example for blacks to move into leadership positions. Arrington serving as the mayor has made it easy for other blacks to move into other visible positions. Having Dick Arrington as mayor made it easier for Walter Harris to be appointed school superintendent."

In other words the election of blacks to high positions of public responsibility not only benefits blacks generally by improving their individual and group self-esteem, but also makes it easier for whites to accept blacks in other positions of public responsibility. Thus, the benefits that blacks have achieved in the symbolic realm have substantially improved their social status.

The substantive benefits that blacks in Birmingham and New Orleans have received from their increased participation in the political process have significantly improved their social and economic conditions. The increased executive appointments and municipal employment opportunities are examples of the substantive benefits that have accrued to blacks in the two cities. These benefits plus the symbolic benefits have collectively enhanced the social and economic conditions of blacks.

It is more difficult to show that improvements in the economic status of blacks follow directly from the benefits blacks have obtained from city government, because so many other factors are involved. In New Orleans the percentage of black middle-class families increased from 10 percent in 1970 to 31 percent in 1985. It is likely that gains in municipal employment have contributed to improved economic conditions for blacks generally by opening up significant, stable employment opportunities that would not have existed otherwise for them.

BIRACIAL COALITIONS: RECENT AND FUTURE DEVELOPMENTS

In both Birmingham and New Orleans the major politically oriented groups consist of blacks, liberal whites, the white business community, and the remainder of the white populace. In New Orleans, organized labor is another center of power. In both cities no one center of power is ascendant over all the major policy issues. Even the strong biracial coalition consisting of blacks and upper-income liberal whites, which has controlled elections in Birmingham since 1967 and which controlled elections in New Orleans from 1969 to 1986, has not won all or even most policy issues. The same is true for the white business community, which is generally acknowledged to be the most influential group once elections are decided.

The least identifiable of the groups—the amorphous remainder of the white populace, which principally consists of low-income conservative whites—has not fared poorly in either city.[2] Arrington reports that he has given more city services to the conservative white areas of the city than any other mayor in Birmingham's history despite the fact that whites in these areas do not vote for him. The wisdom of Arrington's actions is supported by recent political developments in New Orleans.

In the mayoral election of 1986 in which the two principal candidates were black, blacks divided their vote, and whites, now a minority in New Orleans, decided the outcome of the election by voting overwhelmingly for the candidate perceived to be less threatening to their interests. In other words whites are now in the exact same position as blacks were prior to their becoming the majority population. The election result has the potential to stimulate low-income conservative whites to become more organized for political action. If that happens, it would clearly be a significant development, given that low-income whites generally demonstrate little interest in political organizations.[2]

The election result also means that the biracial coalition that controlled election outcomes in New Orleans between 1969 and 1986 is in all likelihood moribund. Mayoral elections in New Orleans are likely to continue to be contested by at least two viable black candidates, and as long as that condition holds, the once-powerful coalition will not be able to function. Thus, the character of biracial politics in New Orleans is changing, evolving into two biracial coalitions split along ideological lines—a liberal coalition and a conservative coalition. The liberal biracial coalition is composed of a large black majority and a small white minority. The conservative biracial coalition is composed of a white majority and a significant black minority. Two points are relevant here. One, having the population of a city align on the basis of two contending biracial coalitions based on ideology is better than having an alignment based on race alone. Two, blacks are strongly incorporated in both coalitions and therefore stand to gain from whichever coalition wins.

---

[2]This "group" is the least identifiable of the political groups in both cities because it is not nearly as organized as the other groups discussed. In fact it is more of a latent group than a group in the traditional sense of interest group pluralism. That low-income whites are not as politically organized as other groups, including low-income blacks, is consistent with prior research findings on black and white participation rates (Verba and Nie, 1972; Shingles, 1981).

In Birmingham the influence of the liberal biracial coalition over electoral outcomes does not appear to be threatened. Arrington is so firmly entrenched in his informal role as the leader of black politics in the city that it is not likely that he will face significant black opposition in future mayoral races. That means that any significant opposition will come from white candidates, which will ensure the continuance of the biracial coalition as the most powerful force in the city's electoral politics.

SUMMARY AND CONCLUSIONS

Black organizations in both cities had enough political resources to successfully energize blacks to increase their participation in politics despite opposition from white individuals, groups, and political leaders who possessed greater political resources. The principal resource that black organizations used to increase their voting strength was protest activity. Specifically, the protest activities of the civil rights movement in the South resulted in national policies and actions that fully extended the franchise to southern blacks. After southern blacks obtained the full franchise in the middle 1960s, black organizations and political leaders used increased black voting as the principal resource to extract favorable policies and actions from city government in Birmingham and New Orleans.

Increased black political participation and power are positively associated with blacks receiving an increased proportion of resources allocated by city government in both Birmingham and New Orleans. The benefits in increased executive appointments and municipal employment opportunities were significant. That black political participation has not been able to significantly increase the number of city contracts awarded to black businesses in either city illustrates a limitation of black political participation in producing private sector benefits for blacks.

The benefits that blacks have received from their increased participation in the political process in both cities have contributed significantly to improving the social and economic conditions of blacks. To those who would criticize the impact of increased black political participation because it has not revolutionized the social and economic conditions of blacks, an appropriate response is that such an expectation was unrealistic. Moreover, there is no precedent for political participation producing revolutionary outcomes for any group in American urban politics or American politics generally. Given the limitations of political participation as a medium for social and economic change, blacks in Birmingham and New Orleans have gained significant results from their incorporation in the political process.

REFERENCES

Barker, Lucius J. 1987. Ronald Reagan, Jesse Jackson, and the 1984 Presidential Election: The Continuing American Dilemma of Race. In Michael B. Preston, Lenneal J. Henderson, and Paul Puryear, eds., *The New Black Politics: The Search for Political Power*, 2d ed. New York: Longman.

Browning, Rufus P., Dale Rogers Marshall, and David H. Tabb. 1984. *Protest Is Not Enough: The Struggle of Blacks and Hispanics for Equality in Urban Politics.* Berkeley: University of California Press.

Perry, Huey L. 1983. The Impact of Black Political Participation on Public Sector Employment and Representation on Municipal Boards and Commissions. *The Review of Black Political Economy* 12:203–217.

Perry, Huey L., and Alfred Stokes. 1987. Politics and Power in the Sunbelt: Mayor Morial of New Orleans. In Michael B. Preston, Lenneal J. Henderson, and Paul Puryear, eds., *The New Black Politics: The Search for Political Power*, 2d ed. New York: Longman.

Shingles, Richard D. 1981. Black Consciousness and Political Participation: The Missing Link. *American Political Science Review* 75:76–91.

Strong, Donald S. 1972. Alabama: Transition and Alienation. In William C. Havard, ed., *The Changing Politics of the South.* Baton Rouge, La.: Louisiana State University Press.

Verba, Sidney, and Norman H. Nie. 1972. *Participation in America: Political Democracy and Social Equality.* New York: Harper and Row.

PART V

Latinos

CHAPTER 9

Hispanic Ascendancy and Tripartite Politics in Miami

Christopher L. Warren, John G. Corbett, and John F. Stack, Jr.

Editors' Note

Miami is a medium-sized city with a Hispanic majority. It has a Cuban American mayor and complex triethnic politics heavily influenced by upheavals in the Caribbean. It shares local government authority with a metropolitan government (Dade County) in the reform tradition. Recently it has undergone the most dramatic ethnic transformation of any American big city because of the rapid influx of Latin refugees. These features make racial politics in Miami unique.

How have these special ingredients shaped the mobilization and incorporation of blacks and Latinos? Warren, Corbett, and Stack show that in Miami Hispanics, unlike blacks and unlike Latinos in many other cities, have achieved rapid economic gains, and that the expanding ownership, wealth, and business success of Cubans in particular have led to rapid political incorporation.

When Hispanic political incorporation stems from rapid economic progress and Hispanics constitute a majority of the population, the coalition that institutionalizes their incorporation is not likely to include blacks, nor is it likely to be especially liberal. If such a coalition does not emerge, what happens to the political position and policy interests of blacks or of low-income Hispanics?

See the Introduction (p. 3, note 1) for an explanation concerning different usages among Latino (Hispanic) groups, especially with reference to Cubans in Miami.

While claims of uniqueness can be made with regard to any city's politics, there are aspects of Miami's political environment that place issues of minority mobilization and incorporation, as well as the resultant questions of coalition building and local government responsiveness to minority policy agendas, in a context quite different from those of the other cases discussed in this book. Three features of the Miami setting are especially noteworthy for the ways they shape the area's minority politics:

1. Miami's distinctive political geography, particularly the governmental structure, the ethnic diversity of its population, and its neighborhood settlement patterns.
2. Heightened group consciousness and conflict resulting from the respective roles played by each of the area's three major ethnic groups (non-Hispanic whites, blacks, and Hispanics) in determining election outcomes and influencing local government policy-making.
3. Growing system complexity, as evidenced by the intrusion of international affairs in local politics and the need for the system to manage conflict over policy issues as diverse as bilingualism, neighborhood redevelopment, police violence, white flight, and local anticommunism.

The following discussion analyzes the substance of Miami politics in light of these features with the goals of explaining (1) the basic contours of black and Hispanic political mobilization and incorporation, (2) the area's well-publicized political and social upheaval (for example, massive immigration and riots), and (3) possible scenarios for the future of minority politics in Miami.

THE POLITICAL GEOGRAPHY
OF METROPOLITAN MIAMI

Two elements of metropolitan Miami's political geography are of particular relevance to minority politics. First, the area has a unique metropolitan form of government, combining the mechanisms of a strong county government with those of the area's 26 municipalities. Second, this governmental structure is, in turn, superimposed on a paradoxical neighborhood settlement pattern that variously concentrates and disperses minority populations, dramatically affecting the relative influence of blacks, Hispanics, and non-Hispanic whites (often referred to locally as "Anglos") in the different municipal and county jurisdictions.

Unlike metropolitan areas such as Boston, Chicago, or Atlanta, where central cities with a clear sense of identity are the dominant governmental structures, Miami's metropolitan government is fragmented, both structurally and in the public consciousness, which blurs jurisdictional lines as well as governmental responsibility and accountability. The very name Miami can be a source of confusion. In common usage and for purposes of this chapter, "Miami" refers to the entire metropolitan area, which is coterminous with Dade County. The city of Miami is the largest municipality in the county and is the core city of the SMSA. Hialeah, Miami Beach, and Coral Gables are but the largest of the remaining 26 cities. Some of the smaller municipalities are as little as a square mile in area and have populations under 1000. Therefore, although the actions of the Dade County and city of Miami governments are highlighted throughout the chapter, the complexities of Miami's political structure are such that this discussion must encompass events in several other municipalities as well.

Metro's Structure

In 1957 Miami-Dade County established the first metropolitan form of government in the United States. Larger and more complex than most city governments, Metropolitan Dade County (popularly referred to as "Metro") provided for a two-tiered system that coordinated the workings of the county and city governments, at the same time, granting the county new powers over the cities. There is also a large unincorporated section of the county with an area and a population greater than that of the 26 municipalities combined. A county-level Metro Commission holds policy-making authority in matters of areawide concern (for example, mass transit, public health, and parks and recreation) and sets minimum performance standards for those services still provided by the municipalities. Metro is also the sole local governing authority for the large unincorporated area. The municipalities retained the authority to maintain their own police departments, set municipal taxes, and exceed county standards in zoning and service delivery, among other narrower powers (Mohl, 1983, p. 80).

Metro uses a council-manager form of government in which eight commissioners and a mayor (who is also a council member) are elected countywide in at-large, nonpartisan elections. The commissioners' 4-year terms are staggered so that elections are held every 2 years in order to fill one-half of the seats. As a ninth member of the commission, the county mayor possesses few powers distinguishing him or her from the other members. Administrative authority is held by a county manager who is appointed and fired by majority vote of the commission. Many of the municipalities use government structures similar to Metro's. The city of Miami, for instance, has a five-member council (including the mayor) elected on an at-large, nonpartisan basis and a city manager who possessed administrative powers. However, some of the other cities, such as Hialeah, have used the more traditional strong-mayor plan in structuring their governments.

With regard to virtually every aspect of its current structure, Metro stands as a model of reformed local government. The reform model has its roots in the American progressive reform tradition. Structurally and functionally the model has been characterized by (1) home rule; (2) the council-manager form of government; (3) the adoption of nonpartisan, at-large elections; (4) reliance on merit-based hiring; (5) an emphasis on economy, efficiency, and other professional bureaucratic criteria in service delivery; and (6) recognition of an "at-large community interest" in local government policy-making, and a deemphasis of party, neighborhood, ethnic, or class-based interests (Banfield and Wilson, 1963, pp. 138–203). Motivated by the goal of promoting a communitywide public interest, Metro has sought to limit the intrusion of what it considers to be narrow political interests in matters of policy-making and administration. In the context of Metro's reformist values, minority and neighborhood interests are frequently dismissed as being contrary to the notion of a broader public good, and Metro's structure acts as a buffer against attempts to use minority and neighborhood based political power to influence public policy. At-large elections, in particular, have worked to dilute minority power in county and many city elections.

The mechanisms of Metro's reformed government have also discouraged the emergence of strong political leaders with close ties to minority groups. Even in the face of the county government's considerable powers, in the recent past, Metro Commission races have rarely attracted more than a few candidates and have not been followed very closely by the public. Many incumbents have run virtually unopposed or else faced token opposition from poorly financed perennial candidates or those with only a neighborhood political base. As a result, until the 1988 election, there had been little turnover in Metro Commission seats during the past 10 to 15 years, despite the fact that there have been dramatic changes in the ethnic makeup of the voting population. Moreover, examinations of lists of campaign contributors to Metro races show a high degree of uniformity in the support received by incumbents from local private sector and civic elites. In close races, it is common for some of those same contributors to give to each of the major candidates running for the same seat—known in the local campaign vernacular as CYA (Cover Your Assets) (Soto, 1988). Unless minority candidates are able to attract similar financial backing, and combine it with policy stands that can be expected to cultivate broad public support, they have little chance of winning office. In effect, Metro's structure dissuades candidates from running as strong advocates of minority political interests.

The results of the 1988 county elections suggest some change in the previously stable electoral patterns described above. Of the five commissioners who faced re-election, three incumbents were defeated. While all three new commissioners are non-Hispanic white, one of the new members campaigned hard on the issue of charter reform and the need for district elections. Since that time, several other commissioners have expressed themselves as at least being open to the question of district elections—a sharp departure from earlier commission sentiment. Given that such pressures for district elections for both Metro and city of Miami races have been mounting over the past 8 years, it is reasonable to intimate an association between the debate over charter reform and the rising levels of conflict among Dade County's three major ethnic groups during the same period of time. Indeed, it has usually been in the immediate wake of racial violence or other ethnic conflict that charter reform has been given the greatest attention in Dade County.

Ethnic Diversity and Neighborhood Settlement Patterns

The internationalization of Miami's population and its unusual neighborhood settlement patterns are phenomena that have had significant impact on Miami politics over the past generation. The better known of these occurrences has been the rapid emergence of Miami as an area with one of the most ethnically diverse populations in America. The combined forces of immigration and "white flight" have resulted in Dade County undergoing the single most dramatic ethnic transformation of any major American city in this century (Metro-Dade Planning Department, 1986). As Table 9.1 shows, the triethnic makeup of the population is a post-1960 phenomenon, largely precipitated by the Cuban Revolution and resultant influx of refugees. However, it is important to realize the extent to which the three ethnic designations mask significant intragroup divisions along such lines as national origin, economic status, language, and religion. For instance, about 20 percent of the over 370,000 blacks in Dade County are of Haitian, Bahamian, or Jamaican background. Yet their uncertain immigration status, lack of citizenship, or feelings of separateness from American blacks, bars them from adding much to black political strength.

While Cuban immigrants compose close to 70 percent of the Hispanics in Dade County (down from over 80 percent in 1983) there are also substantial numbers of Puerto Ricans, Nicaraguans, Colombians, Mexicans, and other nationalities (Strategy Research, 1988, p. 21). Today, once post-1980 immigration is taken into account (especially over 100,000 Cubans who came during the Mariel boatlift), the county's Hispanic population can be estimated at almost 876,500, or about 46 percent of the total. In the late 1980s, a less dramatic but steady flow of refugees from Central America have come to Miami. Nicaraguans in particular have been attracted by the area's already established Nicaraguan community concentrated in the city of Sweetwater. In the city of Miami, Hispanics constitute a clear majority, having surpassed 60 percent of the total (see Table 9.2). Of the other cities analyzed in this volume, only San Antonio has a Latino majority, although in that city the

TABLE 9.1. POPULATION OF DADE COUNTY 1960–1988

Year	Black Number	%	Hispanic[a] Number	%	All others[b] Number	%	Total Number	%
1960	137,300	14.7	50,000	5.4	747,700	79.9	935,000	100.0
1970	189,700	15.0	299,200	23.6	778,900	61.4	1,267,800	100.0
1980	261,900	15.7	683,900	41.1	717,000	43.2	1,662,800	100.0
1985	342,000	19.3	768,000	43.3	661,000	37.4	1,771,000	100.0
1988	374,300	19.6	876,500	46.1	653,000	34.3	1,903,800	100.0

[a]Hispanic is not a race category. Figures are adjusted based on Dade Planning Department estimates in order to avoid overlap.
[b]The "All others" category is at least 94 percent non-Hispanic white. (*Sources: Strategy Research Corporation, "Prospectus of Dade County Growth, 1980"; Dade County Planning Department, 1989.*)

TABLE 9.2. POPULATION OF CITY OF MIAMI 1970–1988

Year	Black		Hispanic[a]		All others[b]		Total	
	Number	%	Number	%	Number	%	Number	%
1970	73,700	21.9	151,900	45.3	110,500	32.8	334,900	100.0
1980	83,300	24.0	194,100	55.9	69,500	20.1	346,900	100.0
1988	95,000	25.0	239,400	63.0	45,600	12.0	380,000	100.0

[a]Hispanic is not a race category. Figures are adjusted based on Metro Planning Department estimates in order to avoid overlap.
[b]The "All others" category is at least 93 percent non-Hispanic white. (*Sources: Metro Planning Department estimates based on U.S. Census; City of Miami Planning Department.*)

population is primarily Mexican and the extent of their economic and political incorporation has been more constrained (see Chapter 10).

Even the so-called Anglo population is far from homogeneous, ranging from significant numbers of retirees, many of them Jewish, to middle-class professionals, to smaller, white ethnic populations.

The second demographic phenomenon shaping minority politics in Miami is the extent to which this diverse population has been superimposed on static municipal boundaries, resulting in several cities that respectively are predominantly Hispanic, black, or non-Hispanic white. At the same time, the rapid growth of the unincorporated population has worked to marginalize the influence of the municipal governments and expand the county's role in the community's affairs. Even the city of Miami plays a very different role than it once did; having encompassed almost 65 percent of the county population in 1940, the city's share as of 1985 was just 20 percent of the total.

Black settlement patterns have had a profoundly negative effect on efforts at political mobilization. Historically, due to both the legacy of southern racism and the conscious placement of some black settlements in unincorporated areas (Mohl, 1987), blacks played an almost insignificant role in the politics of the municipalities. Although the City of Miami has always had a substantial black population, and while there has been some black resettlement into other Dade municipalities, especially Opa Locka and Florida City, over 60 percent of black Miamians live in unincorporated sections of the county.

Overall, there are about a dozen identifiable black neighborhoods spread throughout the metropolitan area, from the densely populated public housing developments in Liberty City (which is not a city at all, but a mostly unincorporated area, bordering the city of Miami in northwest Dade), to the more sparsely settled black neighborhoods in the southern agricultural sections of the county. This settlement pattern, and the extent to which it undermines black influence in the municipalities and complicates grass-roots organizing, stands as a formidable barrier to political mobilization. These factors, along with the at-large county and city of Miami elections, combine in compounding the obstacles faced by blacks in shaping public policy in Miami.

Such patterns are quite unlike those found in most of the other cities discussed in this volume, where contiguous black neighborhoods have often provided a foundation for political mobilization and electoral competition. Even in Florida City and Opa Locka, the only two Dade municipalities with black majorities, black electoral success has always been tempered by the marginal roles played by these cities in the metropolitan area's affairs. The use of these two cities as a base for the articulation of black interests is even more profoundly limited by the severe economic problems they face. Both cities are among the poorest of all suburban incorporated areas in the country (Johnson, 1987).

Although Hispanics also live in unincorporated Dade in sizable numbers, more than 70 percent reside in the various municipalities. The cites of Miami, Hialeah, West Miami, Hialeah Gardens, and Sweetwater all have populations that are mostly Hispanic. Hispanic settlement patterns also differ from those of blacks in that they have resulted in a largely uninterrupted string of Latino residential areas, extending west of the City of Miami's Little Havana section. This strong neighborhood base has facilitated the emergence of Hispanics as important participants in both county and municipal politics.

Meanwhile, the non-Hispanic white population is rapidly declining, both relatively and absolutely, falling from about 80 percent of the county total in 1960, to less than 35 percent in 1988. While several of the smaller municipalities have predominantly non-Hispanic white populations, the important bases of Anglo power are the county government and the downtown business section (located in the heart of the city of Miami). The downtown section serves as home to the Metro government offices and most of the larger business, legal, civic, and media institutions that are involved in community affairs—most of which have primarily been run by non-Hispanic whites.

In short, in the complex political geography of Miami, the three major ethnic groups are not spread uniformly across the metropolitan area, but instead reside in a mixed pattern of enclaves and neighborhoods, the locations of which determine the respective bases of power and possible arenas for effective political participation.

THE TRANSFORMATION OF POLITICS IN MIAMI

The emergence of what is usually referred to in Miami as triethnic politics is premised on a distinctive mix of historical, political, economic, and international elements. To state the case briefly, non-Hispanic whites are seeing their influence in electoral politics gradually decline, while they still remain very powerful in the county government as well as in the major nongovernmental, media, and business institutions. However, even in the nongovernmental area, not only have some Hispanics and blacks been brought into the leadership ranks of prominent local organizations that historically have been bastions of Anglo power, but parallel business and civic institutions, controlled by Hispanics and blacks have emerged, such as the Latin Builders Association, the Spanish American League Against

Discrimination, and the Black Lawyers Association. In fact, there are three local chambers of commerce—each primarily representing one of the three major ethnic groups (Freedberg and Soto, 1989). Yet, for the most part, the story of Miami's black community has been one of struggling to overcome numerical and structural obstacles to effective political mobilization, gaining a foothold in local political affairs, and then fighting to preserve what has been won in the face of tremendous demographic and political-economic change. Hispanics, on the other hand, have effectively combined economic incorporation with ascendancy in electoral politics, forging what many feel will become the new dominant force in Miami's political affairs. However, for reasons discussed below, this change does not promise to produce public policies that are substantially at variance with those of the present, especially with regard to the limited potential for major redistributive policy initiatives.

The Changing Nature of Non-Hispanic
White Dominance

From the time of Miami's founding in the late 1800s, whites remained totally dominant in local electoral politics. As late as 1960, so few blacks had been able to register to vote that although they constituted about 15 percent of the population, blacks usually accounted for less than three percent of the voter turnout (Sofen, 1961, p. 21). The Hispanic population, which was about 5 percent of the total in 1960, played an even less significant role in electoral politics insofar as the exodus from Cuba was only just beginning and few Latin residents were citizens.

Because of the decline in the non-Hispanic white population, their electoral dominance has slipped considerably in the 1980s, especially in cities with Hispanic and black majorities. Changes in the makeup of the city of Miami Commission have been dramatic. In the early 1960s, all five Miami city commissioners were American-born whites. In the mid-1960s, the first black won a seat on the commission. Gradually, several Hispanics won seats, at times defeating and replacing one another, until as of the early 1980s only one non-Hispanic white commissioner remained. These shifts have closely paralleled the growth in Hispanic population and voter registration in the city of Miami illustrated in Tables 9.2 and 9.3.

On the Metro Commission, non-Hispanic whites still hold seven of the nine positions, including the mayor's seat. The remaining two seats are held by a black and a Hispanic. However, the fact that Hispanics already make up a plurality of the county population (46 percent), but only about 27 percent of the registered voters, suggests that as more Hispanics are enfranchised, new Hispanic commissioners are likely to be elected, even under the at-large system.

While electoral politics in Miami is extremely important as it relates to issues of group representation, local policy-making has also usually reflected the priorities of Miami's major business, legal, media, and civic interests—all of which were, for many years, essentially closed to minority participation.

Historically, private sector influence in Miami was linked to the growth and needs of the city's downtown business section and its tourism-based economy. With rapid growth came new demands for roads, water, sanitation, and schools. The area's wildly fluctuating economy, occasioned by boom and bust periods, needed to be stabilized. The community also had to find a balance between the segregationist sentiments in the white community and the need for easy access to black labor for the vitally important hotel and service industries. All these issues had important economic underpinnings and therefore served to facilitate business leadership in community affairs. As Mohl has documented (1987, p. 11), even social programs, such as slum clearance in the 1930s, were shaped by "the hidden agenda of the downtown civic elite," which sought to expand the business section into black neighborhoods.

By the 1950s, population growth, the proliferation of local governments, and resultant fragmentation and inconsistencies in local policy-making all served to demonstrate that despite the city of Miami's centrality in local affairs, its government lacked the capacity to deal with pressing policy concerns in any comprehensive fashion. Local white elites began to explore the development of new government institutional arrangements, giving rise to the effort to establish a metropolitan government in Dade County. Endorsement of the concept of metropolitan government was forthcoming from a variety of "good government" groups, local elite law firms, professional public administrators, the *Miami Herald*, and many of the larger business interests (who wanted to work with a more centralized government, especially in matters of development and zoning). This pro-Metro coalition became and has generally remained the dominant force in shaping the community's basic political-economic agenda (Sofen, 1966; Mohl, 1984). Even in the wake of dramatic demographic changes, Sofen's observations in 1961 regarding Miami's power structure remain essentially valid.

> In the case of Miami, the lack of countervailing organizations in the form of either cohesive labor or minority groups, has meant that the business community had no real competitors in the political arena. Moreover, since the cause of "good government" groups coincided with the desires of the more powerful Miami business organizations, the latter were quite content to allow the newspapers, professional groups, the university professors, and the League of Women Voters to assume the positions of catalytic leadership in civic affairs. (Sofen, 1961, p. 21)

In the 1980s this structure of power has become even more formal and institutionalized through the establishment of organizations such as the "Non-Group" (an informal association of Miami's top business and civic leaders), the Beacon Council (a publicly sponsored organization chartered to encourage business development), and various appendages of the mostly Anglo Greater Miami Chamber of Commerce. Each has served as an important vehicle for the formation and articulation of the policy preferences of local, private economic interests. While the major business associations have not denied the existence of minority policy concerns and have brought some minority members into their ranks, they remain important bases of non-Hispanic white power, and they have continued to be central in articulating what the broader "public interest" is in terms of local government policy—a public interest that has remained remarkably consistent with what was good for Miami's larger and most powerful private sector institutions.

Although business can be expected to play a pivotal political role in almost any major metropolitan area (Fainstein et al., 1986), it is also clear that without the slightest suggestion of collusion between business and local government officials, in Miami, business interests and reformist governmental structures and values converge, creating an environment in which issues of primary concern to minority groups and their neighborhoods are frequently dismissed as not being in the best interest of the community as a whole. In short, the idea that advancement for minorities might require policies contrary to the interests of influential economic institutions is simply not considered.

Black Mobilization: The Limitations of Enfranchisement

When the City of Miami was incorporated in 1896, 162 of the 368 persons who stood to be counted in support of the establishment of the new municipality were black laborers (Porter and Dunn, 1984, p. 2). In 1920, blacks still constituted 31 percent of the city's population. Despite this early, albeit passive, participation, black political mobilization was virtually nonexistent during the six decades that followed. Between 1940 and 1960, the county's black population more than doubled, but it shrank as a percentage of the total. Demands for equality, adequate housing, services, and jobs intensified, but blacks lacked both the direct leverage and the political allies necessary to shape and promote a coherent program geared to reorienting local public policy to meet their needs.

As in most areas of the country, the late 1950s and 1960s seemed to promise a positive political future for Miami's black population. The civil rights movement and the resultant federal government involvement, especially through the 1964 Civil Rights Act and the 1965 Voting Rights Act, encouraged local efforts to mobilize. Although the local movement lacked the high level of organization and intensity found in some other southern cities during the same period, especially with regard to protest activity, substantive gains were made through efforts aimed at desegregation of public and private facilities and voter registration.

Efforts aimed at political mobilization in general and protest activity in particular were difficult to organize given the geographic isolation of several black neighborhoods. However, during the 1950s and 1960s there were sporadic protest actions aimed at desegregating lunch counters and stores in the downtown business district. Additional efforts were made to "open up" the public beaches, the Orange Bowl football stadium, and the Dade County auditorium. Yet, from the point of view of becoming involved in local politics, no development was as important as increased black voter registration. Black registration rose from 6.8 percent of the county total in 1960 to 12.3 percent in 1970 to 19.3 percent in 1989, progressing closer to and finally matching the percentage of black residents. Black registration is 94 percent Democratic, but non-Hispanic whites and now a few Hispanics have remained dominant in local party leadership positions.

Once black registration increased, election and appointment to local political office followed. Since the late 1960s blacks have consistently held one seat on both the city of Miami and Metro Commissions. In the 1970s, a black was first elected to the Dade County School Board, and a black superintendent was hired. In April 1981, Howard Gary, a man who had grown up in Liberty City, became the first black to serve as city manager for the city of Miami, a position he held until late 1984, and which is still considered by many to be the most important and influential ever held by a black in Dade County. In the last 20 years, blacks have also won election to other offices and assumed some important administrative positions, including state legislative seats and several other commission and city manager seats in some of the smaller municipalities. The city of Opa Locka's city council is now all black.

Substantive advancement for blacks can also be seen in the areas of local government employment and government contracting with minority businesses. As of 1987, blacks held approximately 35 percent of the close to 20,000 county jobs and 31 percent of the 3850 positions in the city of Miami (Hispanics held about 25 and 35 percent, respectively). Critics, however, maintain that too many of the government jobs held by blacks are lower-level clerical and maintenance positions. Both police departments have also increased the numbers of black police officers, although in the face of strained relations between the police and the black community, recruitment has been difficult. The number of black police officers on the city of Miami force has increased from about 10 percent of the total in 1974 to approximately 18 percent in 1988. In addition, Dade County and the city of Miami have passed ordinances requiring that building contractors receiving government business use specified percentages of minority subcontractors. However, here too there have been problems with implementation, insofar as contractors have frequently complained that the lack of black-owned businesses in south Florida make meeting the requirements difficult. Moreover, recent federal court decisions have ruled against similar minority set-aside policies in other localities.

**TABLE 9.3. VOTER REGISTRATION IN DADE COUNTY
AND CITY OF MIAMI, MARCH 1989**

	Dade		Miami	
	Number	*Percentage*	*Number*	*Percentage*
Black	135,440	19.3	34,756	31.1
Hispanic[a]	187,092	26.8	46,078	41.3
All other[b]	376,700	53.9	30,840	27.6
Total	699,232	100.0	111,674	100.0

[a]The "Hispanic" category only contains those Hispanics born outside the United States or in Puerto Rico.
[b]The "All other" category is estimated to be 93 percent non-Hispanic white. (*Source: Metro-Dade Elections Department.*)

While advances for blacks in voter registration, elections, appointment politics, and public sector employment have provided important opportunities for the articulation of black concerns in the policy-making arena, their incorporation falls short of the parity—the ratio of the proportion of minority office holders to the proportion of minority population—described by Browning, Marshall, and Tabb (1984, p. 20). Of even more profound importance is the extent to which the gains made by blacks in electoral and appointment politics are limited by the Metro system's highly fragmented structure or are in danger of being eclipsed by rapid Hispanic incorporation. Holding one seat on several commissions or holding a majority of the seats in the two poorest municipalities has not resulted in incorporation that has proven very meaningful in policy terms. The notion that blacks are losing ground to Hispanics was also dramatically reinforced when black city manager Howard Gary's firing in 1984 came at the hands of the Miami city commission's three Hispanic members. Two Cuban Americans have subsequently been chosen to hold the city manager's office. The black incumbents on the city of Miami and Metro commissions have also faced Hispanic opponents in recent elections. In short, gains have been made in black mobilization and incorporation, but the gains are fragile in the existing political environment.

Although there is no formal, written policy agenda for blacks in Miami, most of the concerns voiced by black civic leaders and the black press fall into one of three categories. The perceptions and the realities of limited progress on these issues is indicative of the limitations of meaningful political incorporation for black Miamians. Perhaps the most visible and frequently cited issue is that of the need for greater community control over police behavior and the demanding of stronger measures to reduce and punish police violence against black citizens. Under the Metro charter, incorporated areas maintain their own police departments, while unincorporated areas such as much of Liberty City are policed by the county force. A long history of friction between blacks and police has been a particular problem in the unincorporated neighborhoods and in the city of Miami, and it was a major factor in each of the four riots that have taken place in the Miami area in the 1980s, the most recent of which was in January 1989 (Porter and Dunn, 1984).

The black neighborhoods of Liberty City (which experienced, what was by some measures, the most violent riots of the century in May 1980) and Overtown (where there were several nights of disorder in December 1982, in the spring of 1984, and again in January 1989) have come to replace Watts and Detroit as the contemporary symbols of racial upheaval in America. In each of the four riots, it has been events associated with the separate killings of black men by Hispanic or non-Hispanic white officers of the Dade County and city of Miami police departments that most directly ignited the violence. Indeed, there are those who view the pattern of rioting as symbolizing a host of fundamental problems faced by the black community, leading some to describe the riots as a "rebellion" (Marable, 1980).

Although two blacks have successively served as chief of police in the city of Miami, and both Miami and Metro have instituted new administrative procedures for dealing with police shootings, the attitudes of many blacks toward local police continue to harden. But in this publicity-sensitive community, still economically dependent on attracting large numbers of tourists, many business and civic leaders quickly act to relegate these recurrent incidents to history. The fact that the latest riots coincided with Miami's hosting of the Super Bowl made civic leaders that much more anxious over national perceptions, prompting the president of the Beacon Council to say, "If it wasn't for the fact that the Super Bowl is down here it (the riots) wouldn't be more than a blip in the news. . . . We still have a good product to sell, and we still need to be selling it more than ever before" (Resnick and Croghan, 1989). Just as the influx of Mariel and Haitian refugees closely coincided with Miami's 1980 riots, the racial violence of January 1989 accompanied the arrival of thousands of Central American refugees. The coincidence of such events reinforces the contention that in Miami, black attempts to mobilize politically are frequently undercut by the ever-growing numbers of Hispanics and the immediate needs of the most recently arrived refugees, who are often thought to receive more concentrated assistance than many blacks do in finding work and housing.

A second significant agenda item for many in Miami's black neighborhoods is the need for improved housing and neighborhood revitalization. Public housing, particularly that administered by Dade County's office of Housing and Urban Development ("Little HUD"), has recently come under severe criticism as a result of the innumerable building-code and health violations discovered by investigators. The housing problem is in turn linked to a broader issue, that black Miamians frequently lack the power to shape events that directly affect their own neighborhoods. For example, beyond the slum clearance program of the 1930s, which sought to relocate blacks outside of the Overtown neighborhood, the same area has continued to be disrupted through efforts to improve access to and expand the downtown business district. In the 1960s, massive freeway construction dissected the neighborhood at several angles. The latest Overtown redevelopment effort, only now being implemented, resulted in the construction of a basketball arena and hundreds of units of middle-class housing and shops in the area. At each juncture, policymakers have justified their efforts in terms of the broader public interest and the spin-off benefits for blacks in terms of expanded job opportunities and better overall living conditions. Many blacks remain skeptical of these justifications, insofar as they are premised on seemingly contradictory logic: that improved circumstances for blacks are linked to the gentrification of black neighborhoods and the possible dislocation of current residents. Policies geared to improving black neighborhoods themselves have been few in number and of low visibility.

The same basic patterns of local government action and ensuing justifications have been apparent in other initiatives that involved black neighborhood interests. For instance, following the 1980 riots, the Metro Commission blocked an effort to incorporate the Liberty City area. A major impetus behind the proposal was the desire to establish a Liberty City police department and assume more localistic control over policies affecting the area in general. The Metro Commission, deciding that such a change would not be cost-effective, refused to place the proposal before the voters. The commission has also been at odds with one of Dade County's few middle-class black neighborhoods. Residents sought to block the construction of a new Miami Dolphins football stadium and business complex on the fringe of their area because it was felt that the facilities would disrupt and destabilize the neighborhood. Efforts to unseat one of the Metro commissioners who voted to approve the site selection, as well as efforts to stop construction through court action, have failed.

The third category of policy concerns relevant to Miami's black community is directly linked to the need for greater economic opportunity. Black Miamians have been conspicuously left out of the dramatic economic growth witnessed in the area. Blacks continue to confront the worst living conditions in the Miami area. They possess the lowest median income, the largest percentage of families in poverty, the worst housing conditions, and double the rate of white unemployment. When the city of Miami was designated in the 1980 census as the sixth poorest large city in the United States on the basis of the percentage of the population living below the poverty line, it was largely because the black neighborhoods of Overtown, Little Haiti, Coconut Grove, and a portion of Liberty City are all contained within the city limits. In sharp contrast to Latinos, blacks are not in a position to use economic clout as a means of enhancing their political status. There are few black-owned businesses, and of those, fewer than 20 percent provide employment for anyone other than the owner (Luytjes, 1979).

Across this broad array of issues, black leaders have argued that the only way to truly get at the problems faced by blacks in Dade County is for blacks to gain greater control over their neighborhoods, especially over police protection, development, and service delivery, and to secure greatly expanded programs that promote economic opportunities. To critics, however, such an agenda calls for both localistic control and outside economic assistance (a combination that has numerous political obstacles) and reflects the group-centered, localistic perspective Metro was organized to combat.

Yet, in that broader, countywide context, the problem of issue articulation for blacks is compounded by the fact that most successful black candidates for Dade County and city of Miami offices are very moderate in their politics and well connected with prominent Anglo and Hispanic officials and business leaders. Strong advocacy of minority interests risks the loss of support from elites who fund campaigns as well as from nonblack voters. Lacking sufficient numbers, strong political leadership, supportive coalitions, and a tradition of well-organized protest, black enfranchisement since the 1960s has produced uneven results. Even the pledges of public and private support that were forthcoming after the 1980 and 1982 riots have been short-lived. The Metro–Miami Action Plan (MMAP), which was to be the centerpiece of a coordinated public and private revitalization effort has all but folded after 5 years of operation. Virtually all corporate involvement has stopped, and now the county and city governments have gradually cut back on their support. As one former MMAP board member stated, "MMAP has been abandoned by almost everyone. There is not a sense of urgency about black problems. . . . A lot of prominent corporate leaders began to disappear after the second year. In Miami, you only get the corporate world to react in times of crisis. There's not a conscience that endures'' (Dugger, 1987).

The Political and Economic Dimensions of Hispanic Incorporation

Standing in a city that has been described as ''the capital of Latin America'' (Levine, 1985), it is difficult to appreciate that 29 years ago Hispanic influence in Miami was practically nonexistent. After the Cuban Revolution of 1959, Miami's rapid internationalization and penetration by Latin culture became a remarkable case study in socioeconomic and political change. The first waves of Cuban immigrants were not the dispossessed underclass of that country, but accomplished professionals, who combined personal initiative with an ''open armed'' immigration policy and U.S. economic assistance in establishing themselves in Miami. Subsequent waves of immigrants throughout the 1960s brought a large portion of the Cuban middle class as well as an upwardly mobile working class to Miami. While a myth of the ''Golden Cuban'' (that all Cubans are wealthy) persists, even in the face of a somewhat modest standard of living for many more recently arrived refugees, Cuban immigration has been accompanied by rapid economic incorporation and a number of dramatic success stories. Overall, national census figures show that as of 1986, the median income for Cubans was $26,770, as opposed to $14,584 for Puerto Ricans and $19,326 for Mexicans (Marquis, 1989; Warren, 1984).

Between 1960 and 1982, Cubans founded more than 25,000 businesses (compared to approximately 3000 black-owned businesses in Dade), including banks, television and radio stations, restaurants, and a wide variety of service and industrial enterprises (Luytjes, 1979; Arboleya, 1980). Los Angeles is the only city in the United States with more Hispanic-owned businesses, but it also has a larger Hispanic population, and the Miami-based enterprises tend to be larger, encompass more capital and wealth, and employ more people. While initially Latin businesses provided the foundation for a vibrant, self-contained enclave economy, the Cuban presence and their economic successes also attracted Latin American tourists and capital and has resulted in scores of multinational corporations locating their Latin American offices in Miami. Also, while some Latins in Miami feel they are still excluded from the very top management positions in local American companies, there has been considerable movement into the ranks of management in this sector as well.

The poverty that is so frequently associated with new immigrant groups was conspicuously absent in the Cuban immigrant experience until the arrival of the Mariel refugees in 1980. The Marielitos, as they were called locally, were more likely to be poor, nonwhite, and unskilled than previous Cuban entrants. That the Cuban government seized the opportunity provided by the Mariel boatlift to rid their country of an estimated 10,000 to 15,000 of their criminal and ''antisocial'' elements also resulted in a precipitous rise in Miami's crime rate. Thus, class and racial divisions, as well as the bad publicity that followed the Mariel refugees, have tested the durability of nationalistic ties. However, such divisions within the Hispanic community in general, and within the Cuban population in particular, have yet to manifest themselves in politically significant ways. Nor has the recent influx of Central Americans, especially Nicaraguans, yet resulted in an identifiable alternative Hispanic agenda in Miami. Ultimately, it is the numerical, economic, and political force of the middle- and upper-class Cuban community that has the greatest impact on Miami politics.

As prospects for the quick overthrow of the Castro government faded, increased numbers of Cubans began to apply for citizenship and register to vote. From 1973 to 1989, Hispanic registration rose from 6.3 percent of the county total to 26.8 percent. As more recently arrived immigrants become citizens, Hispanic electoral clout will continue to increase relative to that of blacks and non-Hispanic whites (see Tables 9.2 and 9.3).

Twelve years ago four Hispanics held local elected office in the Miami area. Today there are over forty Hispanic officials, including six mayoralties, city commission majorities in Miami, Hialeah, West Miami, and Sweetwater, and ten of the twenty-eight positions in the Dade delegation of the Florida legislature. Although there is still only one Hispanic on the Metro Commission, there have been other victories in countywide elections, such as for seats on the Dade County School Board. Additionally, a tendency toward higher-than-average voter turnout, bloc voting in support of Cuban American candidates, and the settlement patterns discussed earlier all contribute to Hispanic ascendancy. About 75 percent of those Hispanics in Dade who are registered to vote are Republicans, so the mechanisms of the previously underutilized local Republican party organization have also facilitated Hispanic mobilization. While there can be no guarantee that solidarity within the ranks of Hispanic voters will continue indefinitely, for all of the reasons cited above, there can be little doubt that Hispanics will soon emerge as the dominant force in Miami's electoral politics.

In the area of appointive politics, Hispanic incorporation has progressed just as rapidly. In what is no doubt the capstone in political ascendancy, Hispanic now hold the positions of county manager, city manager in the city of Miami, and superintendent of the Dade County schools. Moreover, county and municipal employment for Hispanics also progresses apace these other developments.

While the immigrant experience, support for the Reagan administration's Latin American foreign policy, and other more localistic factors have channeled Miami Cuban politics in particular directions, it is a mistake to view their efforts as monolithic. Some political rivalries were transplanted from Cuba, there are few leaders behind whom Cubans are truly united, and Cubans running against Cubans is a growing phenomenon in local elections. Most revealing of such cleavages is the fact that in the 1987 city of Miami election, the mayor (a Cuban) allied himself with influential Latin business leaders in a campaign to unseat a fellow commissioner of Cuban background who was best known for his injection of demagogic anticommunism into even the most local and parochial of issues. More recently the local

Republican party organization has been divided by bitter in-fighting in a power struggle between two Cubans seeking the top party post.

Most important, the long-term impact of Hispanic incorporation on policy-making is still uncertain, largely because of the unusual nature of their accompanying policy agenda. In addition to issues of service delivery and business development, Miami's Cubans have frequently emphasized more symbolic issues, such as anticommunism and organized efforts to oppose the anti-Hispanic sentiments expressed by some Anglos and blacks. While anticommunist sentiments certainly fit into the mainstream of American political values, it is its injection into Miami's local elections, city commission votes, and referenda that has been particularly apparent in distinguishing the Cuban policy agenda from that of blacks or non-Hispanic whites. During the 16-month period preceding May 1983, the Miami City Commission passed at least eighteen formal resolutions and motions dealing with U.S. foreign policy, most of which were strictly symbolic expressions of Latin anticommunism. The Hialeah City Commission severed its Sister City ties with Managua, Nicaragua, and the city of Sweetwater declared Fidel Castro persona non grata. Free speech has also become an issue in Miami as a result of sometimes violent disruptions of public speeches, political rallies, and even plays and films thought to be too radical by segments of the Cuban community. But expressions of anticommunism in local politics have by no means been limited to the Cuban community; partly because of the presence of a rapidly growing Nicaraguan population, Miami has also been a center for the organization, support, and execution of U.S. policies supportive of the Nicaraguan Contras. Thus, in some local campaigns, support for the Contras has served as a litmus test of sorts. Several non-Hispanic white candidates seeking Latino support have also relied on anticommunist rhetoric in attempting to gain Cuban support for their campaigns (Warren and Stack, 1986).

Most recently, however, some Cuban leaders have been trying to gradually distance themselves from such emotional or symbolic issues, suggesting a new-found confidence in the power and influence they have gained. Some refer to this transformation as constituting a shift from more militant and internationally oriented exile politics, to more mainstream, domestic ethnic politics. A 1987 proposal to overturn the county's 1980 antibilingual ordinance, which prevents the conducting of county business in any language other than English or the spending of county money in the promotion of foreign languages or cultures, was quickly short-circuited by Latino business and civic leaders. Although the antibilingual ordinance has been viewed by most Hispanics as a slap in the face of the Spanish-speaking population, the effort to repeal it was put aside in the interest of not further alienating the non-Hispanic populations.

Of even more critical significance is the extent to which Hispanic economic and political incorporation in Miami has not raised policy issues that challenge the power of the traditionally influential downtown business elites. Although Latin political successes have displaced a number of non-Hispanic white officials, the Latinization of the economy has proven to be functional for the major Anglo business interests (especially the area's largest financial, real estate, tourism, retail, and service institutions), providing the international linkages that have been instrumental in the area's economic growth. The overlap of Hispanic and Anglo economic interests reduces the non-Hispanic white elite's anxieties over the growing political strength of Latins, diminishing any motivation to enlist black support in a non-Hispanic political coalition. This process differs from the political and economic co-optation of minorities described in some cities (see Chapter 7) and represents more of a genuine convergence of economic and class-based interests between Miami's private sector establishment and the Latino middle and upper classes.

White flight has not had much of a destabilizing effect on Miami's economy. Unlike other migrations of whites out of cities such as New Orleans or Detroit (see Chapter 8; Rich, 1986), in Miami, the phenomenon has not resulted in a decline in the overall population, an exodus by business, or erosion of the tax base. Many middle-class whites have left Miami, but the continued vitality of the Latin community has offset many of the economic dysfunctions commonly associated with white flight.

Overall, Hispanic incorporation in Miami contradicts most generalizations made about other cities with large Hispanic populations in five important ways. First, the makeup of Miami's Hispanic population differs from that of most other cities, being predominantly Cuban and generally more affluent. Second, the economic incorporation of middle- and upper-class Hispanics in Miami has facilitated their political incorporation. Third, Hispanic incorporation in Miami has preceded rather than followed the incorporation of blacks. Fourth, whereas black and Hispanic mobilization and incorporation may be complementary processes in some cities, in Miami, the political and—just as important—economic incorporation of Hispanics is widely perceived as not benefiting blacks. Fifth, Hispanic incorporation in Miami has generally not been associated with the building of more liberal coalitions, but has generally had the effect of complementing rather than challenging the agenda of downtown business elites.

INCREASING SYSTEM COMPLEXITY

The outstanding feature of Miami politics during the last three decades is the increased number and complexity of factors affecting local policy-making. The multiplicity of policy demands coming from new and more assertive minority groups, coupled with the inability of the existing system to thoroughly address them, means that numerous unresolved conflicts persist along both ethnic and socioeconomic lines. As detailed above, there has been great variation in the respective struggles of blacks and Hispanics in Miami, resulting in neither common patterns of mobilization nor a convergence of political-economic and policy interests. In Miami, zero-sum perceptions among all three ethnic groups often prevail. Unlike the gradual, incremental working out of different stands on policy issues discussed by Peter Eisinger (1980), ethnic conflict in Miami has shown signs of growing brittleness and intransigence in an atmosphere of group polarization. Not only have black and Hispanic political mobilizations often been at cross purposes, as in the New York scenario described by Mollenkopf (see Chapter 4), but, unlike New York and most other cities, Hispanic incorporation in Miami has superseded that of blacks in every respect. However, given the coincidence of ethnic and class divisions in Miami, juxtaposing middle- and upper-class Hispanics and non-Hispanic whites with poorer blacks and more recently arrived immigrants, the substantive policy implications of Hispanic incorporation are very different for non-Hispanic whites and blacks, respectively. In short, while Hispanic incorporation has injected new issues into the community, it has not presented a fundamental challenge to the community's essential conservatism in matters of local government policy. In Miami, one simply cannot equate minority politics with poor people's politics or with liberal politics.

As the complexities of Miami's politics and the turbulence of its recent history suggest, a thorough assessment of possible scenarios for the future could fill an entire volume. However, based on recent events, it is possible to highlight certain political possibilities relevant to the ongoing efforts by Miami's diverse minority populations to have their disparate interests effectively represented in local policy-making.

Political Prospects

Browning, Marshall, and Tabb (see Chapter 1; 1984) have discussed the respective roles of both *electoral politics* and *demand–protest* in effective minority-group mobilization. They have also underscored the importance of *coalition building* between minorities and supportive whites in challenging more conservative groups in the influencing and making of policy. The emphasis placed on the respective roles of electoral mobilization, protest, and coalition building is appropriate in assessing the future of Miami politics. By distinguishing what seems accomplishable in the context of these factors, as opposed to what might otherwise be viewed as ideal, one is able to focus on those political possibilities that seem most likely to emerge in the near future.

Electoral Politics. The most important determinant in the future of Miami's electoral politics will continue to be the area's governmental structure. Developed at a time when blacks were disenfranchised and Hispanics were few in number, the structure of the Metro system simply was not designed with effective minority participation in mind. As it is presently structured, Metro remains largely detached from those segments of the community most dependent on the electoral process in shaping public policy, especially blacks.

For blacks, the system frequently seems to combine the worst of both worlds, from the point of view of attaining elected office at either the municipal or county level. Even in the predominantly black municipalities, the needs of those populations can become isolated from the rest of the metropolitan area or require responses that exceed the capacities of the respective city governments. At the county level, those same needs are diffused or simply lost in a system that otherwise attempts to impose a ''one best community interest'' on a heterogeneous, faction-ridden political environment. Blacks seem to have come close to exhausting the electoral possibilities the current Metro system offers. Thus, considerable hope has been placed in attempts to establish a system of district elections through charter reform, especially in the Metro and city of Miami contests.

As of the late 1970s and early 1980s, proposals for district elections drew considerable support from both black and Hispanic groups. Indeed, such proposals represented one of the few substantive policy goals supported by both minority groups in Miami. However, as more Hispanic candidates have been successful in at-large county and city elections, enthusiasm among Latinos for such reforms has diminished somewhat. Presently, the prospect of combined black and non-Hispanic white support for district elections seems more likely, insofar as there has been growing concern over trying to guarantee non-Latin white representation on various commissions in the face of Hispanic voters becoming more dominant.

In the immediate wake of the January 1989 riots, a shift to district elections in city of Miami and Metro commission contests, has become a much more likely prospect. In early February, in what was the most dramatic and effective use of protest tactics by any group in Miami in recent years, 900 black citizens, led by more than a dozen black organizations, converged on a Miami City Commission meeting and effectively took control of the meeting's agenda. A list of demands presented to the commission by the demonstrators was topped by a call for a November 1989 referendum on district elections. The commission immediately voted to appoint a charter review committee to write a proposal that would be placed on the November 1989 ballot.

A week later, the tactic was repeated before the county commission, and although no immediate decision was made to place a district election proposal on the ballot, the action strengthened those newly elected Metro commissioners who support district elections. Thus, although the charter reform forces had suffered a major setback in October 1988 when a federal judge ruled that Dade County's system of at-large elections did not discriminate against blacks and Hispanics, as of this writing the prospects for a vote on district elections (or perhaps a hybrid combination of at-large and district seats) in both Metro and city of Miami contests seem very likely. Should a charter revision be placed on the county ballot, blacks could play a decisive role in the decision, but until recently they have lacked the capacity to force the issue. In the absence of such reforms, black incorporation will remain marginal and vulnerable.

As suggested by all of the preceding discussion, Hispanics are clearly becoming numerically dominant in Miami. In the future, however, more significant than the numbers of Latin voters will be the question of cohesiveness within the Hispanic bloc. Increased diversity in the makeup of the Hispanic population and the growing number of electoral contests between Hispanic candidates provide at least some new political possibilities. In the 1985 city of Miami mayor's race, for instance, one of the two Cuban American candidates actively sought and attained a significant number of black votes, even though there was a serious black candidate running. While the Hispanic candidate did alienate many Latin voters in the process of cultivating black support, he was able to generate sufficient support from blacks and non-Hispanic whites to get into a run-off. While such a campaign strategy is not likely to become typical, it does point to the possibility of there being more voting across ethnic lines in the future—a development that could provide some foundation for coalition building, at least in the support of individual candidates for office.

Protest. Given the often spontaneous and opportunistic nature of political protest, it is difficult to estimate what its role in Miami politics will be in the future. Of the three major ethnic groups in Miami, blacks have used protest most frequently (especially in the mid-1960s, and now in the immediate wake of the January 1989 riots). The absence of a sustained and demonstrably effective protest tradition among blacks is probably a contributing factor in the cathartic racial violence Miami has experienced in the 1980s. Porter and Dunn (1984) report a broad base of sympathy among blacks for the rage displayed in the 1980 Liberty City riot (although not necessarily for the killings of whites which were a part of it). Also, the recurring riots have resulted in a number of responses from the local, state, and federal governments. However, many of the responses have been symbolic gestures (for example, the appointment of numerous study commissions to examine the problems of Miami's black community), have involved the commitment of few resources, or have resulted in inadequate follow-through. The lack of substantive policy results, combined with the fueling of fear and resentment toward blacks as a result of the rioting, has amply demonstrated the limitations of rioting as a policy lever.

Protest and even outbreaks of violence have drawn attention to grievances, but they have been ineffective in assuring a sustained response from government or the private sector. In keeping with Browning, Marshall, and Tabb's observation that "protest is not enough" (1984) in seeking representation for minority interests, it is clear that incomplete and ineffective mobilization in both electoral and protest politics will continue to be the most significant obstacle to the further incorporation of blacks into Miami's policy-making apparatus.

Protest has been used less frequently by Hispanics and non-Hispanic whites. Both groups have had considerably more success in using traditional electoral mechanisms. On occasion, groups of angry residents from a particular neighborhood will turn out in large numbers at a commission meeting to oppose proposed changes in neighborhood zoning, and there have been instances of demonstrations by Hispanics over immigration policy as well as in displays of anticommunist sentiment, but all such examples fall short of protest that is used as a tool to shape local government policies. Notwithstanding the recent demonstrations at city of Miami and Metro commission meetings and the distinct possibility of new outbreaks of violence in the black community, it seems unlikely at present that protest will play a substantively different role in the future of Miami politics.

Coalition Building. The entry of new groups and issues into Miami's political process over the past several years might otherwise have been thought to provide numerous opportunities for the emergence of new political coalitions. However, while Miami politics has become much more complicated than it ever was, there actually seem to be fewer opportunities for the possible formation of political coalitions that could be expected to support liberal minority agendas on government boards and commissions. For years, the city of Miami and Metro systems had made policy according to a fixed, if not always gladly accepted, set of rules. Anglo and private-sector-elite dominance in the political arena seemed unchallengeable. In the 1960s, efforts at black mobilization and the earlier phases of Latin immigration suggested emergent divisions in the community, transforming Miami's black–white racial setting into a much more complex triethnic, indeed multiethnic, political environment.

Yet, while such changes have increased the number of groups and actors participating in the community's politics, there has not been a subsequent emergence of new coalitions able to bring about a major shift in the content of local public policies. The divisions between blacks and Cubans, especially, are so steeped in economic and group differences, as well as cultural and ideological sensitivities, that finding acceptable compromises between them seems difficult under the best of circumstances. Nor have white liberals played a determinant role in the formation of new coalitions. Liberal political organizations in Miami are few in number, and local government has lacked mechanisms, such as partisan elections, that could bring liberals from various groups together in support of particular candidates or policy initiatives.

As suggested earlier, increased voting across ethnic lines does present some opportunity for the creation of new coalitions within the ranks of the electorate. However, the ad hoc character of Miami elections, with no role for political parties, and the highly individualistic nature of campaigning in an at-large system severely limit the opportunity for the building of lasting coalitions between officials on policy-making bodies.

CONCLUSIONS

In the attempts of social scientists to understand black and Hispanic struggles for power and equality in urban politics, the case of Miami is particularly important in suggesting a scenario of increased division between the nation's two largest minority groups. With regard to both substantive and symbolic issues, zero-sum perceptions may widen the gulf between blacks and Hispanics, as well as between both groups and non-Hispanic whites. While the analogy is exaggerated to be sure, former city of Miami Mayor Maurice Ferre's description of Miami as the "Beirut of the West" suggests the depth of the cleavages that have existed.

Those who remain most optimistic about the future of ethnic group relations in

Miami must be careful not to become blinded by mere civic boosterism. In the absence of policy-making institutions that are capable of *both* thoroughly representing group interests and providing an arena for the working-out of differences between blacks, Hispanics, and non-Hispanic whites, continuing polarization and even violence, manifested in numerous ways, seem inevitable.

The political and social problems faced by blacks in Miami require particular attention. Reforms in governmental structure aimed at boosting black representation and providing more direct linkages between black officials and the problems of black neighborhoods do not, by themselves, guarantee substantive changes in local public policy. Yet such reforms—especially district elections, a role for political parties in local politics, and the institution of a strong-mayor form of government—present themselves as the most obvious first step in securing enduring representation for each group on local government policy-making bodies and in strengthening political leadership.

Miami's experiences may also point to the possibility of Hispanics emerging as a dominant force in the politics of some cities. With the rapid growth of Latin populations, especially as a result of new immigration, Hispanics may increasingly achieve political power on their own, without support from white or black coalitions. Such a pattern may prove to be especially evident in cities like Miami, where Hispanic economic and political incorporation are complementary.

Finally, although it is a new twist in the urban politics literature, the alienation and even the underrepresentation of white residents in cities with large minority populations, and the phenomenon of white flight, will likely demand increased attention from policymakers and students of urban politics alike. While such problems are in many ways different in character and degree from those of groups that historically have been disenfranchised in American politics, they nonetheless relate to the continued viability of our cities and the representative nature of their governments. The somewhat related issues of private economic power, the deference that should or should not be accorded it by local government, and the role of business in shaping important public policies are even more complex, and involve questions of political-economic alternatives not encompassed in this analysis. Ultimately, while each urban area faces its own unique circumstances relating to minority political mobilization and incorporation, Miami may represent a microcosm of change, conflict, and adaptation which could rapidly alter previous explanations of minority politics in America's cities.

REFERENCES

Arboleya, Carlos J. 1980. *The Cuban Community 1980: Coming of Age as History Repeats Itself.* Miami: Barnet Bank.
Banfield, Edward C., and James Q. Wilson. 1963. *City Politics.* New York: Vintage.

Browning, Rufus P., Dale Rogers Marshall, and David H. Tabb. 1984. *Protest Is Not Enough: The Struggle of Blacks and Hispanics for Equality in Urban Politics.* Berkeley: University of California Press.

Dugger, Celia W. 1987. MMAP Losing Punch. *Miami Herald*, July 17, p. 1C.

Eisinger, Peter K. 1980. *The Politics of Displacement.* New York: Academic Press.

Fainstein, Susan S., Norman I. Fainstein, Richard Child Hill, Dennis R. Judd, and Michael Peter Smith. 1986. *Restructuring the City: The Political Economy of Urban Redevelopment.* New York: Longman.

Freedberg, Sydney P., and Luis Feldstein Soto. 1989. Miami Splinters in Three Parts. *Miami Herald*, February 13, p. 1B.

Johnson, Dirk. 1987. The View From the Poorest U.S. Suburbs. *New York Times*, April 30, p. 10.

Levine, Barry B. 1985. The Capital of Latin America. *The Wilson Quarterly* (Winter): 46–69.

Luytjes, Jan B. 1979. Black Entrepreneurship in Dade County. Miami: College of Business, Florida International University.

Marable, Manning. 1980. The Fire This Time: The Miami Rebellion, May 1980. *The Black Scholar* 11 (July): 2–18.

Marquis, Christopher. 1989. Cubans Still Better Off Than Other Latins. *Miami Herald*, February 6, p. 1B.

Mohl, Raymond A. 1983. Miami: The Ethnic Cauldron. In Richard M. Bernard and Bradley R. Rice, eds., *Sunbelt Cities: Politics and Growth Since World War II.* Austin: University of Texas Press.

Mohl, Raymond A. 1984. Miami's Metropolitan Government: Retrospect and Prospect. *Florida Historical Quarterly* (July): 24–50.

Mohl, Raymond A. 1987. Trouble in Paradise: Race and Housing in Miami During the New Deal Era. *Prologue* 19:7–21.

Metro-Dade Planning Department. 1986. *Hispanic Profile: Dade County's Hispanic Origin Population.*

Porter, Bruce, and Marvin Dunn. 1984. *The Miami Riot of 1980: Crossing the Bounds.* Lexington: Lexington Books.

Resnick, Rosalind, and Lore Croghan. 1989. After the Storm. *Miami Herald*, January 22, p. 1F.

Rich, Wilbur C. 1987. Coleman Young and Detroit Politics: 1973–1986. In Michael B. Preston, Lenneal J. Henderson, Jr., and Paul L. Puryear, eds., *The New Black Politics: The Search for Political Power*, 2d ed. New York: Longman.

Sofen, Edward. 1961. Problems of Metropolitan Leadership: The Miami Experience. *Midwest Journal of Political Science.* 5(1):18–38.

Sofen, Edward. 1966. *The Miami Metropolitan Experiment*, 2nd ed. New York: Doubleday Anchor.

Soto, Luis Feldstein. 1988. Donors Hedged Their Bets. *Miami Herald*, October 10, p. 1B.

Strategy Research Corporation. 1988. The 1989 South Florida Latin Market.

Warren, Christopher L. 1984. Hispanics. In Manning J. Dauer, ed., *Florida's Politics and Government*, 2d ed. Gainesville, Fla.: University Presses of Florida.

Warren, Christopher L., and John F. Stack, Jr. 1987. Immigration and the Politics of Ethnicity and Class in Metropolitan Miami. In John F. Stack, Jr., ed., *The Primordial Challenge: Ethnicity in the Contemporary World.* Westport, Conn.: Greenwood.

CHAPTER 10

Coalition Politics in San Antonio and Denver: The Cisneros and Peña Mayoral Campaigns

Carlos Muñoz, Jr. , and Charles Henry

Editors' Note

Like Miami, Denver and San Antonio present cases of Latino political mobilization and the election of Latino mayors. But the Latino populations of Denver and San Antonio, unlike Miami, are almost entirely Mexican American. In San Antonio, persons of Mexican descent are actually a majority of the population; in Denver, Latinos constitute only 19 percent of the population. These variations suggest a number of questions. Are Cuban American and Mexican American politics different or similar? How is it possible that Federico Peña could be elected mayor when the Latino population of Denver is so small? Why did it take so long for a Mexican American to be elected mayor in San Antonio?

When Mexican Americans do gain the mayor's office, what sorts of programs emerge? What difference does it make to the nature of a Latino-led coalition when a majority of the population is Latino, as in San Antonio, versus the much smaller percentage in Denver? Muñoz and Henry's answers to these and other questions suggest both that black and Latino politics are different and that different Latino groups produce different politics. Muñoz and Henry also argue that rainbow coalitions, which are class-based and multiracial, are necessary to produce programs which significantly reduce social and economic inequality.

The election of African American and Mexican American mayors in big cities during the past decade has provided the opportunity to critically examine the role of minority mobilization and coalitions. The focus of this study is on the election of Henry Cisneros in San Antonio in 1981 and Federico Peña in Denver in 1983. The pioneering study by Browning, Marshall, and Tabb (1984) highlights the significance of minority mayoral elections in the context of the struggle for political equality. We have placed our analysis in the context of the three central questions underscored in their theory of political incorporation: How open are urban political systems to minorities? How does minority political incorporation occur? Does political incorporation make a difference for minority interests? Although the cities we examine are different in some respects from the Northern California cities covered by Browning, Marshall, and Tabb, their findings are generally applicable with modifications.

SAN ANTONIO

How Open Is the System?

San Antonio, Texas, is a unique city. It is unique in being the only "Mexican" large city in the United States. Whereas Los Angeles has the largest population of people of Mexican descent in the country and Chicago has more Latinos, those populations do not constitute the majority as in the case of San Antonio. It is also a unique city because although it has been a city with a majority population of Mexican descent, Mexican Americans historically have not been able to control it. Political change has taken place in recent years. The election of Henry Cisneros as mayor of San Antonio is evidence of it. It had been 140 years since a person of Mexican descent was the mayor of the city.

Historically, San Antonio has had a closed political system. City government had been dominated by political machines controlled by white local business elites. Mexican Americans and later African Americans were systematically excluded from meaningful participation in both the electoral process and within the apparatus of the political machine. The percentage of the African American and Mexican American population has declined over the centuries although it has grown numerically. When San Antonio was founded, 70 percent of the population was of Mexican origin. At the time of the election of Cisneros, it was 54 percent. The African American population was 8 percent, for a total nonwhite population of 62 percent (Brischetto and de la Garza, 1985).

How Did Incorporation Occur?

From the 1880s until approximately the 1940s, white political machines were able to maintain power through various tactics and mechanisms. Foremost was the system of patronage. Mexican American workers were bought off by the machine when they were given low-paid jobs for their votes. The system lasted until military bases were built in San Antonio during World War II. Those bases opened up jobs controlled by the federal civil service system and not the political machines. Poll taxes, complicated voter registration requirements, and lack of opportunities in education and in professions kept Mexican Americans "in their place." In 1951, the last political machine, the Good Government League (GGL), was created, and it successfully controlled city politics for over two decades. The GGL worked closely with a small and select group of Mexican American small businessmen for the purpose of running token candidates at election time. One or two at most were elected to the city council that was always dominated by a white majority. In 1965, as a direct result of the Voting Rights Act of 1965, the GGL supported the election of the first African American to the council.

Control of the electoral process was largely maintained through a system of at-large elections. In spite of the majority Mexican American population, whites always outnumbered them in the ranks of the registered voters and most important, they always had higher turnouts at the polls (Brischetto and de la Garza, 1985).

The first challenge to the GGL came from the Mexican American Youth Organization (MAYO) during the late 1960s and early 1970s. MAYO was largely a student organization and part of the Chicano Power Movement. It eventually evolved into the La Raza Unida Party, a Chicano political party that first took power in Crystal City, Texas, in 1970. Mexican American candidates supported by MAYO or those independent from the GGL were never able to win elections. But MAYO's presence in San Antonio politics contributed to the increasing militancy and political awareness among Mexican Americans of their political inequality. When MAYO and La Raza Unida Party declined in influence in the Mexican American community, another organization, the Communities Organized for Public Service (COPS), took their place and was able to mobilize Mexican Americans against city hall and the GGL. COPS was created in 1974 by organizers trained by Saul Alinsky and funded by the Catholic Church of San Antonio. COPS departed from the radical orientations of the former organizations and was not even defined as a civil rights or protest organization but as a "coalition of pressure groups dedicated to the pursuit of concrete improvements in the everyday standard of living" (Booth, 1983). Compared to the other groups, COPS grew out of the discontent "among many lower-middle class homeowners and other residents of the largely poor west side with their substandard public services" (Booth, 1983). The organization became a potent political force in city politics when it contributed to the passage of a referendum restricting further expansion and growth of the northern part of the city. COPS called into question the policies advocated and implemented by the city council designed to further the aims of the white business elite.

The GGL began to lose its grip on city government in 1971 primarily because of internal splits among the city's white businessmen. In 1973 the GGL candidate for mayor lost the election for the first time. Despite its declining power, the GGL continued to be central to city politics until 1977, when the city electoral process was changed from an at-large to a single-member district system as a result of lawsuits instigated by the Mexican American Legal Defense Fund under the Voting Rights Act. This change in the rules of political representation was the final blow to the GGL because it made possible a takeover of the city council by a minority coalition of Mexican Americans and African Americans in the election of 1977. However, the coalition lost its majority on the city council 2 years later when a Mexican American councilman narrowly lost his reelection bid to his white challenger. At the time of Cisneros's mayoral victory in 1981, the council was composed of 50 percent white and 50 percent minority (one African American and four Mexican Americans).

Has Incorporation Made a Difference?

Henry Cisneros was one of the city councilmen who played a central role in the transformation of the city's electoral process. He had been elected to the city council in 1975 as the Mexican American candidate of the GGL. Cisneros, however, did not prove to be the typical token Mexican American candidate of the GGL. He had become part of the GGL slate in the 1975 election primary as a result of family connections to the political machine. After losing the mayor's race for the first time in 1973, the GGL leadership had been searching for new bases of power and was willing to accept newcomers to their slates who did not necessarily conform to the GGL's style (Diehl and Jarboe, 1985).

Cisneros, elected with 52 percent of the total vote, received more votes from whites than he got from Mexican Americans. Once on the city council, however, he proved himself adept at working with both GGL interest groups and COPS. He allied himself with COPS on several key issues related to improvements in those communities represented by the organization. In the 1977 election, Cisneros was reelected to the council with 92 percent of the total vote. But by the time he ran for mayor, the alliance with COPS no longer existed. When he announced his candidacy for Mayor of San Antonio, Cisneros had established himself both in the Mexican American community and in the white business community. As a city councilman he had preached and practiced a politics of compromise and consensus. He made clear that he did not see the role of minority politicians as "dealing exclusively with social programs, voting rights, and police brutality but instead . . . concentrating their energies on economic development in the private sector" (Diehl and Jarboe, 1985).

Cisneros' ability to get wide support from white business elites proved to be the significant factor in his victory over his opponent, white millionaire John Steen. He was able to raise $247,000 for his campaign, but most important, he blocked Steen's strategy to label Cisneros as an antibusiness candidate.

On April 4, 1981, Henry Cisneros was elected mayor with 61.8 percent of the vote. He received nearly 100 percent of the Mexican American vote and 45 percent of the white vote. He became the youngest mayor at age 33 in the history of the city, the first Mexican American mayor of a major city, and most important, the first mayor to win as a result of the most diverse coalition in city history that included

Mexican Americans, African Americans, whites, conservatives and liberals, environmentalists, and expansionists. His victory was not a major blow against the GGL, since that political machine had been defeated years prior, but it did represent a final step in the direction of minority political incorporation in San Antonio.

Did the election of Cisneros translate into actual Mexican American political power? It did not for two primary reasons. In the first place the mayor of San Antonio does not have any real power to make changes. City government is a weak mayor–strong city council system with a city manager. Cisneros inherited a white city manager with his own agenda and priorities for the city of San Antonio. Second, outside of the Mexican American community, Cisneros does not promote either his Mexican American identity or the specific interests of that community.

DENVER

How Open Is the System?

In contrast to San Antonio, Denver has never been a Mexican city. Mexican Americans have not been the dominant population nor have they had much access to the corridors of political power through the doors of the city council. Historically, the Denver political system has been closed to minorities.

In 1971 as a direct consequence of the Voting Rights Act, the all-white Denver city council designed a plan for redistricting in the interest of maximizing minority representation on the council. Four new districts were created. Eight and eleven were designated "black districts" and three and nine were called "Mexican American districts." The first city election under the new redistricting plan took place in May of 1971. Two African Americans were elected to the city council but two whites were elected to the "Mexican American seats" on the council.

A study of the election provided several explanations for the failure of Mexican American candidates to win their two council seats (Lovrich and Marenin, 1976). They did not win, because Mexican Americans had lower rates of voter registration and turnout than did white voters. Second, compared with African Americans, Mexican Americans who did vote did not do so as an ethnic bloc. In District Three, the white candidate received 45 percent of the Mexican American vote and in District Nine, he received 35 percent of the Mexican American vote.

In short, the data showed that African Americans were better politically mobilized than Mexican Americans. African American voters preferred the expression "black identity" over the term "Negro" by 52 percent to 29 percent, thus reflecting a certain amount of militant or protest-oriented political consciousness. Mexican American voters, in comparison, reflected a complete lack of consensus over any particular ethnic label. They identified themselves with terms ranging from the militant Chicano label to Mexican, Mexican American, Hispano, Spanish, and Spanish-American. Of all those terms, "Chicano" was least mentioned. Whereas 41 percent of African American voters identified themselves as "liberal," an overwhelming number of Mexican American voters declined to state their ideological orientation. More effective electoral mobilization in the Mexican American community eventually overcame the results of the 1971 election. Three Mexican Americans were subsequently elected to the thirteen-seat city council.

How Did Incorporation Occur?

When Federico Peña decided to run for mayor in 1983, few if any politically astute observers of Denver politics predicted that a Mexican American could ever be elected mayor. Mexican Americans had difficulty enough getting elected to the city council in their own districts. The odds were therefore against any Mexican American winning a citywide election when only 18 percent of the city's population was of Mexican descent. Peña, a 36-year-old Mexican American lawyer, nevertheless won the election by a narrow margin of 51 percent to 49 percent over his opponent, Dale Tooley. His victory was proclaimed a political miracle by the chairman of Denver's Democratic Party.

Why did Peña win? In contrast to Cisneros, Peña was not the beneficiary of a successful grass-roots organization like COPS in San Antonio. The Mexican American vote was not the result of mass mobilization in the community either before or after Peña announced his candidacy. There has not been a strong Mexican American organization in the Denver area since the late 1960s and early 1970s. Mexican American political leadership in Denver has been historically fragmented. In fact, Peña did not receive the endorsement of some of the established Mexican American politicians and community leaders. He did, however, receive a high percentage of the Mexican American vote because of his proven track record for them in the state legislature. Although he did not campaign as a Mexican American candidate and his identity did not play a role in his campaign, it was obvious that he was a Mexican American to the people of his community.

It was during the time he served in the state legislature that Peña planted the seeds for his eventual victory. He established his credentials with liberal legislators and in particular with influential figures like Governor Richard Lamm and U.S. Senator Gary Hart. He was elected as minority leader of the Colorado state legislature in his second and last term of office, thus reflecting his immense popularity with white elected officials. It was from the liberal sector of the statewide Democratic party that Peña was to receive encouragement and support for his candidacy. The key personnel of his campaign, including the campaign manager, came from the Lamm and Hart organizations.

Peña won also because Denver was ripe for a change. The city was in a period of profound transition in its values and issues. The incumbent administration was perceived as old, tired, stale, and of closed-mind about expansion and growth. In contrast, Peña's supporters epitomized the young professionals committed to the modernization of Denver. Second, elections being nonpartisan, the Democratic party could not officially endorse any one candidate from the party. Several prominent party candidates ran and therefore split the vote enabling the newcomer Peña to make the runoff.

The Peña campaign reflected a viable coalition of diverse groups. In addition to Mexican Americans, it was composed of representatives from labor, the elderly, the physically disabled, gays, women, and environmentalists. He was also supported by the incumbent mayor's brother, white millionaires such as oilman Marvin Davis and land developer Lee Ambrose, and after the primary, the coalition expanded to include African Americans. The African American mayoral candidate Wellington Wells was one of the six candidates defeated by Peña in the primary. Peña was endorsed by the local conservative newspaper *Rocky Mountain News* and generally received excellent coverage from all of the media.

Peña's campaign strategy was to stress broad-based issues and project himself as the candidate of all of the people. The themes of his campaign were "leadership," "vision," and "Denver as an open city," captured in his campaign slogan, "Imagine a Great City." Peña projected a "fresh approach" as contrasted to the "good old boy" approach of his opponent, Dale Tooley. The specific issues that Peña spoke to were the building up of the neighborhoods, access to city government for all people, the reorganization of the police department for better policing of the streets, the reorganization of six city agencies with jurisdiction over economic development policies and enforcement, the need for increased state aid for the city, and the review of city contracts and investment policies. Although these issues were relevant to Mexican Americans and African Americans, Peña did not address them as ethnic issues.

Has Incorporation Made a Difference?

In his victory speech, Peña stated that "Denver was not Chicago" because "race was never an issue." No doubt, however, he was aware of exit polls that in fact reflected anti-Mexican attitudes. This awareness, coupled with the fact that Mexican American and African Americans together comprise only 30 percent of the city's population and even less of the city's registered voters, made it difficult for him to initially appoint minorities to his cabinet, although he did appoint them eventually. To four out of eight cabinet positions he appointed three women (one Mexican American and two white) and one African American. He also appointed one Mexican American male and one white woman to serve on two out of four sub-cabinet positions.

Did the Peña victory signal the incorporation of Mexican Americans into the city's political system? Have conditions for them and African Americans improved with the administration of a Mexican American mayor? The answers remain unclear. Like San Antonio, Denver is now a more open city, but it remains to be seen if the previously powerless minorities will take advantage of this new access. If the Mexican American leadership continues to be fragmented, it will not make a difference. If Mayor Peña does not address the reality of Mexican American social and political inequality in Denver, it also will not make a difference. As with Cisneros, it is unlikely he will do so since to maintain power he must address the interests of the Denver white business elite. Nevertheless, he does have more power than Cisneros to make changes since Denver's city government is a strong mayor system.

Elections of 1987

Both Cisneros and Peña won reelection in 1987. Cisneros won a fourth term handily by a margin of 67 percent to his challenger's 31 percent. Peña, on the other hand, had to fight for his political life. He came in second in a field of eight mayoral candidates and narrowly beat his Republican opponent by a margin of 51 percent to 49 percent in the run-off election.

Why did Peña have a more difficult time getting reelected? In contrast to Cisneros, Peña has been the mayor of a strong mayor type city government. He therefore was held directly accountable by the voters for all the problems of the city during his first tenure in office. Cisneros as a weak mayor in a strong city council–city manager system was not held to the same level of accountability from San Antonio voters. He has enjoyed consistently favorable press coverage at the local, state, and national political levels. Even his opponents in the Mexican American COPS organization praised him for the job he has done in steering the city "away from deep racial and economic rifts" and, in particular, for promoting a "politics of inclusion" (LaFranchi, 1988).

Although a powerless mayor, Cisneros has done an excellent job of public relations for the city of San Antonio and has been given credit for many of the city's improvements over the years. His critics accurately state that Cisneros has the "best image-builders money can buy" (Cantu, 1987). Texas as a whole has been in an economic crisis because of the decline of production in the oil industry. But San Antonio has enjoyed relative prosperity in the face of hard times elsewhere. During Cisneros' tenure "the largest volume of construction in the city's history" has taken place (Cantu, 1987). The projects under construction were packaged by Cisneros as part of his "Target '90: Goals for San Antonio." Under construction were 200 street improvements, a new downtown luxury hotel, a "giant Sea World theme park and a shopping mall with a stream running through the middle" (Cantu, 1987). His supporters have ignored the high cost of these projects reflected in substantial local tax increases.

San Antonio has also prospered as a result of Cisneros' promotion of the city's image as the tourist and hospitality capital of Texas. The city has also been given the reputation as a "model of peaceful race relations" (Cantu, 1987). In short, Cisneros enjoyed a relatively stable three terms before his 1987 reelection. No doubt his success also can be attributed to his ability to maintain good standing with both white business elites and the Mexican American community.

Peña's near defeat reflected the fact that he happened to be the mayor during the severest economic downturn in recent Denver history. Peña was not able to garner the support necessary from political and economic elites to turn the tide against a depressed city economy created by the slump in oil prices. His efforts to build a convention center and new airport as part of his plan for the city's economic recovery met with stiff opposition from both economic elites and the city council. At the time of his first election, Denver's economy was booming and his campaign slogan of "Imagine a Great City" generated high expectations for his tenure in office. Instead, the office vacancy rate in downtown Denver increased by 31 percent, among the highest in the nation, and unemployment rose to 9.1 percent, the highest on record (Knudson, 1987).

Peña lost the support of important Democratic Party leaders and never had a majority of the city council behind him. The city's two major newspapers, which endorsed him in his first election, endorsed his Republican opponent. In short, Peña was blamed for Denver's problems. His coalition of white professionals, gays and lesbians, labor, Asian Americans, African Americans, and Mexican Americans, minus some white business elites, proved to be strong enough at the end to make a narrow reelection victory possible. After his victory, Peña strengthened his coalition by replacing two top whites in his administration with one African American and one Mexican American administrator. Those he replaced were the main targets of criticism by the business sector who opposed his reelection. Thus, he also took a significant step in the direction of mending fences with those business elites who had withdrawn their support and bringing them back into his original coalition.

PROSPECTS

What are the prospects for strong rainbow coalitions in San Antonio and Denver? In Denver, it remains to be seen whether African Americans will continue to be a central component of the Peña coalition. So far, Peña has made some efforts to integrate African Americans and Mexican Americans into the city's power structure. But the Peña coalition continues to be dominated by white political and business elites, although he lost some of their support in his bid for reelection.

In San Antonio, Cisneros has the option of building an organization in the minority community that could result in African Americans and Mexican Americans becoming a dominant force in the Cisneros coalition. However, past experience and Cisneros' own political ambitions indicate he will continue to reach out for white support. It seems likely that white business elites will continue to be the dominant force in his coalition. In 1988, Cisneros announced that his fourth term as mayor would be his last and that his plans for the future included employment in the corporate sector. The potential for a viable rainbow coalition in San Antonio after the departure of Cisneros nevertheless exists as it does in Denver. Given the reality of business domination of the existing mayoral coalitions in those two cities, it is unlikely that Mexican Americans in those coalitions will move in that direction. For example, neither Cisneros nor Peña endorsed Jesse Jackson for the Democratic Party presidential nomination in 1984 or 1988. In 1984 Cisneros was a Mondale man and Peña a Hart supporter. They both supported Dukakis in 1988.

There is also the reality of basic mistrust among African Americans and Mexican Americans, which has been exploited by both liberal and conservative politicians. In general, African Americans perceive Mexican Americans as white and not as fellow people of color. Most Mexican Americans do not identify themselves as nonwhite, as shown by their growing preference for the term "Hispanic." According to the dictionary meaning, "Hispanics" refers to those who "are lovers of Spain and Spanish culture." There is nothing in the term that relates to any of the nonwhite indigenous cultures of the Americas, Africa, and Asia, which historically have produced multicultural and multiracial Latino peoples in Latin America and the United States. The term "Hispanic" also ignores the complexities of a multitude of different cultural groups, each with its own unique history, class realities, and experience in the United States. Most may share the common denominator of the Spanish language, but not share the same extent of racial and class inequality. Most Latino politicians have historically promoted a white identity for Latinos and this has contributed to a lack of interest in building rainbow coalitions. In addition, the complexity of the Latino racial identity, in contrast to that of African Americans, has made it difficult to mobilize Latinos along racial lines. The racial complexity notwithstanding, the majority of Latinos are nonwhite, and the prospects for coalition building with African Americans will be enhanced if they are accurately perceived as people of color (Munōz, 1989, pp. 8–12).

COMPARISONS

The findings of the Browning, Marshall, and Tabb study are generally applicable to the two cities we have examined. In turn, our findings appear to support their theory of political incorporation with some modifications. In both cases, Mexican American mayors were elected as a direct result of effective liberal coalitions. As their theory posits, the relative size of the minority population, liberal white support, and the organizational development and political experience of African Americans and Mexican Americans were critical minority resources for electoral mobilization.

Denver and San Antonio also deviate somewhat from the experience of the Northern California cities covered by Browning, Marshall, and Tabb. As pointed out in our analysis, Peña was not the product of minority electoral mobilization or of demand–protest. Established Mexican American politicians did not endorse his candidacy. Peña did receive the majority of the Mexican American and African American vote, but the crucial support for his campaign came from the white liberal sector. Peña's election more closely resembles that of Wilson Goode in Philadelphia in 1983. Like Peña, Goode had gained the support of influential white liberal politicians in his bid for mayor. Just as Peña benefited from his identification with Governor Lamm and Senator Hart, Goode was linked to a liberal reform tradition that began in 1951 with Joseph Clark as mayor and carried through to Goode's predecessor William Green, Jr. Although both Philadelphia's African American and liberal white communities were alienated from the white ethnic machine that brought former Police Chief Frank Rizzo to power in 1971, Goode was more identified with the liberal white opposition than with such African American leaders as Charles Bowser and Lucien Blackwell. Nonetheless, African Americans as well as liberal whites supported Goode's candidacy.

In San Antonio, Cisneros has the base to create a nonwhite dominant coalition similar to that of Harold Washington in Chicago. Washington relied on an extremely large African American voter turnout along with Latino support to defeat the remnants of the Daley machine. However, Chicago has a strong-mayor system, which gave Washington resources Cisneros lacks. Moreover, as noted, Cisneros has larger political ambitions that would be jeopardized by any coalition that excluded influential neoliberal or neoconservative whites.

In both Denver and San Antonio, Mexican Americans have achieved stronger incorporation than African Americans. The relatively small size of the latter population in both of these cities is no doubt a factor for this deviation from the Browning, Marshall, and Tabb findings. But in both cases, it was the white vote and not the African American vote that was critical to the election of Peña and Cisneros. In the case of the Northern California cities, African American support was more important than white support for Latinos.

CONCLUSION

Our evidence suggests that the political systems of Denver and San Antonio have reached a level of openness as a result of substantial minority political incorporation. African Americans and Mexican Americans have indeed achieved a measure of direct access to the policy-making process by virtue of the election of minority mayors. We agree with Browning, Marshall, and Tabb that this represents a major step forward toward eventual political equality. Whether full equality for minorities is possible within the confines of a capitalist democracy remains to be seen. Liberal reforms to date have not significantly contributed to the reduction of socioeconomic inequality. Racial, gender, and class oppression continues to be a fact of life for most Mexican Americans and African Americans. The struggle for equality will continue, and given the limited options available to minorities, the electoral arena is no doubt an important place to wage the struggle. Whether it be demand–protest or electoral politics or both, it will be crucial for people of color to continue efforts to develop biracial, multiracial, and multiethnic coalitions. Rainbow coalitions will be crucial if minorities are to wage a successful struggle against conservative policies at the local, state, and national levels.

REFERENCES

Booth, John. 1983. Political Change in San Antonio, 1970–1982: Toward Decay or Democracy? In David R. Johnson, et al., eds., *The Politics of San Antonio*. Lincoln: University of Nebraska Press.

Brischetto, Robert R., and Rodolfo O. de la Garza. 1985. *The Mexican American Electorate: Political Opinions and Behavior Across Cultures in San Antonio*. Occasional Paper No. 5. San Antonio: Southwest Voter Registration Project.

Browning, Rufus P., Dale Rogers Marshall, and David H. Tabb. 1984. *Protest Is Not Enough*. Berkeley: University of California Press.

Cantu, Tony. 1987. Cisneros Decision Not to Seek Statewide Texas Post May Be Only a Detour En Route to National Office. *The Wall Street Journal*, September 10, 1987, p. 4.

Diehl, Kemper, and Jan Jarboe. 1985. *Cisneros: Portrait of a New American*. San Antonio: Corona Publishing Co.

Knudson, Thomas J. 1987. *The New York Times*, May 15, 1987.

LaFranchi, Howard. 1988. Cisneros Bows Out—for Now: San Antonio Mayor Has Been One of US's Leading Hispanics. *The Christian Science Monitor*, September 14, 1988, p. 3.

Lovrich, Nicholas P., Jr., and Otwin Marenin. 1976. A Comparison of Black and Mexican American Voters in Denver: Assertive versus Acquiescent Political Orientations and Voting Behavior in an Urban Electorate. *The Western Political Quarterly*, 29 (June): 284–294.

Munõz, Carlos, Jr. 1989. *Youth, Identity Power: The Chicano Movement*. London: Verso Press.

PART VI
Strategies and Prospects

CHAPTER 11

Biracial Coalitions in Big Cities: Why They Succeed, Why They Fail

Raphael J. Sonenshein

Editors' Note

Politically excluded groups often debate the best strategies to improve their position. Should they go it alone or form coalitions? If they enter into coalitions, will an appeal to shared ideology be sufficient to hold the coalition together, or will it be necessary to make major concessions to the material interests of the other members? For example, will biracial liberal coalitions be able to increase black employment in city government rapidly, or will it be necessary to protect the employment interests of whites in order to retain white support? More generally, can minorities trust liberal whites to support a bi- or multiracial coalition if white interests are adversely affected by the coalition's commitments to its minority members?

Working out—and reworking—the terms of a coalition are the central tasks of leadership. The terms of a coalition determine its membership, shape the thrust of its policy commitments, and set its chances of success. The nature of the concessions that minority groups have to make to secure white support is at the core of the broader question: Can the political incorporation of minority groups secure anything more than modest benefits, limited to the middle-class and elite members of those groups?

Contrary to the conclusions reached by some students of these matters, Sonenshein argues from the evidence of New York, Chicago, and Los Angeles that shared ideology may indeed form the core commitment of successful biracial or multiracial coalitions. A common ideological vision, properly nurtured and articulated, may dampen at least some of the destructive potential of conflict over interests. On the other hand, the structure of group interests and the way in which emerging issues engage them and make them salient can also undermine a coalition and bring about its demise.

Sonenshein advocates a two-part strategy—organizing around black interests but also maintaining ideological links with liberal whites: "Goodwill alone is not enough, but neither is cold self-interest" (p. 204). His analysis of leadership, group interests, political vision, and the management of issues holds many lessons for activists and leaders alike.

We believe that political relations are based on self-interest: benefits to be gained and losses to be avoided. For the most part, man's politics is determined by his evaluation of material good and evil. Politics results from a conflict of interests, not of consciences. (Carmichael and Hamilton, 1967, p. 75)

Liberals on race issues are very different from conservatives, and ideology has an important influence on the nature and outcome of the minority struggle for access to local government. (Browning et al., 1984, p. 248)

The debate over the viability of biracial coalition politics has been an enduring and intensely argued one. Should blacks go it alone and bargain with the larger society, or do they need to form alliances as a result of their minority status? And if they make alliances, with whom should they link their fate?

On the more specific subject of biracial coalitions between blacks and white liberals, there are optimists and pessimists. The optimistic view calls for efforts to strengthen links between blacks and white liberals in addition to the need for black mobilization. The pessimistic view suggests that blacks should aim primarily at black unity and mobilization and be wary of alliances with white liberals.

During the civil rights movement of the 1950s and 1960s, the optimistic view of an alliance based on shared beliefs in racial equality was widely accepted. However, after the rise of bitter racial conflict in the mid-1960s, liberal biracialism fell under serious challenge. Racial troubles in northern cities where support had been strong for the southern civil rights movement suggested to some that even liberal white allies could not be trusted to maintain the coalition if their own interests were threatened. The most powerful statement of this pessimistic position was made by Carmichael and Hamilton in their book *Black Power* (1967). Persistent racial division over black mayoral candidacies added to the bleak picture portrayed for liberal biracialism (Kleppner, 1985; Bullock and Campbell, 1984).

Arguments have still been made for biracial politics. While pessimists have cited black unity as the key to black mayoral victories, optimists have noted the margin provided by white liberal support for the same black candidates (Cole,

1974). The difference in defining these identical events shows the opposed perspectives on biracialism. In a major formulation of a moderately optimistic view, Browning, Marshall, and Tabb (1984) argued that white liberals hold significantly different racial views from white conservatives and that the presence of active white liberals in a community greatly enhances black (and Latino) political success. In their study of ten northern California cities, Browning, Marshall, and Tabb found that black political success depended on a combination of black numbers and mobilization and white liberal support.

While the debate over biracial coalitions is highly political and pragmatic, it is also an argument over a *theory* of biracial coalitions. The optimists focus on the role of *ideology* and emphasize the enduring and solid character of biracial coalitions based on common beliefs. The pessimists tend to see *interest* as the glue of coalitions and to view biracial coalitions as at best short-lived tactical compromises between self-centered groups.

An active scholarly debate on racial issues divides along roughly the same lines. One school of thought suggests that preexisting racial attitudes deeply influence perception of racial issues; in this sense, racial politics is at its root ideological (Kinder and Sears, 1981). Regardless of the political situation, some whites are more racially liberal than others and this attitude shapes their political actions. A contrasting view holds that racial conflict can be understood as a realistic power struggle between groups. As whites identify with other whites in the face of a black challenge, they protect their group interests through racial hostility (Giles and Evans, 1986). In this view, political actions are affected by the political situation of individuals and groups. Thus the study of biracial electoral coalitions between blacks and white liberals can be seen as a test case in a more general debate about the roots of racial conflict and cooperation.

It is not easy to separate ideology and interest. Kinder and Sanders (1987), for example, interpreted realistic group conflict as ideological because it is ''symbolic'' and unrelated to individual self-interest. This chapter, however, seeks to maintain a line between interest and ideology. Ideology is a set of beliefs that influence political actions regardless of the political situation. Interest is an incentive to action that varies with the realities of group or individual competition. This approach is true to the spirit of the debate over black–liberal coalitions: *goodwill* versus *practical calculation.*

This chapter argues that the success of a biracial electoral coalition between blacks and white liberals depends primarily on ideology, but with a secondary role for interest. Racial attitudes structure political choices in American politics (Carmines and Stimson, 1982). A person who strongly dislikes blacks is highly unlikely to be a prospective member of a biracial coalition, especially if one of the coalition's explicit goals is black political incorporation. Despite the great variety of political situations from city to city, the white base for black politics seems to be highly consistent.

Whites who support black mayoral candidates tend to be young, well-educated, and liberal on social issues. This tends to be the base for liberal reform as well. Jews are disproportionately represented among those who vote for black candidates (Pettigrew, 1972; Cole, 1974; Ransom, 1987).

In political matters where race is an issue, common economic interest is unlikely to override racial hostility. Davidson's study of Houston, for instance, argued that economic interests would eventually bring blacks and poor whites together into a class-based radical coalition (1972). However, in the face of black candidacies this class alliance collapsed in many southern settings (Murray and Vedlitz, 1978). Eisinger's study of Milwaukee (1976), a city with a large white working-class population, concluded that racial attitudes were so polarized that leaders had limited freedom to create a durable biracial coalition. (One area in which economic interest may override racial attitudes is in the close relationship between black mayor regimes and white business leaders. This chapter separates conservative business leaders from white liberals. In fact, these two groups of whites often operate as direct opponents in city politics.)

While racial liberalism is necessary for the creation of a biracial coalition, it is not sufficient. Like most political coalitions, biracial coalitions are influenced by interest. The interests of white liberals may conflict with black interests. Interest alliance, or at least the absence of interest conflict, is a sufficient condition for creating a strong biracial coalition.

Political coalitions are vehicles created and sustained by leaders on a base of group support (Hinckley, 1981). Leadership therefore is likely to be relevant to biracial coalitions. Leaders and organizers have an impact on how group interests are perceived. The prospects for biracial coalitions depend significantly on the willingness and ability of black and white leaders to create and sustain such coalitions. In racial matters, leaders may find it easier to overcome interest conflicts among ideological allies than to create an interest alliance among ideological foes.

While biracial coalitions between blacks and white liberals are viable on ideological grounds, they are not inevitable. Coalition outcomes are likely to change over time, even within the same community, although there may be a consistent pattern of coalition development.

Ideology, interest, and leadership will be explored in relation to biracial coalition dynamics in the nation's three largest cities—New York City, Chicago, and Los Angeles. Until the sudden death of Mayor Harold Washington in 1987, Chicago represented a black-dominated winning coalition that drew secondary support from Hispanics and a bloc of white liberals (Kleppner, 1985). Contemporary New York City is an example of minority exclusion from the ruling coalition, with blacks, Puerto Ricans, and white liberals mutually isolated and unable to form a challenging coalition (see Chapter 4). Los Angeles has a winning coalition linking blacks and white liberals, with a secondary role for Latinos (see Chapter 2).

The experiences of New York City and Chicago, the first and third most populous American cities, have been particularly important in the debate over biracial politics. What happens in these two cities affects political strategies and attitudes nationwide. In recent years both cities have been used to support the pessimistic view of biracial coalitions. Chicago illustrates the persistence of racial polarization and New York City is often cited to show the limits of black–liberal and black–Jewish relations. The experience of Los Angeles, America's second largest city, has received hardly any attention at all despite the presence of an important alternative model. Since 1973, Los Angeles politics has been dominated by a biracial coalition linking blacks and white liberals, particularly Jews, behind a popular black mayor; this coalition holds leadership in the city council and underlies the other two citywide officeholders (see Chapter 2). What is happening in Los Angeles that is not happening in New York City or Chicago? What can all three cities contribute to a theory of biracial coalitions?

The three cities are particularly useful because they represent alternative urban models. New York City and Chicago are both older cities with traditional party structures deriving from their industrialization period in the nineteenth century. In that sense, they share many qualities with a large number of eastern and midwestern cities. Liberalism and the norms of the welfare state have dominated New York City, while pragmatic governance by a political machine has been the leading force in Chicago.

Los Angeles is a model of the newer western cities developed in the later nineteenth and early twentieth centuries, shaped by midwestern Protestant migrants who hoped to devise an urban alternative to the ''old, corrupt'' cities of the east and midwest (Fogelson, 1967; Singleton, 1979). The antiparty norms of the Progressive movement found their greatest expression in the west (Shefter, 1983), and were central to the development of the Los Angeles political community. Party organization has been virtually nonexistent in Los Angeles (Adrian, 1959; Carney, 1964), representing the polar opposite of Chicago.

Only Chicago has a sufficient black population (nearly 40 percent) to make black mobilization the primary strategy. Both New York City and Los Angeles fall in the middle area of black population—large enough to compete but too small to depend on black mobilization alone. While both New York City and Chicago have large populations of European Catholic immigrant groups, New York City is by far the larger center of Jewish population. Together, metropolitan New York and Los Angeles hold 60 percent of America's Jews (Fisher, 1979).

Los Angeles has the largest Hispanic population (largely Latino) of the three cities and a significant Jewish population; it lacks the numerous working-class white Catholic group so prominent in New York City and Chicago. Its black population is the smallest of the three cities (see Table 11.1).

The three cities therefore provide different models in political culture and

TABLE 11.1. 1980 PERCENTAGE OF POPULATION

Group	New York	Chicago	Los Angeles
Black	25.2	39.8	16.7
Latino	19.9	14.0	27.5
Jewish (est.)	20.0	3.2	7.0

Source: U.S. Census, 1980.

demographics. In light of these differences, how has each city's biracial politics been affected by ideology, interest, and leadership?

IDEOLOGY

The optimistic argument suggests that where white racial liberalism is strongest, both in numbers and in prestige, black political success will be greatest. Where blacks are in a position to compete for power, in this view, white liberals will be essential to victory. Among the three cities, liberal reform has been strongest in New York City and the least imposing in Chicago. Los Angeles is in between.

Liberal reform is weakest in Chicago because reformers there have been unable to mount a significant challenge to the Chicago machine. The Democratic machine long dominated the city's political life. In recent years the Jewish community of Chicago has had a limited impact due to its small numbers and the small role played by liberal reform in the city (Cohen, 1969). By contrast, in Philadelphia, a city with about the same black population percentage as Chicago, a reform tradition created the basis for a strong biracial coalition behind a black mayor and lower racial polarization than in Chicago (see Chapter 3; Ransom 1987).

New York City is the spiritual home of American liberalism. The city operates a university, for many years free to all, as well as a network of public hospitals. It has been in the forefront of welfare services and an innovator in social policy. A high level of party strength has been counterbalanced by an effective, Manhattan-based reform movement that has competed successfully for citywide power.

Liberalism was profoundly weak for many generations in Los Angeles, but in recent decades has made strong inroads. Although the city had a heavy Democratic majority in voter registration, liberalism did not deeply influence Los Angeles until at least the mid-1950s. The vehicle was the biracial liberal coalition; minorities and liberals rose up together. Reform barriers to traditional party strength had the surely unintended consequence of clearing the way for the leadership of reform liberals, black and white. Despite the harder road for liberalism in Los Angeles compared to New York City, the higher prestige of reform (whether liberal or conservative) helped generate a solid base for reform liberalism.

By the standard of ideological politics, the strongest and most successful biracial politics ought to be found in New York City, followed by Los Angeles, and then by Chicago. Regardless of the level of biracial liberalism, black incorporation based on numbers alone ought to be highest in Chicago. Black and liberal numbers should rule New York City. Los Angeles should have the hardest road, because of the small black population and the mixed record of liberal strength. Of course, this is not the case. In fact, the linkage between black politics and white reform liberalism was stronger in Chicago during the Harold Washington era than in New York City.

Harold Washington's victory in the 1983 Chicago mayoral election was helped significantly by a late surge of votes from white reform liberals and his ruling regime depended on the support of a bloc of white liberal aldermen. Education and ideology were key electoral factors: "Whites who held a liberal ideology gave [Washington] over a third of their votes, and those who had attended graduate school gave him nearly half" (Kleppner, 1985, p. 221). Washington received 30.6 percent of Jewish votes in 1983, the highest white support he received.

In Chicago, even a small liberal community in a city with a black near-majority could hold the balance of power in a highly polarized election. (In the 1989 Democratic primary, low black turnout and the shift of liberal voters to Richard Daley's camp sealed Mayor Sawyer's defeat.) The same linkage occurred in Los Angeles, with far fewer blacks. Bradley's election in 1973 was based on a mobilized black community and the widespread support of white liberals. The educated, the politically liberal, and Jews were Bradley's strongest supporters (Hahn et al., 1976; Halley et al., 1976).

In two of the three cities, therefore, an ideological alliance between blacks and white liberals was essential to black political incorporation. There is solid grounding for the ideological explanation in the Chicago and Los Angeles outcomes. But the frequent failure of black political efforts in New York City, where liberal strength should be an asset, suggests a problem.

In this sense, New York City is "the great anomaly" (see Chapter 4). Why has Los Angeles found itself with strong biracial politics, while in New York City, the liberal center, biracial politics has been a mess? Why was there a functioning black regime with significant white liberal input in Chicago, where reform liberalism has low prestige? To more fully explain the situation it is necessary to explore the realm of interest, and the concepts originally presented by Carmichael and Hamilton.

INTEREST

Carmichael and Hamilton suggested that the ideological support given to blacks by white liberals is contingent on self-interest:

> We do not seek to condemn these groups for being what they are so much as we seek to emphasize a fact of life: they are unreliable allies when a conflict of interest arises. Morality and sentiment cannot weather such conflicts, and black people must realize this. (1967, p. 76)

Potential interest conflicts grow out of the nature of the city struggle for power and the extent to which the elected city government controls material stakes. When the minority struggle for political representation directly threatens the interests of white liberals, the odds of biracial politics ought to decline. Conflicts between blacks and white liberals should arise when white liberals hold public jobs, or have already achieved political incorporation when blacks challenge incumbent regimes or public institutions. Even the strongest ideology is unlikely to become a formula for a persistent reduction in self-interest.

The material stakes in city politics are far higher in Chicago and New York

City than in Los Angeles. In New York City, these stakes are the most likely to include the interests of white liberals. Unlike liberals in Chicago and Los Angeles, New York City's white liberals were concentrated in public jobs and heavily incorporated into ruling regimes. Thus the black movement was a much more direct threat to liberal interests.

Table 11.2 compares public jobs in the three cities in 1982. Clearly on a per capita basis, New York City (5.32) dwarfs Chicago (1.51) and Los Angeles (1.36) in its level of city-controlled public employment. Alone among the three cities, New York City's work force includes education and hospitals; these categories account for about one-third of city jobs. Surprisingly, reformed Los Angeles looks very similar to machine Chicago in numbers alone. But in Chicago many more of these jobs are politically controlled.

New York City lacks a central machine like the once-powerful Daley operation, but has a larger number of public jobs at stake due to its huge public investment. As the recent municipal scandals in New York City illustrate, a huge amount of discretion is exercised through city hall, the Democratic party, the borough presidents, the Board of Estimate, and the city council.

Education and hospitals are directly controlled by the city government in New York City, leading to gut-wrenching decisions by the mayor and other political leaders. The schools, for instance, are very much at stake in New York municipal elections and offer a basis for struggle between blacks and white liberals. In both New York City and Chicago, mayors make appointments to the board of education.

While Los Angeles has as many public jobs as Chicago, the level of political influence over the public sector is much lower. Political control of public hiring is limited in Los Angeles both by severe formal strictures and powerful local norms. The mayor controls no more than several hundred public jobs and the city council even fewer. The civil service system covers virtually everybody else, and there is a local premium on bringing people up through the merit system.

The separately elected Los Angeles Board of Education handles such sensitive questions as busing. While Los Angeles liberals hold some conservative opinions on such divisive issues as school busing and racial quotas (Caditz, 1976), busing has rarely been an issue in a mayoral election. Struggles between white liberals and racial minorities over whether schools should be open year-round (Woo, 1987) have thus far remained insulated from city hall.

TABLE 11.2. PUBLIC JOBS, 1982

	New York	Chicago	Los Angeles
Pop. 1980	7,071,639	3,005,072	2,968,579
City jobs	376,512	45,260	40,560
% of Pop.	5.32	1.51	1.36

Source: United States Department of Commerce, Bureau of the Census. 1984. Government Employment (3) (1), Table 2.

There are just not as many material stakes to fuel interest conflicts in Los Angeles or to sustain party machines. In highly polarized Chicago, the material interests of blacks and white liberals have also not been in conflict and their political interests were allied. It is in New York City where the political and economic interests of blacks and potential white liberal allies have seemed to conflict.

The city's very progressivism created a vast network of programs employing many white liberals. As poor and minority people sought to improve their power position in the city, they inevitably came up against liberal people in positions of power over them. Thus, the very success of old-fashioned liberalism in New York City, in that it predated the rise of black consciousness, set up interest conflicts that would ultimately complicate biracial politics. In particular, the large Jewish community, the city's most liberal ethnic group, had been incorporated into ruling regimes and city employment for decades.

The rise of an Italian–Jewish coalition in 1933 behind reform mayor Fiorello LaGuardia brought Jews into high positions of city hall at the expense of the Irish (Bayor, 1978). As a result, Jews moved into all levels of public service, including teaching. In 1970, the Jewish percentage of the city's teachers was estimated at more than 50 percent, and an even higher share of school principals were Jewish (Glazer and Moynihan, 1970). This differed from the role of Jews in other cities: "In New York, as contrasted with cities where the Jewish population is smaller, there is a huge lower-middle class . . . One-seventh of the government employees in New York are Jewish. This is smaller than the Jewish proportion in the city, but much greater than the proportion of Jewish government employees in other cities" (Glazer and Moynihan, 1970, p. 146).

Jews were politically incorporated through the LaGuardia regime, then the Liberal Party, and in recent years through the Reform Democratic movement. While Jews represented the most liberal group in the city, they also had a stake in the establishment—a stake which was severely challenged in the 1968 school strikes.

The strikes began after a black-led experimental school board in Ocean Hills–Brownsville transferred nineteen teachers out of the district, setting off three bitter strikes by teachers (Harris and Swanson, 1970). The 1968 school strikes pitted activist blacks as "outs" against a school bureaucracy led and staffed disproportionately by liberal and moderate whites (including many Jews). Liberals were cast as "ins" in traditionally liberal New York City; it was a strike against institutional liberalism. The high degree of black–Jewish conflict produced by the strikes shifted much of the city's liberal base into a moderate-conservative alliance with white Catholics; this link became the base for the Koch regime (Chapter 4; Harris and Swanson, 1970). The result left blacks without political incorporation. The breakdown of biracial politics did not create either a winning independent black movement or an interest-based alliance with any other group.

Not surprisingly, the other metropolis heavily influenced by liberal political culture, San Francisco, represented one of the Browning, Marshall, and Tabb cities where racial minorities were able to obtain only limited independent political incorporation. Thus, it is possible that *too much* liberalism can be a deterrent to black political incorporation, as well as not enough. An established liberalism could have the paradoxical effect of stifling the development of an independent black political movement, while promoting policies on ideological grounds that could bring some material benefits into minority communities (see, for example, Chapter 4; Browning et al., 1984, p. 162). In such a city, even moderate regimes would have to adopt policies to pre-empt the formation of a potentially popular minority–liberal coalition.

In addition to ideology, however, blacks and liberal reformers can *share* important interests in city politics (a point not addressed by Carmichael and Hamilton). Exclusion from traditional party politics or from conservative regimes creates a common interest in political incorporation. Black mayoral candidates run as liberal antiparty reformers (Tryman, 1974). In most cities, the greater likelihood of white liberals holding professional positions in noncity employment may reduce potential interest conflicts in the allocation of city jobs. Thus affirmative action in city hiring may not generally conflict with white liberal interests. In fact, a black reform regime may multiply the access of white reformers to higher-level, policy-making positions in the new government.

In Chicago, the victory of the Harold Washington coalition brought white liberal reformers their first incorporation into a stable ruling regime. In addition to the ideological incentive of supporting a black mayoral candidate, the white liberal community joined in a coalition that was sympathetic to its goals and interests. White liberals obtained important policy-making roles in the Washington administration, and white liberal aldermen previously isolated in the heyday of the machine became key allies of the mayor. With the death of Harold Washington, this access became uncertain.

In Los Angeles, white liberals and blacks shared major political interests. The Los Angeles biracial coalition originated as an alliance of the "outs"—who happened to be blacks and white liberals. They built a coalition together as outsiders on the basis of shared ideology and a mutual desire for political incorporation. Bradley's victory brought black and white liberal leaders the top political jobs in the city (Sonenshein, 1984).

In a thriving city spread over a huge area, the opportunities for both black and Jewish social mobility were somewhat higher than in eastern cities. As middle-class blacks moved into west-side Jewish areas, Jews were already migrating westward and northward to their current locations in West Los Angeles and the San Fernando Valley (Vorspan and Gartner, 1970). While there was an unusually large and successful black middle class in Los Angeles (a group often amenable to biracial politics), the Jewish population was concentrated in the private sector—not in city jobs.

This is not to say that black–liberal conflict has not been a force in Los Angeles; the Watts riot of 1965 and Bradley's 1969 mayoral campaign aroused a backlash among some Jews. Those Jewish communities closest to black neighborhoods registered the strongest feelings of being threatened by blacks (Wilson and Wilde, 1969), an outcome consistent with an interest explanation. In the mid-1980s, as economic development spread citywide, the interests of white liberals in a particular quality of life were directly threatened by the Bradley administration's probusiness policies. This perceived threat led to a major erosion of support for the Bradley regime, and to the possibility of the coalition's collapse (Boyarsky, 1987). The rise of a number of liberal politicians has raised the likelihood of political competition between blacks and white liberals (Guerra, 1987; Willens, 1980). Recent investigations of Bradley's personal finances for evidence of conflict of interest have added serious new problems for the coalition.

Thus, interest conflicts between blacks and white liberals in New York City help explain the historical failure of the predicted model of black political incorporation through black mobilization and white liberal support. Conflict between blacks and the majority of whites in Chicago did not prevent the formation of an ideological and interest linkage between blacks and white liberals sufficient to bring about black victory and a stable governing regime. In Los Angeles, ideology and interest flowed together, at least until recently, to make possible a strong coalition. It has been argued that the incentives for reform politics are "purposive" (ideological) rather than material (Clark and Wilson, 1961). But even to reformers, non-ideological political benefits provide powerful incentives for political action.

LEADERSHIP

Biracial coalitions depend heavily on the actions of leaders and supporting organizations in both black and white communities. Such coalitions do not arise simply because the "objective conditions" are in place. Biracial leadership has two elements: organizing the black community and building links to white liberals. Strong bi-racial coalitions generally develop out of effective black community politics.

Black mayoral candidates have been important leaders in the development of biracial coalitions. They have had the greatest political stakes in building cross-racial alliances, since in few cases can they win with black votes alone. The key role of black voting unity has made them mobilizers of the black community. The single most important factor in the election of black mayors, regardless of black population, has been the ability of blacks to exceed whites in voting turnout, in Los Angeles as well as in cities with larger black populations (O'Laughlin and Berg, 1977). In pursuing their electoral interests, black candidates have temporarily sealed severe class divisions among blacks. But black mayoral candidates have risen on the backs of massive efforts within the black community.

The evolution of the Los Angeles biracial coalition was marked by sophisticated and unified black political work, from the 1963 nomination by a community convention of a single black candidate (Tom Bradley) to contest a council seat to the highly effective mobilization of the black vote in Bradley's mayoral elections. As a result of this political base, the black influence in Los Angeles is likely to continue after Bradley leaves office, even if the biracial coalition itself fades.

Chicago is a case study in successful black political organization, from a community nominating process to select a black mayoral candidate to a remarkable registration and get-out-the-vote drive in black neighborhoods (Barker, 1983; Preston, 1987). The contrast to Cleveland, where black mayor Carl Stokes left office relatively early and the black movement declined precipitously, is instructive (Nelson, 1987).

In both Chicago and Los Angeles, the black rise to citywide power was preceded by strategic bloc voting by blacks. In 1979, blacks helped defeat the Chicago machine's mayoral candidate by backing Jane Byrne; in 1982 blacks nearly unseated the Republican governor of Illinois. In 1961, Los Angeles blacks provided Sam Yorty's margin of victory over an incumbent mayor. Two years later, three blacks won seats on the fifteen-member City Council.

In New York City, blacks have been unsuccessful in mobilizing as an independent political force. Blacks in New York City have been comparatively reluctant to back black candidates for borough or citywide offices. Unlike black communities in many other cities, New York City's blacks have voted in the 50 percent to 60 percent range for black candidates (Hamilton, 1979). The same complaint is heard in Boston (Chapter 6). In recent years, local observers have bemoaned the lack of black political strength in New York City. Mollenkopf (Chapter 4) notes that New York City's black political leaders are in many cases incorporated into the regular party and do not seek to lead a reform coalition.

To successfully achieve political incorporation, then, blacks in Chicago and Los Angeles have *in actual practice* tended to follow some of the advice of Carmichael and Hamilton. While pursuing this path they have also succeeded in maintaining links to liberal whites, as suggested by the advocates of ideological coalition, and as ruled impractical or unwise by the black-power theorists. It is this two-part strategy, not just population figures, that accounts for the great increase in black political representation since 1967. The loss of the mayoral election by Chicago blacks in 1989 reflected both a lack of black unity and the absence of a biracial coalition. Goodwill alone is not enough, but neither is cold self-interest.

Black power and biracial coalition politics are not incompatible; indeed they are complementary. Once a black base has been established, the task of building links to white liberals becomes crucial. But these links have long been controversial among blacks. Class division among blacks is reflected in attitudes toward biracial coalitions; biracialism has been more often pursued by the black middle class (Unrau, 1971). Biracial coalitions are vulnerable among blacks because of their bourgeois nature, the key role middle-class blacks play in them, the weak appeals made to black solidarity, and the limits of the coalition's economic agenda. This black ambivalence is an important part of the climate within which black leaders operate (although these cross-pressures are not always understood by their white counterparts).

The key to the Los Angeles biracial coalition was a personal link at the leadership level between middle-class black activists and white reformers. Carmichael and Hamilton rightly argued that white reformers often ignore blacks or impose their own interests on them (1967, pp. 64–65). This was true generally of the CDC, the liberal Democratic reform movement in California (Wilson, 1962; Jones, 1962). In fact, the priorities of blacks and liberal reformers in Los Angeles often differed on such issues as the importance of black political representation (Wilson, 1962). Bradley's leadership in the CDC was therefore a major factor in building cross-racial links.

A black religious leader in Los Angeles, Bishop H. Hartford Brookins, has since 1963 been a major force in connecting the electoral interest of blacks to the ideological support of white liberals. In Bradley's 1963 council campaign, Brookins developed a strategy to reach white liberals (Patterson, 1969). In later years, he counseled Bradley to form an alliance with liberal councilwoman Rosalind Wyman (Littwin, 1981). Brookins' close alliance with Bradley has been a major factor in maintaining Los Angeles' biracial liberalism. A loyal network of white liberal CDC activists has also worked closely with Bradley since 1963. They have helped protect his interests in the liberal community and provide a direct, personal link with the Bradley network in the black community. The biracial leadership of the Los Angeles coalition has been highly active in reducing black–liberal tensions whenever they arise in the city, often meeting behind closed doors to air differences (Chapter 2).

The experience of New York City shows that in the presence of interest conflicts, leaders may tend to protect their own group first, and avoid the search for creative, overarching solutions. Leaders in the black and Jewish communities did little to prevent intergroup hostility from arising during the 1968 school strikes. Black anti-Semitism emerged and was not repudiated by black leaders. Teachers' union chief Albert Shanker publicized black anti-Semitic remarks in order to mobilize support for the union's position. The school strikes left deep scars. There has been no real network linking blacks and white liberals in recent years (Chapter 4).

But the human element of leadership also indicates the role of time. Circumstances and leadership change over time, which ought to influence the dynamics of biracial coalitions. After all, if this chapter had been written in 1969, it would be explaining the defeat of a black mayoral candidate in Los Angeles by a racist campaign; the continued exclusion of Chicago's black population from political incorporation; and the re-election of a white liberal mayor backed by racial minorities in New York City. Time demands analytical caution. With all three cities electing mayors in 1989, significant changes could not be ruled out.

For example, New York City's biracial politics could change if liberal reformers, emboldened by the current municipal scandals, build links to the city's minority groups. Although he began his career in the liberal reform wing of the Democratic party, Mayor Koch's regime has been more moderate or conservative. Many liberal reformers have felt unrepresented, along with racial minorities; 16

years of mutual exclusion could stimulate joint efforts. Furthermore, a black candidate for mayor, David Dinkins, could mobilize a reform–minority electoral alliance. A crucial element will be leadership building bridges over a recent history of interest conflict by drawing on ideological affinities.

Los Angeles, of course, could go in the other direction. Bradley's narrow re-election in 1989 shows that his coalition is in transition (Sonenshein, 1989). Equally problematic are the various investigations of Bradley's personal finances. Bradley's eventual retirement and the rise of electoral conflict between blacks and white liberals would certainly change the alignment of forces in the city. The seeds of such conflicts have been germinating for some time (Boyarsky, 1987). In Chicago, the death of Harold Washington was soon followed by the rise of black–Jewish conflict and the replacement of the black-led regime.

Thus leaders influenced the contemporary failure of biracial politics in New York City and its success in Los Angeles and Chicago. While interest and ideology matter greatly, the outcome is not fixed. The presence of a black mayoral candidate and the active creation of biracial networks may make the difference.

CONCLUSIONS AND IMPLICATIONS

In all three cities, the roots of black political incorporation lie in a combination of black mobilization and white liberal support. Ideology remains a central force in biracial politics, providing an important base for liberal politics and minority incorporation. Liberal beliefs matter, and the ability of white liberals to be politically effective is one of the leading factors in the attainment of black equality. But interests and leadership are crucial factors in the success of biracial coalitions.

This analysis also suggests why the road for blacks is so much harder than for other groups. Racial ideology blocks off access to potential allies who share interests. When separated by interest conflict from those who share beliefs, blacks face exclusion. Dependence on liberalism undoubtedly adds to the inherent tension in any coalition.

It would be much too optimistic to generalize from the Los Angeles case, where all three predisposing factors were favorable. The Los Angeles example has been rarely replicated among big cities with black populations between 15 percent and 30 percent. (Of Browning, Marshall, and Tabb's ten cities, only Berkeley showed the same degree of biracial coalition.) Another city where such a coalition has formed is Cincinnati (Lieske and Hillard, 1984). A prescription for basing black political strategy on links to white liberals is handicapped by the low level of white liberal impact in many cities where blacks lack the numbers to take power through mobilization. On the other hand, it would be unduly pessimistic to suggest that if one or more factors are missing in other cities, no productive alliance is possible. Situations can change, and new arrangements can arise. The time factor in political coalitions may make today's situation obsolete in 10 years. Interest conflicts between ideological allies are at least theoretically capable of resolution.

The role of liberal support can be overstated. When black numbers are sufficient, as in Chicago, white liberal support may be secondary to black mobilization and, if possible, links to Latinos. In light of the weakness of liberal forces in many cities with smaller black populations, the prospects are less comforting. In such a setting, blacks will either face exclusion or ally themselves with forces that are anathema to liberal reformers. An example is Cleveland, where blacks are incorporated through co-optation by a conservative mayoral regime (Nelson, 1987).

When blacks have a majority and mayoral elections feature two black candidates (one liberal, one moderate), the balance of power may shift from liberal whites to moderate or conservative whites, as in New Orleans (Poliawsky and Stekler, 1987). Where liberalism is too strong, as perhaps has been the case in New York City and San Francisco, it may inhibit the development of independent minority politics as well. Thus, the health of a black–liberal coalition may depend on a balance of strength.

Ideological politics can break down when conflicts of interest cause groups and their leaders to defend their ground. White liberals ought to understand that many blacks are justifiably cautious about committing themselves to biracial coalitions that may founder when hard, divisive issues arise.

The best biracial politics is not a form of philanthropy; when liberal support seems like charity, baffled liberals may find their hands bitten by the "ungrateful" recipient. As Hamilton (1979) has pointed out, votes provide reciprocity; mutual need can add a reliable and dignified glue to good intentions. While the black-power argument too quickly dismisses the consistent support of white liberals, liberals tend to understate the importance of realistic group conflict and pragmatic cooperation.

Both Los Angeles and Chicago offer strong cases for blacks organizing independently before linking themselves to liberal whites. In fact, in no city has it been practical for blacks to *start off* with biracial politics; rather, black organization precedes any links to liberal whites, as predicted by Carmichael and Hamilton.

Biracial coalitions can mean different things to blacks and white liberals. To blacks, the election of a black mayor is often seen as a group advance; to white liberals, the symbol of the individual black mayoral candidate may be the focus of idealism (Sonenshein, 1984). In urban governance, in fact, white liberals and black mayors may have different policy directions. Like the political machines before them, black mayors have tied themselves heavily to local business (Erie, 1980), often in opposition to liberal antidevelopment views (Eisinger, 1983). Bradley is one of the few black mayors who has managed to balance business and environmental constituencies, but even he is often the subject of criticism from white liberals.

Primarily ideological, but also grounded in mutual interests, biracial coalitions behind black mayors have certain strengths and weaknesses. They are best at developing minority political incorporation, some material changes, and symbolic benefits. A growing body of literature shows their weakness in addressing economic inequality (see, for example, Chapter 7).

Since the blacks most likely to work directly with white liberals are middle class, a policy agenda seeking "status" rather than "welfare" goals may be favored. Status goals include the upward mobility of individual group members and symbolic group recognition, while welfare goals involve the redistribution of money and power to the masses (Wilson, 1960).

While it might seem more effective to ally with groups of the same economic status if blacks are to achieve economic equality, such potential allies are unlikely to favor the black *racial* agenda. Because of the potency of racial ideology, it may be difficult to promote simultaneously a racial agenda and a mass-based economic agenda. Building a progressive mass movement around the minority search for equality therefore requires a flexible, multifaceted approach. Hamilton, for example, has noted the need to use a "deracial" strategy in building an economic coalition for blacks (1977). As Henry asks (1980), what strategies will build alliance with Latinos, a group with comparable economic status to blacks'? As the analysis in this chapter shows, much will depend on the attitudes Latinos hold on the question of race. Future studies might ask why blacks have formed a stronger alliance with Latinos in Chicago than in either Los Angeles or New York City.

Based on ideology, biracial coalitions are vulnerable to public disagreements and moral challenges. The ideological nature of the alliance calls for public determinations of justice and right. A political machine would easily deal with an outsider who intends to fracture the coalition by ignoring jarring words and continuing to pragmatically assign benefits. To an ideological coalition, by contrast, words are supremely important. There is as yet no clear answer as to how this challenge will be met, although the closed-door leadership meetings in Los Angeles may suggest one way (Chapter 2).

The case of biracial electoral coalitions shows that the nature of racial politics depends heavily on the arena of political action. When it comes to choices about school busing, practical calculations of individual interest may be very important along with ideology, and the role of leadership may be slim (Giles and Gatlin, 1980). But biracial electoral coalitions call on ideological preferences before interest calculations enter in, and the role of leaders can be exceptionally important. This suggests that racial politics is a broad phenomenon whose dynamics differ in various situations.

The art of building biracial electoral coalitions calls for leaders who can link the interests and ideologies of groups together in order to win elections, enact policies, and offer benefits. Although highly vulnerable to challenge from both the left and the right, biracial electoral coalitions continue to offer a relatively consistent linkage for minority politics. To the extent that they are not seen as ends in themselves, but rather as a base for further efforts at social change, biracial coalitions will be pursued and developed as tools in the struggle for racial equality.

REFERENCES

The author thanks Alan Saltzstein for his comments on an earlier draft of this paper. This chapter is a revised version of a paper presented at the 1986 annual meeting of the American Political Science Association.

Adrian, Charles, R. 1959. A Typology for Nonpartisan Elections. *Western Political Quarterly* 12:449–458.

Barker, Twiley, W. 1983. Political Mobilization of Black Chicago: Drafting a Candidate. *PS* 16:482–485.

Bayor, Ronald H. 1978. *Neighbors in Conflict: The Irish, Germans, Jews and Italians of New York City, 1929–1941.* Baltimore: Johns Hopkins Press.

Boyarsky, Bill. 1987. Old Alliance Loses Ardor for Bradley. *Los Angeles Times*, July 2.

Browning, Rufus P., Dale Rogers Marshall, and David H. Tabb. 1984. *Protest Is Not Enough: The Struggle of Blacks and Hispanics for Equality in Urban Politics.* Berkeley: University of California Press.

Bullock, Charles S. III, and Bruce A. Campbell. 1984. Racist or Racial Voting in the 1981 Atlanta Municipal Elections. *Urban Affairs Quarterly* 20:149–164.

Caditz, Judith. 1976. *White Liberals in Transition: Current Dilemmas of Ethnic Integration.* Holliswood, N.Y.: Spectrum Publications.

Carmichael, Stokely, and Charles V. Hamilton. 1967. *Black Power: The Politics of Liberation in America.* New York: Random House.

Carmines, E. G ., and J. A. Stimson. 1982. Racial Issues and the Structure of Mass Belief Systems. *Journal of Politics* 44:2–20.

Carney, Francis. 1964. The Decentralized Politics of Los Angeles. *Annals of the American Academy of Political and Social Sciences* 353 (May): 107–121.

Clark, Peter B., and James Q. Wilson. 1961. Incentive Systems: A Theory of Organizations. *Administrative Science Quarterly* 6:219–266.

Cohen, Seymour J. 1969. Patterns of Jewish Voting, 1968: Chicago. *Midstream* 15 (February): 27–31.

Cole, Leonard A. 1974. Electing Blacks to Municipal Office: Structural and Social Determinants. *Urban Affairs Quarterly* 10 (September): 17–39.

Davidson, Chandler. 1972. *Biracial Politics: Conflict and Coalition in the Metropolitan South.* Baton Rouge: Louisiana University Press.

Eisinger, Peter K. 1976. *Patterns of Interracial Politics: Conflict and Cooperation in the City.* New York: Academic Press.

Eisinger, Peter K. 1983. Black Mayors and the Politics of Racial Economic Advancement. In William McCready, ed., *Culture, Ethnicity, and Identity: Current Issues in Research.* New York: Academic Press, pp. 95–109.

Erie, Steven P. 1980. Two Faces of Ethnic Power: Comparing the Irish and Black Experiences. *Polity* 13 (Winter): 261–284.

Fisher, Alan M. 1979. Realignment of the Jewish Vote? *Political Science Quarterly* 94:97–116.

Fogelson, Robert. 1967. *The Fragmented Metropolis: Los Angeles, 1850–1930.* Cambridge, Mass.: Harvard University Press.

Giles, Micheal W., and Arthur Evans. 1986. The Power Approach to Intergroup Hostility. *Journal of Conflict Resolution* 30:469–486.

Giles, Micheal W., and Douglas S. Gatlin. 1980. Mass-level Compliance with Public Policy: The Case of School Desegregation. *Journal of Politics* 42:722–746.

Glazer, Nathan, and Daniel Patrick Moynihan. 1970. *Beyond the Melting Pot: The Negroes, Puerto Ricans, Jews, Italians, and Irish of New York City*, Cambridge, Mass.: MIT Press. 2d ed.

Guerra, Fernando J. 1987. Ethnic Officeholders in Los Angeles County. *Sociology and Social Research* 71:89–94.

Hahn, Harlan, David Klingman, and Harry Pachon. 1976. Cleavages, Coalitions, and the

Black Candidate: The Los Angeles Mayoralty Elections of 1969 and 1973. *Western Political Quarterly* 29 (December):521–530.

Halley, Robert M., Alan C. Acock, and Thomas H. Greene. 1976. Ethnicity and Social Class: Voting in the 1973 Los Angeles Municipal Elections. *Western Political Quarterly* 29 (December): 521–530.

Hamilton, Charles V. 1977. De-Racialization: Examination of Political Strategy. *First World* 1:3–5.

Hamilton, Charles V. 1979. The Patron-Recipient Relationship and Minority Politics in New York City. *Political Science Quarterly* 94 (Summer): 211–228.

Harris, Louis, and Bert E. Swanson. 1970. *Black-Jewish Relations in New York City.* New York: Praeger.

Henry, Charles P. 1980. Black-Chicano Coalitions: Possibilities and Problems. *Western Journal of Black Studies* 4 (Winter): 222–232.

Hinckley, Barbara. 1981. *Coalitions and Politics.* New York: Harcourt Brace Jovanovich.

Jones, William B. 1962. CDC and the Negro Community. *CDC Bulletin* 1 (September): 4–5.

Kinder, Donald R., and D. O. Sears. 1981. Prejudice and Politics: Symbolic Racism versus Racial Threats to the Good Life. *Journal of Personality and Social Psychology* 40:414–431.

Kinder, Donald R., and Lynn M. Sanders. 1987. Pluralistic Foundations of American Opinion on Race. Paper presented at the annual meeting of the American Political Science Association.

Kleppner, Paul. 1985. *Chicago Divided: The Making of a Black Mayor.* DeKalb, Ill.: Northern Illinois University Press.

Lieske, Joel, and Jan William Hillard. 1984. The Racial Factor in Urban Elections. *Western Political Quarterly* 37:545–563.

Littwin, Susan. 1981. Inside Tom Bradley: The Making of a Mayor, 1981 and of a Governor, 1982. *New West* 6:85–89.

Murray, Richard, and Arnold Vedlitz. 1978. Racial Voting Patterns in the South: An Analysis of Major Elections from 1960 to 1977 in Five Cities. *Annals of the American Academy of Political and Social Sciences* 439 (September): 29–39.

Nelson, William. 1987. The Rise and Fall of Black Politics in Cleveland. In Michael Preston, Lenneal J. Henderson, Jr., and Paul L. Puryear, eds., *The New Black Politics: The Search for Political Power*, 2d ed. New York: Longman, pp. 172–199.

O'Laughlin, John, and Dale A. Berg. 1977. The Election of Black Mayors, 1969 and 1973. *Annals of the Association of American Geographers* 67 (June): 223–238.

Patterson, Beeman. 1969. Political Actions of Negroes in Los Angeles: A Study in the Attainment of Councilmanic Representation. *Phylon* 30:170–183.

Pettigrew, Thomas. 1971. When a Black Candidate Runs for Mayor: Race and Voting Behavior. In Harlan Hahn, ed., *People and Politics in Urban Society.* Beverly Hills, Calif.: Sage Publications, pp. 99–105.

Poliawsky, Monte, and Paul J. Stekler, 1987. The Evolution of Black Politics in New Orleans: From Protest to Powerbrokers? Paper presented at the annual meeting of the American Political Science Association.

Preston, Michael B. The Election of Harold Washington. In Preston et al., eds., *The New Black Politics*, 2d ed. New York: Longman, pp. 139–171.

Ransom, Bruce. 1987. Black Independent Electoral Politics in Philadelphia: The Election of Mayor W. Wilson Goode. In Preston et al., eds., *The New Black Politics*, 2d ed. New York: Longman, pp. 256–290.

Shefter, Martin. 1983. Regional Receptivity to Reform. *Political Science Quarterly* 98 (Fall): 459–484.

Singleton, Gregory H. 1979. *Religion in the City of the Angels: American Protestant Culture and Urbanization, Los Angeles, 1850–1930*. Ann Arbor: UMI Research Press.

Sonenshein, Raphael. 1984. Bradley's People: Functions of the Candidate Organization. Ph.D. dissertation, Yale University.

Sonenshein, Rapheal. 1989. The Los Angeles Board of Bi-racial Coalition Politics. *Los Angeles Times*, Opinion Section, April 16.

Tryman, Mfanya D. 1974. Black Mayoralty Campaigns: Running the "Race." *Phylon* 35 (Winter): 346–358.

Unrau, Harlan D. 1971. The Double V Movement in Los Angeles During the Second World War: A Study in Negro Protest. M.A. thesis, California State University, Fullerton.

Vorspan, Max, and Lloyd P. Gartner. 1970. *History of the Jews of Los Angeles*. San Marino, Calif.: The Huntington Library.

Willens, Michele. 1980. The Sudden Rise of the Jewish Politician. *California Journal* 11:146–148.

Wilson, James Q. 1960. *Negro Politics*. New York: Free Press.

Wilson, James Q. 1962. *The Amateur Democrat: Club Politics in Three Cities*. Chicago: University of Chicago Press.

Wilson, James Q., and Harold R. Wilde. 1969. The Urban Mood. *Commentary* 48:52–61.

Woo, Elaine. 1987. Neighborhoods at Odds Over Year-Round Schools. *Los Angeles Times*, October 22.

CHAPTER 12

Has Political Incorporation Been Achieved? Is It Enough?

Rufus P. Browning, Dale Rogers Marshall, and David H. Tabb

In the 21 cities examined in this book, have blacks and Latinos achieved strong political incorporation? Sometimes. Where incorporation has been achieved, have minority-oriented city governments produced gains for minority people? Yes, in significant, but limited, areas. Have these governments achieved the goals of the movement that produced them? No.

In this concluding chapter, we first summarize the findings of the preceding chapters on racial politics in American cities with respect to the explanations of minority mobilization and incorporation developed in Chapter 1. Then we take up questions of the record of minority-oriented city governments, their adequacy, and their possible future agenda.

MOBILIZATION AND INCORPORATION: FUNDAMENTALS

Withholding for the moment judgment about the value of minority incorporation in city governments, we bring together here findings and interpretations about resources for mobilization and incorporation, and barriers to it.

Weak and Strong Forms of Minority Incorporation

Representation alone gained little influence for minorities; minority participation in liberal dominant coalitions led to much stronger minority influence and policy responsiveness; coalitions led by black mayors typically incorporated still stronger minority commitments.[1] As Stokely Carmichael and Charles Hamilton put it in 1967:

> When black people lack a majority, Black Power means proper representation and sharing of control. It means the creation of power bases, of strength, from which black people can press to change local or nation-wide patterns of oppression— instead of from weakness.
>
> It does not mean *merely* putting black faces into office. Black visibility is not Black Power. (1967, p. 46)

Interest Group and Electoral Strategies

Mobilization that produced sustained incorporation built both on interest-group organization, demand, and protest and on electoral effort, including party or partylike coalition formation. While electoral mobilization and coalition were the essential foundation of enduring incorporation, group organization, demand, and protest were the foundation for successful electoral effort, in spite of instances where too intense protest hindered and delayed the formation of coalitions.

Cities in which blacks or Latinos achieved the most powerful participation in electoral coalitions, and subsequently in city governments, were those in which the development of autonomous, solidary minority leadership and organization preceded it, confirming Carmichael and Hamilton's argument:

> The concept of Black Power rests on a fundamental premise: *Before a group can enter the open society, it must first close ranks.* By this we mean that group solidarity is necessary before a group can operate effectively from a bargaining position of strength in a pluralistic society. (1967, p. 44)

The linkage between the achievement of solidarity within the minority group and the achievement of strong incorporation was very close in the cities studied. The early strong incorporation of blacks in Berkeley depended on the usually strong organization of black leadership in the Berkeley Black Caucus; the long delay in the election of a black mayor in Oakland was the result in part of the split between the Black Panther Party and middle-class black leadership (see Chapter 1). Failure to achieve solidarity both within and between minority populations in New York explains in part the failure of blacks and Latinos to obtain incorporation corresponding to their population size in that city (see Chapter 4). Breaking away from the Democratic machine and organizing a grass-roots process to pull black community organizations together, and the inclusion of Latinos in a coalition, were prerequisites for Harold Washington's victory in Chicago (see Chapter 5).

---

[1] Mollenkopf suggest in Chapter 4 that New York may be an anomaly in this regard—that a regime in which blacks are weakly incorporated nevertheless produces substantial benefits for them. We deal with that possibility later in this chapter.

The Importance of Coalitions

Regardless of election system (partisan or nonpartisan), the political incorporation of minorities—the extent of their role in dominant coalitions that controlled city government—depended on their ability to form and maintain cohesive electoral coalitions. In particular, where blacks and Latinos constituted a minority of the effective electorate, their incorporation depended on the formation of bi- or multiracial coalitions that selected candidates, controlled the number of minority candidacies so as to prevent splitting the vote for minority candidates, organized slates, coordinated campaigns, and controlled city councils and departments.

The fundamental resources of the minority populations plus supportive whites formed the basis of these coalitions. Depending on historical patterns of competition and conflict, on leadership, and on the sizes of black and Latino groups and of the supportive white population, coalitions were variously composed of blacks and whites, Latinos and whites, or all three groups.

The Importance of Leadership

Because historical competition and conflict between groups is typical, the structure, size, and timing of new coalitions depended on the ability of leaders to overcome divisions and to shape issues so as to minimize antagonism and sustain joint effort. The flow of issues, partly under the control of coalition leaders, and the willingness and ability of the available leadership to reach out across racial boundaries—a difficult task—shaped the structure of the coalitions that actually formed, won control of city government, and maintained their commitment and position (see Chapter 11). The structure of local leadership, as well as that of group conflict, is shaped by historical experience, such as innovative cooperation that takes hold and becomes accepted practice in a city, as in Philadelphia (see Chapter 3).

GROUP SIZE AND PATTERNS OF MOBILIZATION

Patterns of mobilization that emerged in these cities nationwide correspond well to the expectations about mobilization, given group size, identified in the California cities. Blacks in Atlanta, Birmingham, and New Orleans and Latinos in Miami and San Antonio constituted majorities in 1980 (see Table 12.1); black and Latino mayors in these cities did lead biracial/multiracial coalitions, although they were by then no longer so critically dependent on white support. In Birmingham and New Orleans, as Huey Perry carefully delineates in Chapter 8, biracial coalitions had formed earlier and had first elected racially liberal white mayors, then black mayors.

In a second group of cities, neither blacks nor Latinos constituted majorities in 1980, but the two groups together made up at least 40 percent of city population: Los Angeles, Philadelphia, Chicago, and New York. In all of these cities, a

TABLE 12.1. BLACK AND LATINO POPULATION AND REPRESENTATION IN ELEVEN U.S. CITIES

City	Population, 1980			Electoral system and political structure of city government	City Council, 1988		
	Total (1000)	% Black	% Latino		Size	% Black	% Latino
San Antonio	786	7.3	53.7	10 district since 1977, 1 at-large (mayor)	11	9	29
Denver	492	12.0	18.8	11 district, 2 at-large since 1971, nonpartisan	13	15	23
Los Angeles	2,967	17.0	27.5	District since 1925, nonpartisan	15	20	7
Boston	563	22.4	6.4	9 district, 4 at-large since 1981	13	15	0
Miami	347	25.0	55.9	At-large, nonpartisan, council-manager City: County:	5 9	20 11	60 11
New York	7,072	25.2	19.9	Board of Estimate: citywide/borough Council: district	11 35	9 20	0 9
Philadelphia	1,688	37.8	3.8	10 district, 7 at-large	17	29	6
Chicago	3,005	39.8	14.0	District	50	32	8
New Orleans	558	55.3	3.4	5 district, 2 at-large, nonpartisan	7	57	0
Birmingham	284	55.6	0.8	At-large, nonpartisan	9	67	0
Atlanta	425	66.6	1.4	12 district, 6 at-large since 1973, nonpartisan	18	67	0
Mean	1,653	33.1	18.7		19.3	33.7	13.9

Source: U.S. Department of Commerce, Bureau of Census, Statistical Abstract of the U.S. 1986, Table 19, and authors.

biracial/multiracial electoral alliance with a strong commitment to minority (primarily black) interests had taken control of the mayor's office by 1987. In New York, this was a biracial coalition under Mayor John Lindsay, elected in 1967 and 1971. Thus, the experience in all of these cities was consistent with the simple model, derived from the California experience, that predicts a successful multiracial coalition will form and take control of city government where the minority population plus support from liberal whites approaches 50 percent of the population.[2]

In New York, the subsequent replacement of Mayor Lindsay's regime in 1975 and the ascendancy of a considerably less liberal one led by Mayor Edward Koch is, however, an anomaly in terms of the model, as Mollenkopf argues in Chapter 4.

Denver constitutes a modest anomaly on the other side, with a combined black and Latino population of only 30.8 percent in 1980 but a Latino mayor by mid-decade. But as Muñoz and Henry explain in Chapter 10, Federico Peña's campaign for mayor of Denver fell a good deal short of the model of a multiracial electoral alliance with a strong commitment to minority interests. A Latino mayor was elected, but minority *interests* were not strongly incorporated.

New York since 1975, Boston, and Chicago before Harold Washington (and perhaps after) all exemplify co-optation, in which segments of black and Latino leadership and electoral support are brought into a dominant coalition in which whites play primary roles and which does not make so strong a commitment to minority interests. (In Boston, combined black and Latino populations made up only 29 percent of total population in 1980—probably not enough to support a winning liberal multiracial coalition; or not enough to do so in the face of a well-established party machine, as Travis notes in Chapter 6.[3])

BARRIERS TO INCORPORATION

Urban Machines

Boston, New York since 1975, and Chicago before Harold Washington present characteristics that were not found in the California cities and that constitute

---

[2] The 40 percent minority figure is a rule of thumb—an approximation for circumstances that vary from city to city. An illustration will show its plausibility. Suppose the black plus Latino population is 40 percent; white non-Latino population, 60 percent. Evidence from many cities suggests that typically 10 percent to 20 percent of the white population will support a biracial coalition (see Preston, Henderson, and Puryear, 1987). This amounts to 6 percent to 12 percent of the total population. Combined with a 40 percent minority population, we have a potential coalition of 46 percent to 52 percent of the population, within striking distance of an electoral majority if all the coalition's supporters can be mobilized.

[3] A minority population of about 29 percent was enough to produce a winning biracial coalition in Berkeley in the early 1960s, but only in the presence of an unusually large liberal white population. A minority population of 29 percent, or whatever figure, does not of course necessarily mean that the minority share of the effective electorate is 29 percent. Because of the typically lower voter turnout of low-income groups and the smaller percentage of adults and greater numbers of children in many minority populations, the minority share of the electorate is frequently considerably smaller than the minority share of the population. On the other hand, at periods of peak mobilization around critical elections involving challenges by minority-oriented coalitions, the minority share of the electorate is likely to rise substantially (Browning et al., 1979).

additional barriers to minority mobilization and incorporation. In these three cities, we find a party, or "machine," variant of the co-optation pattern, in which strongly organized urban parties have co-opted minorities into their organizations.

The machines are well-institutionalized coalitions that predate minority mobilization of the 1960s. Not oriented toward reform and determined to protect the power of the organization and the economic interests of its ultimately white leadership and business support, the machine attempts to prevent the formation of multiracial challenging coalitions through co-optation, building on and generating divisions among minority leaders and groups and establishing minority officeholders against whom other minority people find it difficult to run. The machine creates some minority incorporation and produces some minority-oriented policies but prevents the mobilization of a liberal, unified minority-based coalition.

Thus the machine stands as a barrier to the formation and success of reform-oriented coalitions, in which more autonomous minority leadership would play central and dominant roles. Some benefits flow to minority populations from such machines, as they do from co-optive regimes generally—city government employment, for example, and contracts from the city—but they will not undertake efforts to reorient city government across a broad range of policy areas.

In Chicago, unlike New York, a weakened machine was defeated by a multiracial coalition led by black insurgents. Harold Washington's election as mayor and then his success in gaining a council majority show that even a long-entrenched machine and its co-optation pattern can be overthrown, given appropriate leadership, fundamental resources of minority population, and some support outside the minority community.

But the Chicago case also demonstrates the difficulty of accomplishing an overthrow. As Robert Starks and Michael Preston show in Chapter 5, Washington's coalition and leadership were unusual (see also Chapters 4 and 11). The coalition conducted an extraordinary grass-roots mobilization and involvement in the decision to select Washington as the coalition's candidate for mayor in the first place. Washington himself was capable of reaching out across racial lines to Chicago's Latino population, including them as respected partners in his ultimately victorious coalition. Not every leader with the ability to win majority support in his own group also has the will and the credibility to create a liberal biracial or multiracial coalition. (See Chapter 11 for a discussion of the importance of black leadership.)

The fragile dependence of such coalitions on leadership was sadly illustrated when Washington died in office and black candidates competing to succeed him split his coalition, leading to the election of the white machine candidate, Mayor Richard M. Daley, in 1989.

Fragmentation of Minority Groups

In addition to the party machine as a barrier to minority mobilization, New York illustrates also the possibility and consequences of extreme fragmentation of minority groups. The 1980 census counted more than 45 percent of New York's population as black or "of Spanish origin," and these groups probably made up more than half of New York's population by the late 1980s. By the standards of the other cities studied in this book, resources of such size should have been more than ample to found a liberal multiracial coalition that could control city government over a long period of time. A major reason why this has not happened, as seen in Chapter 4, is the extent to which both blacks and Latinos in New York have been divided.

In contrast to the California cities, where most blacks and Latinos have arrived since World War II, New York's black and Latino populations have had a long history of competition, conflict, established leadership, and political division. This is not new clay that a skillful leader can readily mold into a unified force, but a congeries of minority populations between which divisions are deep and solid. Blacks and Latinos in New York are further split within each group by ancestry and nativity—blacks of West Indian birth or origin as well as blacks of southern origin; Latinos of Puerto Rican birth or ancestry but also Dominicans and other Latino immigrant groups—and by place of residence in the boroughs of the city.

Fragmentation of minority populations in New York is not only a result of differences in ancestry and nationality; it stems from a long history of conflict and competition and the habituation of organizations and leaders to that history, as Mollenkopf notes (Chapter 4). This is utterly unlike the experience of black communities in the California cities. Blacks arrived in California mainly during and after World War II. Coming predominantly from the American South, they are not divided by different ancestry. Organizational structure and leadership still emerging, they were mobilized by the civil rights and Black Power movements and were presented with an opportunity to overthrow conservative regimes, if they could coalesce among themselves and with others. For California blacks, the civil rights movement was the formative influence for political mobilization. In contrast, the political fragmentation of New York's black population was well established long before the civil rights movement. Their ability to overcome fragmentation was tested again in the 1989 New York mayoral election pitting Mayor Koch against David N. Dinkins, the black Manhattan borough president, who was trying to form a biracial coalition.

Intense fragmentation between and within minority groups is likely to impede the formation of a multiracial coalition. Anthony Downs draws the lesson:

> In many big cities minorities need to overcome their own fragmentation into conflicting groups and their deliberate cooptation by the white politicians who have long dominated local politics before they can fully control their local government. (1986, pp. 291–292)

Issues, Interests, and the Loss of White Support

The formation and survival of bi- and multiracial coalitions depend in part on the ideological commitment of liberal whites to the minority cause. Mollenkopf's analysis of New York (Chapter 4) and Sonenshein's comparative study of New York, Chicago, and Los Angeles (Chapter 11) delineate the limits of that commitment; the New York case especially illustrates the potential for drastic loss of earlier support and the long-term eclipse of progressive multiracial coalitions.

In some cities, certainly in New York and Los Angeles, Jews have accounted for a large share of white support for blacks, reflecting the experience of Jews with discrimination and their special moral determination to oppose it. Unfortunately for the cause of coalition, blacks and whites generally but Jews in particular have a special potential for conflict of interests around anti-Semitism, city government fiscal problems, residential and labor market succession, and control over city government functions and employment.

Anti-Semitism. A few black leaders express openly anti-Semitic attitudes; the expression of anti-Semitism and the failure of some black leaders to denounce them must reduce support for biracial coalitions among Jews.

Fiscal Problems. In New York, the fiscal crisis of the 1970s turned white supporters away from the problems of minority groups and dominated the agenda of city government for years. As a result, Mollenkopf notes, "social spending lost out to developmental and basic services through the cycle of austerity and recovery between 1975 and 1983."

Residential and Labor Market Succession. In New York in particular, many Jews have been affected in recent years by the transition of Jewish lower-middle and working-class neighborhoods to black or Latino neighborhoods. Such transitions are likely to kindle racial, class, and cultural antagonisms and thus reduce support for coalitions.

Control Over City Government Functions and Employment. In the 1968 school strikes in New York, black activists were

> pitted . . . as "outs" against a school bureaucracy led and staffed disproportionately by liberal and moderate whites (including many Jews). Liberals were cast as "ins" in traditionally liberal New York City; it was a strike against [white] institutional liberalism. The high degree of black–Jewish conflict produced by the strikes shifted much of the city's liberal base into a moderate/conservative alliance with white Catholics; this link became the base for the Koch regime. The result left blacks without political incorporation. (Sonenshein, this volume, Chapter 11)

It is apparent that conflicts arising from these and other issues can destroy or prevent the formation of bi- and multiracial coalitions. Although the issues described above involved conflict between whites and blacks, it is easy to think of tensions and issues that divide blacks and Latinos or whites and Latinos. Thus, the general problem is the management of issues so as to form and maintain an effective coalition, even in the presence of actual or potential conflict with respect to interests.

Rollbacks of minority incorporation can and do occur, not only in New York but also in Philadelphia in the late 1960s and 1970s (see Chapter 3). As the Philadelphia case shows, it is possible to reform a biracial coalition with an enhanced role for blacks if the conservative regime in office is distasteful to liberal whites as well as to blacks and if an attractive black candidate is available (Wilson Goode).

LATINO MOBILIZATION AND INCORPORATION

Latinos are different. They are, first of all, not black except in small numbers; thus they do not suffer the stigma of blackness in American society, and many consider themselves to be whites of Hispanic origin. Second, they are much more diverse than blacks, and the diversities count: Cuban Americans are not Puerto Ricans, who are not Dominicans, and Mexican Americans are not Central Americans, either culturally or in socioeconomic status.[4] Third, they are more likely to be Roman Catholics and less likely to see political action as a preferred means of improvement than blacks are. Finally, although poverty continues to be a major problem in many Latino communities, Latinos on average appear to assimilate economically more rapidly than blacks and are less concentrated geographically than blacks.

They are different in other political respects as well. Warren, Stack, and Corbett (Chapter 9) report that of the Latinos in Dade County, Florida, who are registered to vote, about 75 percent are Republicans. Anticommunism is a central tenet of their political program, even at the local level, and they are strongly growth-oriented and increasingly successful in business.

In San Antonio, with Mexican Americans in the majority but a weak mayor–city manager system, Mayor Henry Cisneros "does not promote either his Mexican-American identity or the specific interests of that community"; he has promoted major development in San Antonio, with considerable success (see Chapter 10).

Federico Peña, mayor of Denver, with a strong-mayor form of city government, was not the product of minority electoral mobilization or demand–protest and was not endorsed by established Mexican American politicians. In a city with only 18 percent Latino population (31 percent black or Latino in 1980, but a smaller percentage of the electorate), he did not emphasize his Mexican American identity in his campaign, but he had a "proven track record" for Mexican Americans and with liberal whites as a state legislator, and was strongly supported by Mexican American voters and the liberal wing of the statewide Democratic party.

With Denver experiencing a severe recession, Peña lost the support of important Democratic party leaders, barely won reelection, and never had control of a majority of the city council. This is clearly not a case of strong minority incorporation, in spite of the election of a Latino to the mayor's office. According to Muñoz and Henry, Peña has made some effort to integrate African Americans and Mexican

---

[4] With respect to socioeconomic differences among Latinos in the eastern United States, see Fitzpatrick and Parker (1981).

Americans into city government, but his "coalition continues to be dominated by white political and business elites" (Chapter 10).

Denver city government has been opened to a modicum of minority participation, but in the absence of organization, solidarity, and mobilization around a minority oriented program, it is unlikely that much policy change will come of it. However, given the relatively small size and weak mobilization of Denver's minority population, perhaps it is surprising that a Latino mayor was elected at all. A somewhat larger Latino population in San Jose has not elected a mayor; but San Jose's black population, which would support a liberal coalition, is very small, unlike Denver's.

Latinos can be mobilized to vote for multiracial coalitions led by whites (Sacramento) or blacks (Chicago), but they are not very likely to generate strongly minority oriented programs and coalitions themselves. This is not to say that they have not done this to some degree in some cities, such as Miami and perhaps San Antonio, or that they will not do so in the future, but if Latino economic assimilation proceeds with reasonable speed, it is unlikely that Latinos as a group will mobilize strongly around demands of the sort articulated by the black power movement.[5]

In the meantime, Latino incorporation, as we see it in the cities studied in this book, is different. It draws more narrowly from the comprehensive socioeconomic goals of the black power movement and has a more limited view of the proper role of government. Latino political leadership has responded to an electoral base that has been more diverse and, typically, more conservative.

The conservatism of Latino mobilization and incorporation has of course implications for the responsiveness of city governments in which Latinos are incorporated—responsiveness to what? To whose demands and interests? To what ultimate goals? We should expect Latino-run city governments to end discrimination in hiring, certainly, in the routine administration of city affairs, and in the award of government contracts to minority owned businesses. Should we expect such governments to equalize the delivery of city services and improvements generally? Perhaps somewhat, alleviating the most glaring inequities; but not much, if it means significantly reallocating municipal resources toward low-income neighborhoods, their residents, and their businesses.

The studies reported in this book confirm the difficulty of forming multiracial coalitions including blacks and Latinos. The tensions between these groups are often high as they compete both in labor markets and for political position and governmental benefits. The obstacles seem greatest in New York and Miami, where the two groups are in direct conflict, but political relationships are problematic in Los Angeles as well. The most successful black–Latino coalition seems to have

---

[5] William Julius Wilson (1985, p. 148) raises the possibility that rapidly growing urban Latino populations, with both continued immigration and high birth rates, might experience a worsening of their social and economic conditions, including an increase in joblessness, crime, teenage pregnancy, female-headed families, welfare dependency, and ethnic antagonism directed toward them.

been Harold Washington's in Chicago. The process of coalition formation in that city should be a model for similar efforts elsewhere.

HAVE BLACKS ACHIEVED POLITICAL INCORPORATION?

To summarize, we list all of the twenty-one cities in a rough ranking of the extent of black incorporation:

Black Incorporation

Strong (bi/multiracial coalition; black mayors)

Berkeley	1971–1985	Warren Widener, Jr., Gus Newport
Atlanta	1973	Maynard Jackson, Andrew Young
Los Angeles	1973	Tom Bradley
New Orleans	1977	Ernest Morial, Sidney Barthelemy
Oakland	1977	Lionel Wilson
Birmingham	1979	Richard Arrington
Chicago	1983–1987	Harold Washington
Philadelphia	1983	Wilson Goode

Fairly strong (bi/multiracial coalition, white leadership or weak-mayor system)
Sacramento, CA
Richmond, CA

Weak (black representation, not in dominant coalition)
New York
San Francisco
Denver (coalition controls mayor's office but not council)
San Jose (very small black population)
Boston
Stockton, CA
Miami

Very weak (little or no black representation)
San Antonio
Hayward, CA
Vallejo, CA
Daly City, CA

New York is especially difficult to classify. While blacks are not well incorporated in Mayor Koch's administration, they are incorporated in the party organizations of the boroughs, and the organizations, with great influence at the state as well as the local level, are surprisingly supportive on key issues (see Chapter 4). Blacks in New York might well be termed fairly strongly (but unevenly) incorporated once the complexities of political organization are taken into account, in spite of Mayor Koch's rhetorical tendencies. They are in fact represented in the party organizations, which are multiracial coalitions with white leadership but commitments to at least some black interests.

What should we conclude from this listing? Of course such a classification is changeable—conservative coalitions may arise and win control of city governments where blacks are now strongly incorporated, and vice versa. At this writing, black incorporation is weaker than we might expect on grounds of black population alone in New York, Miami, and Boston. If we had to point to a single limiting factor in those cities, we might note that black and Latino populations in New York and Miami are especially divided, and that Boston's minority population overall is relatively small compared to cities in which blacks have achieved that especially strong form of incorporation, the bi- or multiracial dominant coalition led by a black mayor.

With the important exceptions of New York, Miami, and Boston, blacks appear to be well placed in dominant coalitions in the eight cities in this set in which they constituted at least 20 percent of city population in 1980. They have not achieved stronger incorporation in three large cities, and they have not carved out stronger roles in numerous cities where they are smaller proportions of the population. These are significant limitations. Nevertheless, there is no denying the enormous change from the virtual exclusion of blacks 30 years ago to positions of governmental authority and leadership in 1988.

IS INCORPORATION ENOUGH?

No one who favors political equality objects in principle to the formation of multiracial coalitions or to minority officeholding. The question is, what do minority officeholders and coalitions *do* with their positions? Do they make city government responsive to the demands and interests of minority communities? Especially, do they use the powers of city governments to pursue the broader aims of the black power movement, including expansion of assistance and provision of employment to economically marginal populations, largely black, and redistributive allocation of the resources of city governments?

There *is* "an inherent value in officeholding. . . . A race of people who are excluded from public will always be second class" (McCain, 1981). Officeholding *does* confer legitimacy on a hitherto excluded group, as Perry argues (Chapter 8). These are symbolic but nonetheless terribly important considerations.

Still, some of the authors of this book set forth criticisms of some largely black regimes and some black leaders, criticisms that lean toward a conclusion that they are not as active as they should be in redistributive efforts; that they are less powerful than their political positions imply, because of the pervasive systemic power of white business interests and a progrowth ideology that may simply ignore the needs of ordinary citizens; and that they are too narrowly self-interested, too focused on their own interests, the interests of the black (and white) middle and upper class.

Clarence Stone, writing on Atlanta in this volume, concludes that the city's black middle-class political leadership is in a "tight alliance with the white business elite"; he reports the remark of one activist that a meeting of black and white leaders in Atlanta "is nothing but a roomful of people trying to cut a deal." The city's biracial coalition leaves out a range of lower-class interests, including neighborhood organizations and affordable-housing groups. The dominance of the governing biracial coalition replicates the extreme inequalities in the socioeconomic sphere—Atlanta is second only to Newark in poverty rate among U.S. cities—and the mass of black constituents remains effectively excluded (Chapter 7). The moral prestige of former civil rights leader Mayor Andrew Young renders the regime all the more invulnerable.

We see the possibility that we might hope eagerly for black political incorporation, but when it arrives, find that it is an obstacle to achievement of a broader set of goals. Even if we do not conclude that incorporation is *only* a sham, *only* the illusion of empowerment, we might still suffer a profound ambivalence toward it.

The authors of this book do *not* conclude that black incorporation is only a sham. They agree by and large that biracial regimes have accomplished some good. What has been accomplished varies from city to city.

HAVE MINORITY REGIMES BEEN RESPONSIVE?

By "minority regimes," we mean city governments dominated by bi- or multiracial coalitions in which blacks or Latinos play significant, usually leading, roles. Primarily these are black regimes.

City Government Employment

All of the minority regimes studied in this book have effectively reduced discrimination in city government employment. Often they have created strongly affirmative recruitment and hiring practices that have resulted in minority work forces close to or above parity with the size of minority populations. Even governments like New York's, with limited minority incorporation, have pushed ahead rapidly with minority hiring (Chapter 4). All of the minority regimes have greatly increased minority representation in professional, managerial, and executive positions, including department heads.

Some commentators deride city government employment as the weakest of weak rewards, "a few government jobs" with which elites buy off minority protest. We do not agree. One analysis concludes that

> about 55 percent of the increase in black professional, managerial, and technical employment between 1960 and 1976 occurred in the public sector, and employ-

ment in social welfare programs accounted for approximately half of that increase. (Murray, 1984, citing Brown and Erie, 1981, p. 308)

This suggests that city government employment gains probably contributed significantly to middle-class black employment gains generally during this period. Our own analysis of city work forces in the ten California cities showed that minority employees of city governments ranged from 2 percent to 6 percent of total minority residents in the work force, more in the older, larger cities with the highest proportions of black residents, again not an insignificant contribution to total minority (especially black) employment.

The argument is also sometimes made that the advantages of city government accrue almost entirely to middle-class blacks and Latinos; but the pattern varies a great deal from city to city. Older cities with broader governmental functions also hire large numbers of blue-collar workers. Bolstering the employment opportunities of middle-class *or potentially middle-class* minority persons is obviously not the same from an antipoverty perspective as enhancing employment opportunities for low-income persons; on the other hand, support for a nascent minority middle class is not to be scoffed at, either.

Police–Community Relations

Establishment of civilian police review boards was one of the points at which minority incorporation in the ten California cities did make a difference, and some of the authors in this volume report progress along these lines. Police review boards are, of course, only one of several strategies for reducing the use by police of often lethal force against minority people. Minority hiring onto police forces and changing top leadership are common and probably more effective steps taken by minority regimes. Reviewing the literature on black regimes, Adolph Reed concludes:

> Black regimes generally have been successful in curbing police brutality, which often has been prominent among black constituents' concerns. . . . Not surprisingly, black regimes have made substantial gains in black police employment, which contributes to the reduction in police brutality. (Reed, 1988, p. 156)

Development of Minority Businesses

''Development'' is typically supposed to be accomplished by set-asides or other special efforts to channel city spending for supplies and services to minority-owned businesses, thus encouraging the growth of the minority-owned and operated private sector. The record of minority regimes in this area is murky. Perry reports little or no progress in New Orleans and Birmingham (Chapter 8), and the record in other cities is mixed. Minority contracting is sometimes distorted by favoritism for a few firms with special ties to the regime (Stone, Chapter 7), as governmental contracting frequently is. In some cities, some minority contractors have been found to be paper corporations, fronts for white-owned businesses. There may actually be success stories of city government support for minority businesses, but the evidence for them is hard to come by. Recent Supreme Court decisions are likely to make set-asides more difficult to implement, even when city governments are willing to develop strong programs.

Appointments to Board and Commissions

All of the minority regimes studied in this volume have made substantial numbers and proportions of minority appointments to city boards and commissions. No doubt the significance of these appointments varies enormously. In some cities, they may be entirely symbolic; in others, they are key steps in the extension of control over city government and associated agencies. In Oakland, for example, minority control of commissions with real governmental authority was essential to the establishment of minority control over city departments and over public authorities associated with the city, such as the Port Authority. This in turn allowed the dominant coalition to change the policies of those organizations to emphasize direct minority hiring, employment-related development, increased provision of facilities and services to minority residents and neighborhoods, and coordination with other minority oriented programs of city government.

In these respects, the minority regimes studied here have typically been responsive. We simply do not have sufficient evidence in this volume about other areas of need in which they may or may not have made substantial progress. Adolph Reed, reviewing the available evidence, concludes that "the presence of a black mayor or regime has some, but less than dramatic, racially redistributive effect on allocation of public resources" (1988, p. 139). Several authors of this volume note that the regimes they studied had done little to meet the needs or even heed the objections of lower-income minority populations. Yet worsening poverty and other signs of social breakdown in inner-city populations would seem to be critical conditions that a city government must deal with, certainly a government that purports to be responsive to its minority population, as minority regimes do.

Unfortunately, it is extremely difficult for city governments to have much impact on poverty. Due to cutbacks in programs instituted in the sixties and seventies, the federal government can no longer be depended upon to lead the effort to reduce poverty, and city governments lack both the fiscal resources and the structural capability to do so, even if they were willing to take up where the federal government left off.

THE STRUCTURAL LIMITS OF MINORITY REGIMES

The painful truth is that many of the forces shaping the conditions under which the mass of low-income minority people live are not under the control of city governments, even governments run by minority regimes (Peterson, 1981). Big cities with large minority populations are undergoing two radical transformations that have been under way for several decades and are continuing (Kasarda, 1985; Wilson, 1985; Downs, 1985). One of these transformations is economic: the shift from manufacturing and distribution activities to administration, information, and other services, many highly technical in nature. The number of low-skill jobs in such cities is dropping.

Big-city populations are being transformed as well: as blacks and Latinos, mainly poor and unskilled, increase in number, whites are leaving, partly for racial reasons but also as the continuation of long-term trends.

> This transformation is occurring in part because of the white majority's deliberate policy of segregating itself from both poor and nonpoor minority group members. Such segregation . . . operates by excluding nearly all poor households and most minority households from new suburban areas. Segregation is less evident in workplaces, although residential segregation also produces massive racial separation jobs. . . .
>
> Confronted by a triple handicap of shrinking job opportunities, poor education, and low-quality neighborhoods [and increasing competition for low-skill jobs from new immigration and from high birth rates in the inner city], these minority citizens are caught in a situation from which there appears to be no escape. (Downs, 1985, p. 285)

Not only the white population but also its taxable wealth is being suburbanized; so at the same time the minority populations of big cities are facing increasingly severe and intractable problems, their cities are losing resources to cope with them.

The roots of this knot of problems and constraints are many; again, they are not easily controlled by city governments. National policies that fight inflation by keeping interest rates high increase demand for the dollar, thereby raising the exchange value of the dollar, raising the prices of U.S. goods and leading eventually to the closure of older manufacturing plants—deindustrialization—often, in big cities. Construction of new regional freeways leads to additional suburban development relative to the central city. The income tax deduction for mortgage loan interest increases the demand for new homes, which must be built in the suburbs.

The forces operating against big cities and their minority populations are so powerful and manifold that it is difficult to see any direct way out of their dilemmas.

WHAT CAN BE DONE?

City governments are not, however, entirely without resources. Where blacks or Latinos have political control of city government, the legal control of city government over private development greatly increases the bargaining power of minorities in relation to major property owners who pay taxes, and increases their political power in Congress and the state legislatures" (Downs, 1985, p. 291).

Minorities need allies, not only to win elections but to mobilize to the fullest extent possible the resources of the community to improve education and job training. Whereas in earlier decades supporters of minority demands for improved education and job training were powerful at the federal level, that is no longer true. Today, as Downs puts it:

> The best natural allies are those who stand to lose most if the minority community cannot produce competent workers. That means businesses locked into the city itself, such as downtown property owners, nonbranching banks, or newspapers. They might support more ghetto enrichment as a quid pro quo for further integrated core development benefiting them. (Downs, 1985, p. 292)

Adolph Reed emphasizes the advantageous location of big-city black regimes in cities that are national or regional economic and administrative centers:

> Those regimes should be capable of generating and enforcing measures aimed at channeling some of the proceeds of growth to address the needs of their electoral constituency. So far, however, none of the black regimes seems to have made genuine strides in that direction. (Reed, 1988, p. 165)

This means "neither a reflexive opposition to economic growth nor an adversarial relationship with concrete business interests." Rather, the goal is to use "public authority to articulate policy agendas that accommodate economic growth as much as possible to the needs of the municipality and its citizenry rather than vice versa" (Reed, 1988, p. 167). A major technique is the use of planning mechanisms to shape desirable private development and link it to an appropriate vision of the urgent problems and future of the city and its people. Downs and Reed both emphasize the leadership role of the minority community and minority mayors in particular. Reed suggests that regimes use the "cultural authority of office to draw attention to unpalatable conditions that affect constituents but are beyond the scope of municipal control." They can also engage in forms of official protest, such as

> passing unconstitutional tax ordinances, to dramatize existing inequities, thereby opening them to public awareness and debate and providing opportunities for political mobilization. Along each of these dimensions of advocacy for justice and equity, the record of black regimes is poor (Reed, 1988, p. 168).

Downs too stresses possibilities for effective advocacy that go beyond the current political efforts to minority regimes. One tactic that might be effective "is constantly emphasizing that spending more on educating minority group children is investing in the city's future, not just aiding the poor." Another tactic "would be launching a series of nonviolent demonstrations in white areas and schools about the poor quality of minority schools," resembling civil rights protests of the 1960s (1985, p. 292). Such advocacy might lead eventually to metropolitan tax sharing or other measures to channel state or local funds to inner-city schools, investment, and employment programs. Minority regimes could do more to organize and publicize demands on suburban governments in metropolitan regions and on state and national governments for resources and programs to alleviate their problems. Downs emphasizes self-help efforts in minority communities:

- More internal discipline and leadership than most of them have shown up to now, both politically and socially. . . .
- Elements of any solution must come from within minority communities themselves, just as happened with other ethnic groups in the past. . . .
- Self-help efforts can make a huge difference in the welfare of both groups and individuals in a relatively open society. (Downs, 1985, p. 292)

Minority regimes can play an important leadership role in this area and with relatively modest governmental resources or private support, also can organize community self-help activities that involve recyclable financial resources. Leadership in self-help efforts would be an effective tactic politically as well as for the direct help it generates, because it would assure nonminority people that minority communities are doing what they can to help themselves.

This is not a comprehensive list of tactics, and we have scarcely scratched the surface of Reed's complex and eloquent analysis. The fundamental point is that many minority regimes, even with the constraints they operate under, could undertake significant new efforts. These efforts could make a difference in revenue and program development. For this to happen, however, may require "greatly increased and informed pressure from the black electoral constituency" (Reed, 1988, p. 196) and from liberal whites, which in turn implies broad public debate on the issues—a debate that is not now heard.

Thus minority regimes should also undertake new efforts in the realm of political mobilization. Incorporation cannot be the limit of minority governmental effectiveness. Minority regimes—and prospective challengers to the leadership of those regimes—possess unique resources with which to pursue renewed mobilization and advocacy, so that issues of poverty, employment, housing, isolation, and inadequate education, for disadvantaged whites as well as for people of color, again find their way onto local, state, and national agendas. Understanding the histories of leadership, mobilization, coalition formation, and incorporation described in this volume will, we hope, help people of color and their white allies, both present and potential, fashion the vision and the coalitions that will carry to a new plane the historical struggle to build democracy out of the centuries-long practice of racial domination.

REFERENCES

Brown, Michael K., and Stephen P. Erie. 1981. Blacks and the Legacy of the Great Society: The Economic and Political Impact of Federal Social Policy. *Public Policy* 12 (Summer): 299–330.

Browning, Rufus, P., Dale Rogers Marshall, and David H. Tabb. 1979. Minorities and Urban Electoral Change: A Longitudinal Study. *Urban Affairs Quarterly* 15 (2):206–228.

Carmichael, Stokely, and Charles V. Hamilton. 1967. *Black Power*. New York: Random House.

Downs, Anthony. 1985. The Future of Industrial Cities. In Peterson, Paul E., *The New Urban Reality*. Washington, D.C.: The Brookings Institution.

Fitzpatrick, Joseph P., and Lourdes Traviesco Parker. 1981. Hispanic Americans in the Eastern United States. *Annals of the American Academy of Political and Social Science* 454:98–124.

Kasarda, John D. 1985. Urban Change and Minority Opportunities. In Peterson, Paul E., *The New Urban Reality*. Washington, D.C.: The Brookings Institution.

McCain, Tom. 1981. Quoted in American Civil Liberties Union *News*.

Murray, Charles. 1984. *Losing Ground: American Social Policy 1950–1980*. New York: Basic Books.

Preston, Michael B., Lenneal J. Henderson, and Paul Puryear, eds. 1987. *The New Black Politics*, 2d ed. New York: Longman.

Reed, Adolph, 1988. The Black Urban Regime: Structural Origins and Constraints. In Michael Peter Smith, ed., *Power, Community and the City. Comparative Urban and Community Research*, Vol. 1. New Brunswick, N.J.: Transaction Books.

Wilson, William Julius. 1985. The Urban Underclass in Advanced Industrial Society. In Paul E. Peterson, ed., *The New Urban Reality*. Washington, D.C.: Brookings Institution.

Index